The Communicator's Commentary

Mark

THE COMMUNICATOR'S COMMENTARY SERIES

Lloyd J. Ogilvie

General Editor

The Communicator's Commentary

Mark

David L. McKenna

WORD BOOKS, PUBLISHER • WACO, TEXAS

First Printing, November 1982
Second Printing, April 1983
Third Printing, January 1984

Library of Congress Cataloging in Publication Data
Main entry under title:

The Communicator's commentary.

Includes bibliographical references.
Contents: v. 2. Mark/David L. McKenna.
1. Bible. N.T.—Commentaries—Collected works.
I. Ogilvie, Lloyd John. II. McKenna, David L.

BS2341.2.C65   225.7'7   81-71764
ISBN 0-8499-0155-3 (v.2)   AACR2

Printed in the United States of America

To
my co-authors
at
Seattle Pacific University

Trustees
Faculty
Students
Staff
Alumni

&

Fellows

Contents

Editor's Preface

God has called all of His people to be communicators. Everyone who is in Christ is called into ministry. As ministers of "the manifold grace of God," all of us—clergy and laity—are commissioned with the challenge to communicate our faith to individuals and groups, classes and congregations.

The Bible, God's Word, is the objective basis of the truth of His love and power that we seek to communicate. In response to the urgent, expressed needs of pastors, teachers, Bible study leaders, church school teachers, small group enablers, and individual Christians, the Communicator's Commentary is offered as a penetrating search of the Scriptures of the New Testament to enable vital personal and practical communication of the abundant life.

Many current commentaries and Bible study guides provide only some aspects of a communicator's needs. Some offer in-depth scholarship but no application to daily life. Others are so popular in approach that biblical roots are left unexplained. Few offer impelling illustrations that open windows for the reader to see the exciting application for today's struggles. And most of all, seldom have the expositors given the valuable outlines of passages so needed to help the preacher or teacher in his or her busy life to prepare for communicating the Word to congregations or classes.

This Communicator's Commentary series brings all of these elements together. The authors are scholar-preachers and teachers outstanding in their ability to make the Scriptures come alive for individuals and groups. They are noted for bringing together excellence in biblical scholarship, knowledge of the original Greek and

Hebrew, sensitivity to people's needs, vivid illustrative material from biblical, classical, and contemporary sources, and lucid communication by the use of clear outlines of thought. Each has been selected to contribute to this series because of his Spirit-empowered ability to help people live in the skins of biblical characters and provide a "you-are-there" intensity to the drama of events of the Bible which have so much to say about our relationships and responsibilities today.

The design for the Communicator's Commentary gives the reader an overall outline of each book of the New Testament. Following the introduction, which reveals the author's approach and salient background on the book, each chapter of the commentary provides the Scripture to be exposited. The New King James Bible has been chosen for the Communicator's Commentary because it combines with integrity the beauty of language, underlying Greek textual basis, and thought-flow of the 1611 King James Version, while replacing obsolete verb forms and other archaisms with their everyday contemporary counterparts for greater readability. Reverence for God is preserved in the capitalization of all pronouns referring to the Father, Son, or Holy Spirit. Readers who are more comfortable with another translation can readily find the parallel passage by means of the chapter and verse reference at the end of each passage being exposited. The paragraphs of exposition combine fresh insights to the Scripture, application, rich illustrative material, and innovative ways of utilizing the vibrant truth for his or her own life and for the challenge of communicating it with vigor and vitality.

It has been gratifying to me as Editor of this series to receive enthusiastic progress reports from each contributor. As they worked, all were gripped with new truths from the Scripture—God-given insights into passages, previously not written in the literature of biblical explanation. A prime objective of this series is for each user to find the same awareness: that God speaks with newness through the Scriptures when we approach them with a ready mind and a willingness to communicate what He has given; that God delights to give communicators of His Word "I-never-saw-that-in-that-verse-before" intellectual insights so that our listeners and readers can have "I-never-realized-all-that-was-in-that-verse" spiritual experiences.

The thrust of the commentary series unequivocally affirms that God speaks through the Scriptures today to engender faith, enable adventuresome living of the abundant life, and establish the basis of obedient discipleship. The Bible, the unique Word of God, is unlimited in its resource for Christians in communicating our hope to others. It is our weapon in the battle for truth, the guide for ministry, and the irresistible force for introducing others to God. In the New Testament we meet the divine Lord and Savior whom we seek to communicate to others. What He said and did as God with us has been faithfully recorded under the inspiration of the Spirit of God. The cosmic implications of the Gospels are lived out in Acts and spelled out in the Epistles. They have stood the test of time because the eternal Communicator, God Himself, communicates through them to those who would be communicators of grace. His essential nature is exposed, the plan of salvation is explained, and the Gospel for all of life, now and for eternity is proclaimed.

A biblically rooted communication of the Gospel holds in unity and oneness what divergent movements have wrought asunder. This commentary series courageously presents personal faith, caring for individuals, and social responsibility as essential, inseparable dimensions of biblical Christianity. It seeks to present the quadrilateral Gospel in its fullness which calls us to unreserved commitment to Christ, unrestricted self-esteem in His grace, unqualified love for others in personal evangelism, and undying efforts to work for justice and righteousness in a sick and suffering world.

A growing renaissance in the church today is being led by clergy and laity who are biblically rooted, Christ-centered, and Holy Spirit-empowered. They have dared to listen to people's most urgent questions and deepest needs and then to God as He speaks through the Bible. Biblical preaching is the secret of growing churches. Bible study classes and small groups are equipping the laity for ministry in the world. Dynamic Christians are finding that daily study of God's Word allows the Spirit to do in them what He wishes to communicate through them to others. These days are the most exciting time since Pentecost. The Communicator's Commentary is offered to be a primary resource of new life for this renaissance.

Dr. David L. McKenna is one of America's finest communicators. He exemplifies the quality of communication I have been describing. Dr. McKenna is a distinguished scholar, excellent Biblical preacher, dynamic teacher, talented educator, and revered leader of evangelical Christianity. During his years as President of Seattle Pacific University, he led students and faculty in being a Christ-centered, biblical community of faith and learning. Now as President of Asbury Theological Seminary, he is focusing his leadership gifts on the equipping of articulate, contagious, and creative communicators of the Gospel.

Dr. McKenna's commitment to Christ and his unswerving dedication to biblical exposition has made him a communicator's communicator. He is emulated and quoted. Utilizing his immense intellectual gifts coupled with a profound faith, he is both informative and inspirational. Students admire his love for truth and scholars are pressed deeper into the adventure of learning.

Here is a communicator who knows his Bible and his times. He is in touch with the deepest questions and most urgent needs of our day. This provides his preaching and teaching with empathy and sensitivity. The lucid flow of his thought comes from the well of study, awareness of the issues of our culture, and careful preparation. His remarkable ability to tackle a text or theme with gusto involves the listener or reader. Ordered thought, clear outline, and vivid illustration are the obvious secret of his excellence. He speaks to tough issues with boldness, complex problems with clarity.

This volume of the Communicator's Commentary Series on Mark expresses David McKenna's talents and gifts under the guidance of the Holy Spirit. I have read dozens of commentaries on Mark's Gospel over the years. This one is the finest I have ever studied. It combines penetrating scholarship and powerful exposition. Dr. McKenna catches the intent and style of John Mark. His explanation of thought gives valuable tools to every conscientious communicator. But more than that, he exposes the mind of Jesus as the Master Communicator. This volume will endure through the years for the way the author clarifies the basic principles of how to communicate. It should be a guide for teachers and preachers and a must in any curriculum for a contemporary course on communicating and leadership. Throughout the commentary you will sense that one of our nation's leading educators has opened the treasure-chest of years of learning and experience.

But that's only one aspect of the value of this volume. Not only are we provided with a fresh approach to the exposition of the first Gospel to be written, but we are given an outline of Mark's thought which equips us to prepare for our own teaching or preaching of his Gospel. And then, in each section the division of thought exemplifies how to tackle a text for exciting communication. The reader's first reaction will be, "That will preach!" and then on reflection McKenna's excellence will challenge us to our own originality spurred on by his creativity.

Another stunning dimension of this commentary is the use of illustration. I have known Dr. McKenna over the years both by reputation and personal friendship. But I know him in a new depth from reading this outstanding work. His illustrations from his own personal adventure with Christ introduce us to a sensitive, caring, and growing contemporary disciple. That would be enough, but added to the exposure of his own pilgrimage are perfectly selected illustrations and quotes from classical and contemporary literature. And yet, the most important contribution to the communicator of the Gospel is the way he allows the Bible to speak with a unified voice. The use of corollary passages opens the text at hand to the witness of the entire Bible.

This volume provides a moving experience of the life and message, death and resurrection, reigning power and indwelling strength of the living Lord. It will help every communicator in introducing people to Christ and will be the basis of teaching essential Christianity for people who want to move on in obedient discipleship. You will see how Mark can be preached and taught, but you will find yourself personally refreshed in your own quest to know and do the Lord's will.

Most commentaries become resource books for insight and wisdom on particular passages we want to teach or preach. Seldom is one of the quality that keeps us reading on beyond the immediate research we are doing. Here is one that does. It will become a devotional classic for daily reading as well as a source of scholarly insight for communication.

By this time, you have sensed my great enthusiasm for this work on Mark. When the vision for the Communicator's Commentary Series was birthed in my mind, what Dr. McKenna has accomplished in this volume was exactly what I envisioned. But the accolades go not just to this exemplary contemporary communicator, but to Mark whose mind he has captured and especially to the Savior whose story he tells. And I know that the prolonged study and careful writing which this volume represents will be rewarded by the gratified readers through the decades who meet the Savior in a new and exciting way through Dr. McKenna's eyes and picturesque pen.

LLOYD OGILVIE

Introduction

If you were commissioned by God to send a letter of hope to Christians facing martyrdom, what would you write? Mark, under the inspiration of the Holy Spirit, answers this question by writing a Gospel that demonstrates how to communicate with compassion, precision, urgency and hope to people in need. Rather than laboring with the elaborate details of history as Matthew does or weaving through the intricacies of Jesus' teaching as Luke does, Mark drives straight to the communicator's questions, "Who?" "What?" "When?" "Where?" "How?" and "Why?" By asking these same questions about the Gospel of Mark, we will discover a dramatic setting and a moving stage for our study of the book.

Who is Mark? Out of the struggle of his own life, Mark identifies with people who are tempted to give up under pressure or persecution. Son of Mary, a wealthy and prominent Christian woman of Jerusalem, John Mark bears the double name of a Jewish and Roman heritage. By inference, he enjoys all of the creaturely comforts of a large and affluent home which becomes the Jerusalem base for the Apostles after Pentecost. Night after night, he listens to reports about the growth of the Gospel, feels the tears of concern for companions in Christ who are being persecuted, and watches the flame kindle in the eyes of the men of God as they lay plans to "Go therefore and make disciples of all the nations . . ." (Matt. 28:19).

Mark appears as a companion of Barnabas and Paul on their first missionary journey. Trouble, however, brews at Perga when Paul's fervor for the Gospel leads him to propose going beyond their goal and into the uncharted and untested spiritual wilderness of Asia Minor. Mark demurs, perhaps from fear or homesickness, and returns to Jerusalem.

Paul does not forget easily. When he and Barnabas are planning the second missionary journey, Mark wants to go again. Cousin Barnabas pleads his case, but to no avail. Quitters have no second chance with the strong-minded Apostle, so in a flurry of harsh words, Paul and Barnabas split up. Paul takes Silas, and Barnabas chooses Mark.

Mark's ministry with Barnabas disappears into the hidden history of the Acts of the Apostles until suddenly he surfaces in the most unexpected of places. From his Roman prison cell, Paul informs the Colossians that Mark is with him! Through the love of God, two brothers in Christ have been reconciled as comrades. In his brief letter to Philemon, he includes Mark on the roster of his fellow laborers in the Gospel. When Paul is approaching death, he asks that Timothy, his most beloved son, come to him in the Roman prison bringing Mark, ". . . for he is useful to me for ministry" (2 Tim. 4:11). Grace has turned their relationship full circle, and Mark, whom Paul once denounced as a quitter, becomes his trusted companion, effective co-worker and indispensable servant.

What does Mark communicate? Christian tradition and Biblical scholarship generally concur on four facts about the Gospel of Mark. *First,* Mark is the author of the Gospel that bears his name. Even though he does not claim authorship in his own writing, the internal and external evidence leads such distinguished scholars as Papias, Eusebius, Irenaeus, Clement of Alexandria, Tertullian and Origen to accept the fact that he is, indeed, the writer of the Gospel.

Second, the Gospel of Mark is the earliest of the three Gospels which are called *synoptic* because they "see together." Evidence shows that Matthew and Luke use Mark's writing as a primary source.

Third, even though disputed, the Gospel of Mark has unity. Scholars have raised questions about sections of the Gospel which might lead to the conclusion that more than one author is involved in the writing. They have also detected an appendix after the last eight verses of the Gospel which does not appear in the earliest manuscripts. Nevertheless, the differences do not distort the essential message of the Gospel and its example of effective communication.

Fourth, Mark's source of information for his writing is the eyewitness account of the Apostle Peter. The earliest church fathers give the Gospel of Mark full credibility as an authentic document in which Peter is the eyewitness and Mark is the interpreter.

Among all of these generally accepted conclusions, none is more important for understanding the value of the Gospel of Mark than the fact that it is accepted as an accurate report of Peter's eyewitness account of the life and ministry of Jesus Christ. Peter puts his relationship with Mark into perspective when he calls him, ". . . Mark my son" (1 Pet. 5:13). Here, Mark is pictured as a young man sitting at the feet of a great Apostle and hearing him recall the graphic events of Jesus' life. Hour after hour, Peter talks while Mark writes. Day after day, Mark follows the Apostle to his preaching stations in order to capture the high moments of fiery inspiration as they complement their calm and reflective conversations.

Probably Mark completes his inspired work after Peter's death. The product is what William Barclay has called the ". . . most important book in the world."[1] Not only is it the earliest of the Synoptic Gospels and the first written account of the life of Jesus that we know, but it is accepted in the courts of tradition and scholarship as admissible evidence from an eyewitness who was there when Jesus served and suffered, lived and died, arose from the dead and ascended into heaven. As a fair and accurate reporter who captures both the truth and the tone of Peter's witness, Mark qualifies as a communicator *par excellence.*

When and where does Mark write? Time and location always have a bearing upon the nature of communication. Yet, the exact date for the writing of the Gospel of Mark remains a conundrum. At best, we can set the limits between A.D. 50 and 70. The earlier date reflects the opinion of conservative scholars that Mark is the first of the Synoptic Gospels and the one used as a reference source for the writing of Matthew and Luke. Because these latter Gospels are dated between A.D. 60 and 70, at least the draft of Mark's account would have to be available at an earlier date. Another line of argument places the writing of Mark before Peter's death about A.D. 67 and before the fall of Jerusalem in A.D. 70. Although there is no sure word on the date, the conclusion that it was the earliest of the Gospels and written before the fall of Jerusalem leads us into the time range between A.D. 50 and 70.

With only the exception of Chrysostom, who locates Mark in Egypt when he compiles his notes, scholars concur that the Gospel is written in Rome. The nature of the message, the style of the writing, and even the words that are used tend to confirm this conclusion. So, for date and place, Mark writes the earliest of the Gospels from the city of Rome at a time preceding the apocalyptic period when the Apostles will be martyred and Jerusalem ravaged.

How does Mark write? As a communicator, Mark exhibits a writing style that expresses the personality of Peter and enlarges the impact of his message. His choice of words is not by accident. To express Peter's personality, Mark uses the impulsive, action-oriented words, "immediately" and "straightway," almost thirty times in his Gospel. To take his readers into the depths of Jesus' personality, he writes about His "sighs" (7:34; 8:12), His "compassion" (6:34), His "marvel" (6:6), His stirrings with "anger" (3:5; 8:33; 10:14), His "love" (10:21), His "hunger" (11:12), and His "fatigue" (6:31).

True to Peter's memory as an eyewitness, Mark picks up details that other Gospel writers miss. No one else describes the scene of Jesus "taking" a little child into His arms (9:36) or being "asleep on a pillow" at the back of the ship during the storm at sea (4:38). Mark even captures the native intelligence and the lively imagination of Peter when he alone among the Gospel writers paints the word picture of the people sitting down in groups of hundreds and fifties like flower beds in a garden during the Feeding of the Five Thousand (6:40).

Critics find fault with the rush of words and the kaleidoscope of events that characterize the Gospel of Mark. Another of his favorite words is "and," which is used thirty-four times in the Gospel. A grammaticist would feel as if he were drinking from a fire hose. But, if you consider Peter, the impetuous source, and Mark, the eager young man, "and" becomes a connector for an urgent story and an indication of authenticity as Peter recalls the times when he became fully alive in the presence of Jesus Christ.

Mark has another stylistic technique that lends authenticity to his Gospel. His verbs often spring to life as he chooses to use the "historic present" for events that took place years earlier. One is reminded of the television series "You Are There," as Jesus *says* to them, "Those who are well have no need of a physician, but those who are sick" (2:17); or as, at the end of His life, Judas, one of the Twelve, *comes* "from the chief priests, the scribes, and the elders" to betray Him (14:43). Who can deny the feeling of being present with Jesus at those events? As a skilled craftsman of words, Mark not only conveys with accuracy the eyewitness of Peter, but he also shows the artistic touch that makes all of his readers full and personal participants in the experiences of Jesus Christ.

Why does Mark write? A good communicator is true to his message, artistic with his medium, and sensitive to his audience. Mark meets each of these qualifications, and particularly with his ability to fine-tune his writings on the wave length of those for whom he writes. Scholars agree that Mark speaks in his Gospel to the needs of Roman Christians who are being subjected daily to the barbarous whims of Nero as he tries to use persecution and death as the final resolution for the Christian question. Nero fails, but Mark does not. Wasting no words, he begins his Gospel with the announcement that Jesus Christ is the Son of God, the central truth upon which persecuted Christians can rely. Then, to substantiate this claim, Mark marshals the facts about Jesus as the serving and suffering Son of Man and marches them to Peter's confession, "You are the Christ" (8:29). Or, if his readers number themselves among the heathen, Mark leaves no alternative but the admission of the Roman Centurion before the cross, ". . . Truly this Man was the Son of God!" (15:39).

And then the Resurrection! Mark extols Jesus Christ, the risen Lord. As He has been the Lord who *serves* in the early chapters of the Gospel, and the Lord who *suffers* through the detailed account of His Passion, He is now the Lord who *lives* to give hope to the believers in Rome that they too shall have the power to serve and be recipients of life beyond death if they are called to suffer.

Mark's message is complete. He has fulfilled his role as the first and most exciting communicator of the Gospel of Jesus Christ. To Roman Christians who are daily facing death, he sends a letter of compassion, precision, urgency and hope. Whether he knows it or not, he also writes a Gospel for the ages, inviting us to study his message, confess the Christ, and receive the power of our resurrected Lord.

NOTES

1. William Barclay, *The Gospel of Mark,* rev. ed. (Philadelphia: Westminster Press, 1975), p. 1.

An Outline of Mark

Purpose: Mark presents the facts to prove that Jesus Christ is the Son of God who serves us and the Son of Man who saves us.

I. Establishing His Credentials: 1:1–13
   A. The Prologue: 1:1
   B. Announced by Man: 1:2–8
   C. Affirmed by God: 1:9–11
   D. Acknowledged by Satan: 1:12–13

II. Outlining His Mission: 1:14–39
   A. His Message: 1:14–15
   B. His Men: 1:16–20
   C. His Authority: 1:21–34
   D. His Field: 1:35–39

III. Introducing His Kingdom: 1:40—3:6
   A. Ministry of Compassion: 1:40–45
   B. Ministry of Forgiveness: 2:1–12
   C. Ministry of Hope: 2:13–17
   D. Ministry of Joy: 2:18–22
   E. Ministry of Grace: 2:23–28
   F. Ministry of Mercy: 3:1–6

IV. Defining His Relationships: 3:7–35
   A. Hero of the Masses: 3:7–12
   B. Leader of the Disciples: 3:13–19
   C. Son of Man: 3:20–35

V. Developing His Teaching: 4:1–34
   A. The Universal Message: 4:1–9

CHAPTER ONE

Establishing His Credentials

Mark 1:1–13

THE PROLOGUE

1 The beginning of the gospel of Jesus Christ, the Son of God.

Mark 1:1

Curiosity makes me a collector of the opening lines of great literature. Most often quoted is Charles Dickens' introduction to *A Tale of Two Cities*, "It was the best of times, it was the worst of times. . . ."[1] In contemporary literature, scholars call attention to Ernest Hemingway's genius for piquing his reader's interest and prefiguring the story to come when he begins *The Old Man and the Sea* with the simple sentence, "He was an old man who fished alone. . . ."[2] Neither of these opening lines compares with the profound and awesome Truth of Genesis 1:1, KJV, "In the beginning God created the heaven and the earth."

My penchant for the opening lines of great literature began with a college course in journalism taught by a premier reporter from the *New York Times*. Daily, she drilled into us the discipline of writing "lead" sentences for our stories that would meet two journalistic tests. One test was to limit our opening sentence to twenty-four words; the other was to answer the journalist's questions—"Who?" "What?" "When?" "Where?" and "How?" with those twenty-four words. Only the question "Why?" could be reserved for the second sentence.

Mark would excel in her class. In the opening sentence to his Gospel, he uses twelve words and answers all the questions except "Where?," which he reserves for a later sentence. "When?" is answered by Mark's choice of the opening words, *The beginning of the gospel* (v. 1). A time line for the Gospel is envisioned that reaches back into prophetic history, advances to the dynamic present, and continues on into a glorious future. "The beginning" is not just a moment in time, it is a step in eternity. Consequently, when Mark goes on to relate "The beginning of the gospel" to the fulfillment of the prophecies of Malachi and Isaiah in verses 2 and 3, we know that he is reaching back along the time line that he has established in order to substantiate the current events that he will report and to affirm their promise for the future.

"What?" is answered by the single word *"gospel."* Mark is introducing a concept that has to be inspired by the Holy Spirit. Remember that he is writing to Roman and Gentile Christians whose faith has become a matter of life and death. To them, Mark announces the Gospel, better translated as the "Good News." He dares not be flippant or gratuitous with such an announcement. Too much is at stake. The "Good News" has to be backed up with facts upon which suffering Christians can rely.

A presidential colleague once showed me his collection of crystal goblets. One by one, he took the glasses from the shelf and snapped his finger against the rim. Those that were the most precious rang with tones true and pure; the cheap ones insulted the ears with a dull thud. The sound betrays their value.

Mark is willing to claim the authentic ring for the "Good News" that Jesus Christ, the Lord who serves and suffers, is also the Son of God who lives and gives us life. This Truth, he contends, sounds in human history as the truest and the purest note of grace that man has ever known. Against the dreadful "plunk" of crosses dropping into the ground, there is the music of voices that will not give up the faith. From the dreariest dungeons that Romans can contrive, the night air comes alive with the singing of a joyful hymn. "Bear me out," Mark is saying, "and you will hear the sound of music."

Of course, it all depends upon the question "Who?". Mark answers with the name of Jesus, the personal name for a man with whom we can identify. Mark does not shy away from the full humanity of Jesus. In fact, he makes Him more human than any other Gospel writer. Jesus is the Son of Man who serves and suffers. The life history of Peter and Mark is showing through. One is a denier; the other is a dropout. Like us, they need to know someone who serves and suffers with them. And so their Gospel begins, not with the royalty of Matthew, the perfection of Luke, nor the mysticism of John, but with the humanity of Jesus. Let the truth be known. Peter and Mark speak for all of us.

There is still the question "How?" Jesus must be more than a person with whom we can identify, if there is to be any hope for transcending the struggle of our common humanity. Mark answers the question "How?" by declaring that Jesus is the Christ, the Messiah, the Anointed One of God. With these words, Mark points forward to his emphasis upon the suffering of the Christ as our only hope for salvation. One must never forget that almost one-half of Mark's Gospel is dedicated to the Passion of our Lord. Why not? Mark is writing for Roman Christians for whom faith means suffering. For them he has this message: Jesus Christ has been there, too. Yet His Passion is eminently different because He is the Christ. He suffers and dies for the sin of all men. In Him, and Him alone, we find our hope for righteousness.

Mark does not stop with the Truth that Jesus is the Christ, the servant who suffers for our redemption. In his prologue, he anticipates the Resurrection of Jesus Christ as proof that He is the Son of God. He is the living Lord who conquers death and promises eternal life to all who are called to die with Him. Roman Christians who live in the swirl of intoxicating power find particular hope in the promise that they have a share in the life and power of the Son of God.

In one short and profound sentence, Mark announces his theme and gives the outline of his book. His lead sentence is so potent that some scholars believe that he wrote his prologue after he wrote his book. Their opinion betrays their lack of knowledge about the purpose and the style of a good communicator. Mark knows what he is saying. His opening sentence speaks his purpose. In contrast with Matthew, who starts with a genealogy and needs sixteen verses to announce that Jesus is King of the Jews; in contrast with Luke, who begins with a sentence of eighty-two words in order to tell the story of Jesus as the Savior of all men; or in contrast with John, who introduces his Gospel with a sentence of seventeen mystical and baffling words to show that Jesus is the Son of God, Mark puts it all together in a simple sentence of twelve words. In his brief prologue, Mark promises a book that moves in historical rhythm with the Kingdom of God, sounds the "Good News" of redemptive grace, identifies Jesus with all who serve, claims salvation through the suffering of the Christ, and promises the Life and Power of the Son of God as our ever-present hope.

Mark can now shift from announcer to advocate. In the prologue, he puts his purpose on the line. Can he prove his case? An experienced attorney once advised a newcomer to the profession, "If your facts are strong, hammer on the facts, but if your facts are weak, hammer on the desk." Mark hammers on strong facts. Seldom does he stop to explain what is happening. Instead, he chooses to remain an objective reporter of Peter's eyewitness account, convinced that his readers will identify with the Lord who serves, confess the Lord who suffers, and receive power from the Lord who lives.

Mark's case begins with the presentation of three character witnesses—John the Baptist, God the Father, and Satan the Tempter— whose testimony leaves no doubt that Jesus has the credentials to begin His ministry as the Servant Lord.

ANNOUNCED BY MAN

2 As it is written in the Prophets:
   "Behold, I send My messenger before Your face,
   Who will prepare Your way before You."
3 *"The voice of one crying in the wilderness:*
   'Prepare the way of the LORD,
   Make His paths straight.'"
4 John came baptizing in the wilderness and preaching the baptism of repentance for the remission of sins.

5 And all the land of Judea, and those from Jerusalem, went out to him and were all baptized by him in the Jordan River, confessing their sins.

6 And John was clothed with camel's hair and with a leather belt around his waist, and he ate locusts and wild honey.

7 And he preached, saying, "There comes One after me who is mightier than I, whose sandal strap I am not worthy to stoop down and loose.

8 "I indeed have baptized you with water, but He will baptize you with the Holy Spirit."

Mark 1:2–8

As the transition between his prologue and his text, Mark quotes from the prophecies of Malachi and Isaiah as historical connectors with the coming of John the Baptist, who will introduce Jesus Christ. Mark's choice of the perfect tense for the word "written" carries with it the meaning of prophecies that have been fulfilled in the past, but still stand written in the present. Malachi's prediction refers in history to the Lord coming to His Temple in judgment for the sins of His people; Isaiah's words are preparatory to the coming of the Servant Lord who will deliver His people from their bondage in Babylon. Equally valid in the present moment, however, these same prophecies speak the roles of both John the Baptist and Jesus Christ. John is to be a wilderness preacher, preparing the way for the coming of Jesus by getting people to straighten out their lives. Jesus, in turn, will come, according to the prophets, as Judge in His divine power and as Deliverer in His Servant role.

John the Baptist accepts his role as forerunner. Every detail of his life points toward that grand moment when he will pick a figure out of the crowd and announce, "Behold! The Lamb of God who takes away the sin of the world!" (John 1:29). Most of us find it difficult to identify with John the Baptist. He cuts directly across the grain of self-interest and the glamour of being Number One that continues to plague us. Think of it. If you were asked to choose the dominant symbol for our generation, what would it be? A flag, a cross, a missile, a television antenna, a dollar sign, a test tube, an oil barrel, a bloated belly, a handgun, an automobile, a peace symbol? My choice would be the sight of a forefinger pointed into the air and accompanied by the chant, "We're Number One." The symbol, of course, comes from the world of sports, where winning has come dangerously close to being everything.

More than a game is at stake in the symbol. Number One has come to symbolize the personal and national self-interest of the "me" generation. Christopher Lasch sees these tendencies as self-destructive in his book, *The Cult of Narcissism*. Narcissus is the boy-god of the Greeks who falls in love with his own image in a reflecting pool, withers away with ungratified desire to make love to that image, and eventually turns into a flower. Lasch likens the personality of the "me" generation to Narcissus. Falling in love with our own self-image, we wither away with ungratified desire because self-interest can never be satisfied. Three symptoms follow. First, self-interest so squeezes time into the *radical now* that we lose our sense of the past and can only despair of the future. Second, self-interest forces our human relationships into formal and informal negotiations as we bargain to win for the *radical self.* Third, self-interest endlessly pursues pleasure under the driving force of the assumed right of *radical happiness.*

No wonder that John the Baptist makes us uncomfortable. He has all of the opportunities to be Number One. Luke tells us that John is conceived by a miracle, announced by Gabriel, the archangel, and filled with the Holy Spirit while still in his mother's womb. John the Baptist also has the preparation to be Number One. Scholars identify him as a member of the Nazirites, the Essenes, or the Qumran society. Each group is synonymous with rigid disciplines, such as eating no meat and drinking no wine. John has the image to go with those disciplines. He appears in a hair shirt tied down with a leather belt, and he subsists on a diet of locusts and wild honey. What a character—fitting for a Biblical Bigfoot or a spiritual Sasquatch! Imagine flaming hair, steely eyes, chiseled face, and a wiry body wound as tightly as a coiled spring. What an image—fitting for a prophet and magnetic with a crowd! John the Baptist is perfect for a media age when style is all-important.

Unforgettable though he is, John the Baptist has *substance* to match his style. True to his prophetic heritage, he preaches social justice as the product of repentance. When the Pharisees come out into the wilderness to critique his preaching, he meets them with the scathing indictment, "O brood of vipers!" (Matt. 3:7). When the tax collectors appear, he calls upon them to be honest, and to the soldiers in the crowd, he preaches mercy. Evidently John has never heard the Arabian proverb, "He who tells the truth keeps one foot in the stirrup."

Not only is John the Baptist born to be great and prepared to lead, but he has the *success* to be Number One. Peter is so impressed with the crowds that come out to hear John the Baptist that he tells Mark, "all " of the people of the country of Judea, and "all" of the people of Jerusalem come to hear him and respond to his message. How many is "all"? Scholars estimate that as many as 300,000 converts were baptized by John. Put those numbers into a contemporary perspective. Without advertising, stadiums, amplifiers or satellites, John the Baptist has to be recognized as one of the most successful preachers of all time.

Flattery always follows success. When John's fame peaks, the rumor spreads that he is the Christ. He does not stop for a moment to bask in the reflection of a false impression. Immediately and directly, he answers, "I am not the Christ" (John 1:20).

Never forgetting his prophetic call, John repeats the words of the prophet who identifies his special role in the Kingdom of God, "I am the voice of one crying in the wilderness, 'Make straight the way of the Lord' " (John 1:23). With that unequivocal pronouncement, the man who has been born, prepared, and touted to be Number One steps aside so that Jesus Christ, and He alone, can be exalted. John the Baptist teaches us what it means to be second to Jesus Christ.

To be second, you must have a sense of history. Contrary to the Cult of Narcissism which squeezes all time into the *radical now,* John the Baptist understands his present role in continuity with the past and the future of the Kingdom of God. Even though he has all of the qualifications for being first, he does not succumb to the temptation of assuming that no one has contributed anything to the Kingdom before he came and that no one will contribute anything after he leaves.

To be second, you must be *submissive.* John the Baptist resists the desires of the *radical self* and submits himself to the greatness of Jesus Christ. Imagine being born, prepared, and acclaimed for a singular moment when you stand on the banks of the River Jordan and shout, "Behold! The Lamb of God who takes away the sin of the world!" (John 1:29).

Can one sentence sum up a lifetime? In the purpose of God, it can. Queen Esther is an example. The decisive moment arrives when she can save her people if she will intervene with the king at the risk of her life. Mordecai, her uncle, minces no words when he puts out the challenge, ". . . Who knoweth whether thou art come to the kingdom for such a time as this?" (Esther 4:14, KJV).

To be second, you must be *self-sacrificing.* John the Baptist finds his joy in the glory of Christ by giving up his self-serving right to *radical happiness.* Move forward to the third chapter of John's Gospel in which John the Baptist exalts the Christ. Disciples of The Baptist are jealous because Jesus is baptizing in what appears to be competition with John. Their dismay is revealed in their report, ". . . all are coming to Him!" (John 3:26). John's answer should go down in history as the spirit of being second. After reminding his disciples once again that he is not the Christ, but only the one sent to prepare the way, he now informs them that his work is over and that he must get out of the way. But instead of giving his own funeral oration, he likens his situation to being the best man at a friend's wedding: "He who has the bride is the bridegroom; but the friend of the bridegroom, who stands and hears him, rejoices greatly because of the bridegroom's voice. Therefore, this joy of mine is fulfilled. He must increase, but I must decrease" (John 3:29-30).

What an ego-shaking condemnation of the right to *radical happiness!* Sooner or later, we learn that happiness is neither an inalienable right nor an end in itself. For the followers of Christ, the word is not "happiness," it is "joy"—a Biblical word that is always used in the context of submitting to the greatness and the glory of God.

The story of John the Baptist does not end here. When he says of Jesus, "He must increase, but I must decrease" (John 3:30), he does not know that it means prison and execution for him. Yet, after he has been jailed by Herod for telling the truth about the king's sin, John has his own moments of self-doubt. In the depressing setting of his dungeon, he begins to have second thoughts about being second: Is this the way my life will end? Have I been deluded? Is it worth it?

John sends his disciples to Jesus with a question of honest doubt, "Are You the Coming One, or do we look for another?" (Luke 7:20).

Jesus does not respond directly. Instead, he sends back the evidence and asks that John decide for himself: "Go your way and tell John the things you have seen and heard: that the blind see, the lame walk, the lepers are cleansed, the deaf hear, the dead are raised, the poor have the gospel preached to them. And blessed is he who is not offended because of Me" (Luke 7:22-23).

Jesus' response reads like a code between brothers. He reinforces John's faith, not by soft sympathy but by hard evidence based upon the fulfillment of prophecy. John can now go to his death knowing that his role as a messenger, however brief, is infinitely meaningful to the Kingdom of God and his decision to submit to the Christ is infinitely worthwhile.

Whether John ever heard it or not, Jesus honors him as no other human being when He tells His disciples: "Among those born of women there is not a greater prophet than John the Baptist . . ."

But then He makes room for all of us who are willing to follow John's example and become second to the Person and the power of Jesus Christ: ". . . but he who is least in the kingdom of God is greater than he" (Luke 7:28).

Jesus has been introduced as the Son of God by a great man and a true prophet.

AFFIRMED BY GOD

9 And it came to pass in those days that Jesus came from Nazareth of Galilee, and was baptized by John in the Jordan.

10 And immediately, coming up from the water, He saw the heavens opened and the Spirit descending upon Him like a dove.

11 And a voice came from heaven, "You are My beloved Son, in whom I am well pleased."

Mark 1:9–11

In natural sequence with John the Baptist's announcement, Mark brings Jesus on the scene. It is not a triumphal entry heralded by a trumpet fanfare. Rather, in his matter-of-fact "Who?" "What?" "When?" "Where?" "How?" "Why?" style, Mark reports ". . . *in those days that Jesus came from Nazareth of Galilee, and was baptized by John in the Jordan*" (v. 9). Here again, we see the genius of the author for sorting out events in order to balance the prosaic with the spectacular. By design, Mark brings a man with a common name from a common town to participate in a common experience—*God with us.* "Jesus" will be the name used by Mark until Peter confesses Him as the Christ at Caesarea Philippi (8:29). Nazareth is the town where Jesus lives in obscurity and labors as a carpenter. Whether or not He is fully conscious of His deity is an issue of scholarly debate. Certainly, He does not need to be baptized for His sins, but Mark puts the event in such a sequence with His common name and His common town that the baptism becomes an experience in which He shares our common humanity.

What a lesson for leadership. A friend told me about a miserable moment during his military training. The recruits had been ordered to the rifle range right after a rainstorm. Prone in the mud, they shot round after round. My friend said that he reached back in anger for shells from the soldier who was flat in the mud just behind him. Resentment rammed every shell into the chamber and hate squeezed the trigger. Then, perchance, as he reached back for another round, he caught the face of his companion out of the corner of his eye. It was his Commander! Flat in the mud and passing shells, the Commander was at one with his men. "From that time on," my friend said, "I was ready to follow that man, even to death." With equal insight into human nature, Mark knows that his case for Jesus as the Servant Leader begins with the evidence that He is on our level, beside us, and sharing our experience.

God's anointing of Jesus comes in a contrast that brings us to our knees. No sooner has thundering violence split the heavens in an awesome show of God's power than His Spirit takes the form of a dove to settle with a gentle flutter on Jesus. He is thus anointed as the One who comes, neither by might nor power, but by the tender Spirit of the Lord. Whereas we cannot stand before God's power, we will be saved by His Spirit. As we noted with John the Baptist, the man and the message are one. Stern of countenance and fiery of tongue, John the Baptist takes an ax to the root of the tree and preaches repentance "unto" the remission of sins. He can only prepare the way. But Jesus, common of person and gentle of Spirit, is anointed by God the Father as the Servant who will be made sin "for" the forgiveness of sins.

Affirmation follows the anointing: *"And a voice came from heaven, 'You are My beloved Son, in whom I am well-pleased' "* (v. 11).

Dare I say that all we need to know about our relationships with God and with each other is summed up in this declaration? God affirms His Son by saying, "I claim you, I love you, I am proud of you." How simple! How basic! *To belong, to be loved, to be praised!* Nothing more is needed in our relationship with God, our families and with each other.

To belong. God said to Jesus, "You are My . . . Son." Each of us has a desperate need to belong to someone. If that need is met, we have the strength of self-identity. We know who we are and no one can take that identity from us. But, if our need to belong is not met, we wander as lost and unclaimed souls. Psychiatrists find that the root of emotional disturbance is alienation, which is to be cut adrift from human identity and belong to no one.

An image comes to mind. During a visit to the students from Seattle Pacific University who are volunteers in Cambodian refugee camps, my wife and I are taken on hospital rounds with Dr. Michael Oh. As we enter the pediatric hut, a little girl wraps her arms around the doctor's thigh and hangs on. Her legs are twisted and knobby trunks, her eyes are dull with mental retardation, and her body is a mass of malfunctioning and malaria-filled organs. As if this is not enough, Dr. Oh explains that she is listed among the "unnamed" and the "unclaimed" because there is no trace of her parents or her family. She cannot be resettled, she cannot be returned. She belongs to no one.

Each of us needs a sense of family in order to belong to someone. We know who we are by our family names. For years, my son has been identified by his father's name. Now he has come fully into his own as a professor of psychology in a Christian college. Imagine my shock when the time came that I was introduced to someone who answered, "Oh, yes, you must be Dr. McKenna's father." My mind flipped to the telegram that Dr. O. Meredith Wilson is reputed to have sent to his father on the day that he was inaugurated as the President of the University of Minnesota. The wire from son to father read, "Remember whose father you are."

God sends a similar message to His Son and to the world at the time of Jesus' baptism. To Jesus, He gives the assurance, "You are My . . . Son. I claim you. You belong to Me." To the world, God gives this warning, "This is My . . . Son. Never forget it." Biblical scholars tell us that the *adoptive principle* is at work in these words. Of course, Jesus is the natural Son of God, but beyond that, He is also the chosen Son of God. There is a difference. Each of us is a natural son or daughter of our parents. We belong to them by nature. But not all of us are the chosen sons or daughters of our parents. Some may know the deep hurt of abandonment as orphans and others may feel the wound of rejection even while continuing as a member of the family. I personally know a bit of that hurt and feel some of these wounds. Perhaps that is why my proudest moments are the times when I introduce my children, "This is my son," or "This is my daughter." They are my natural children, but I also want the whole world to know that they are my chosen children. We belong to each other.

When God claims Jesus as His Son by choice as well as by nature, He sets the stage for our adoption. By nature, we are not the sons and daughters of God. Sin so separates us from God that, by law, we are unclaimed orphans and unnamed rejects. Ah, that is what redemption is all about. In Galatians 4:4–7, we read:

> But when the fullness of the time had come, God sent forth His Son, born of a woman, born under the law, to redeem those who were under the law, that we might receive the adoption as sons.

And because you are sons, God has sent forth the Spirit of His Son into your hearts, crying out, "Abba, Father!"

Therefore you are no longer a servant, but a son, and if a son, then an heir of God through Christ.

We are to whom we belong. "You are my son," "You are my daughter," is God's affirmation to us that we belong to Him. With Jesus, we have an identity which no one can take from us.

God also says to Jesus and to the world, *"You are my Beloved Son"* (v. 11). Closely linked with the need to belong is the *need to be loved.* Tragedy stalks any relationship where belonging is without love. Marriages that hang together on legal grounds without love are hells on earth for the partners and the children. The other day, a mature woman told me about her childhood when the only word spoken between her parents was a scream. During the hottest of those hostile days, she remembers running out of the house, up the street, and into her grandmother's arms, sobbing, "Hold me." To belong gives us our sense of identity, but we need to be loved for our security.

In John 15:13, God's love is presented to us as *self-sacrificing.* After Jesus says that He abides in His Father's love, He then tells us what kind of love it is: "Greater love has no one that this, that he lay down his life for his friends."

There is more. God's love for His Son is *unchangeable.* Love gets severely tested in human relationships. When God affirms Jesus with the words "I love you," He sets Him free to be Himself. The risk is obvious. A son may choose to be a prodigal, a daughter may make choices that lead to disaster. Unchanging love will hold when all other relationships have broken down.

Finally, the Scriptures lead us to the *controlling* love of God. In 2 Corinthians 5:14, there are the promising, but provocative words, "For the love of Christ constrains us. . . ." Love is a guidance system for our behavior. Because of love, there are certain things that we will do and certain things that we will not do.

When I was a high-schooler, movies were taboo. One night, I sneaked away to a movie with a friend. A strange twist of coincidence trapped me so that my father found out. The next day, he took me for a ride into the country. I was totally disarmed when he spoke so gently, "Did you enjoy the movie last night?" Bloodied by a clean cut, but unbowed, I gritted my teeth and answered, "Yes." A period of silence followed. Then, even more gently, my father said, "Son, if you choose to go to movies, I only ask that you do not use my money." I was devastated. I wanted to cry out, "Beat me, ground me, chew me out, but don't . . . don't . . . don't punish me with words that say I have betrayed your love." To this day, I remember that episode as the greatest licking I ever took.

There is no greater control over our lives than the control of love. When God tells His Son, "I love you," He puts His *self-sacrificing, unchangeable, inseparable* and *controlling* love on the line. Jesus has the security of a love that is willing to take a risk as well as a family identity that cannot be broken.

Now we come to the most fulfilling moment in a father-son relationship. God must have glowed when He commends Jesus, ". . . in whom I am well pleased." In speaking these words, God completes the triad of *belonging, love, and praise.*

Scripture and psychology reinforce the importance of praise. Jesus Himself says, "Rejoice with those who rejoice, and weep with those who weep" (Rom. 12:15). It is so much easier for us to weep together than to rejoice together. We are quick to cry, but slow to praise. This is particularly true with those who are the closest to us. Because of our own frustrations with our failure to achieve our aspirations, we transfer our dreams to our children as unrealistic aspirations. To compound our error, we either fail to praise them for their own achievements or roundly criticize them for not measuring up to our expectations. Fathers are always in danger of belittling their sons, and mothers are subject to the same temptation with their daughters.

When God says to His Son, "I am proud of you," He commends His character, honors His achievements, and encourages Him for the future. If only we can learn the same truth. Our family, our friends and our colleagues grow faster in the direction of our praise than in the path of our criticism. If only we can learn to give and receive a simple "Thank you," we, too, will release in others the confidence that God releases in His own Son.

Our lesson is simple. God not only anoints Jesus for service, but gives to His Son the strengths of identity, security and confidence when He says, "I claim you, I love you, I am proud of you." Jesus' credentials now include the affirmation of God the Father to go along with the announcement of John the Baptist.

ACKNOWLEDGED BY SATAN

12 And immediately the Spirit drove Him into the wilderness.

13 And He was there in the wilderness forty days, tempted by Satan, and was with the wild beasts; and the angels ministered to Him.

Mark 1:12–13

One more relationship, perhaps the most difficult of all, must be tested before Jesus can qualify for public service. "And immediately the Spirit drove Him into the wilderness" (v. 12). There is no time to bask in the glorious presence of the Spirit of God. Turned in His tracks as soon as He steps out of the water, Jesus finds Himself compelled to leave the glory and the glamour of the cool and crowded banks of the Jordan River for the white heat and hellish loneliness of the God-forsaken desert.

Do you remember the loneliest moment of your life? I was flying in a twin-engined airplane from Kalamazoo, Michigan, to Chicago, Illinois. Just after taking off into a dense fog, the right side of the aircraft flashed fire when the engine exploded. The captain assured us that emergency measures were being taken, but that we would have to turn back for an emergency landing at Kalamazoo. As the plane waffled and shuddered through the soupy sky, I looked around at forty other fear-paralyzed passengers and wrote in my daybook, "Lord, I'm not afraid to die, but I don't want to die alone among strangers." To paraphrase Coleridge, I felt:

> Alone, alone,
> All, all alone,
> Alone in the wide, wide sky.

Loneliness is created by drastic shifts from the emotional highs to the emotional lows of life. Actors and actresses say that the loneliest moment of their celebrated existence comes immediately after the last encore when they sit all alone in their dressing rooms. Jesus rides that roller-coaster from high to low because He has experienced the instant plunge from the shining glory of the presence of God at the Baptism into the dark night of the soul when He suddenly finds Himself all alone in the desert.

A hostile environment adds to the dread of loneliness. According to Mark, the Spirit drives Jesus into a desert peopled only by Satan and wild beasts.

On a trip to Arizona a few years ago, my wife, son and I took our first horseback ride into the desert. As we rode back into the hills, we encountered a silence that we had never known before. Sound seemed to disappear into the unfathomable blue of the desert sky. Even tumbleweeds and lizards moved as if they were partners in a conspiracy of silence. No one spoke a word. Refreshing waves of stillness washed over us. But after a couple of hours, the silence became unbearable. We longed for a human voice, a rushing wind, a cricket's whistle, or alas, even the sound of an auto horn. The dread of being all alone in the desert started to creep up into our beings. I remember thinking, "Imagine being all alone in this silence day after day." The silence that had been so refreshing turned into dread. All alone in the desert for forty days and forty nights, Jesus must have known the madness as well as the magnificence of that silence.

In the evening of the same day, I tested the desert once again. After the sun had gone down, I decided to jog along the winding roads on the edge of town. Once again, I ran into the silence of the desert. This time, the silence had a companion—blackness. I could see nothing at my feet, ahead of me, or around me. When I looked up, however, the stars were poking bright holes in the sky. My soul leaped into praise with the Psalmist, "When I consider thy heavens, the work of thy fingers, the moon and the stars, which thou hast ordained; What is man, that. . . . ?" (Ps. 8:3, 4, KJV).

I never finished. Out of the silence and the blackness came the most soul-piercing, bone-chilling scream that I had ever heard. I stopped dead, paralyzed with fear. Then, when the blood returned to my brain, I realized that I had heard my first coyote howl in the blackness of the desert. It is a close encounter of the first kind—stopping the heart, freezing the brain, and jellying the bones. The experience helps me understand why Mark chose to say that Jesus was all alone in the desert with only wild beasts for company.

There is another reason why Mark goes out of his way to mention "wild beasts." Remember that he is writing for Roman Christians whose unswerving faith is marching them straight into lions' mouths. One can almost hear the first hushed reading of Mark's Gospel among a fear-filled band of Christians who are huddled together around a candle in a catacomb. The phrase that seems so little to us flickers in their imagination and then becomes the bright flame of recognition as they bring together their plight with the hazards of Jesus in the wilderness. If they have to stand before the bared fangs of snarling lions tomorrow, Jesus is with them.

Mark has more to say about the circumstances of Jesus' temptation. A person's physical condition combines with emotional swings and a hostile environment to aggravate the dread of loneliness. Jesus fasts in the wilderness for forty days and forty nights. Psychologists who have studied hunger and starvation find a pattern that affects the mind. At first, the mind clears and food is not important, but as the body slows down, fantasies of sumptuous feasts flash into consciousness. If the person still does not eat, the fantasies disappear and food becomes unimportant once again, but depression sets in. Later on, the individual enters a stage when mental processes are numbed and suggestibility increases until the person becomes vulnerable to brainwashing and mind control. It is a loneliness where no one and no thing really matters. As a human being fasting for forty days and forty nights, Jesus subjects Himself to all of these dangers; particularly to the emotional and spiritual vulnerability that comes from prolonged hunger.

Most of us only know a loneliness that is partial and passing. Jesus knows the ultimate loneliness—total and prolonged. *Emotionally*, He has fallen from high to low; *environmentally*, He has been driven from the cheers of the baptism to the dread of the desert; and *physically*, He has been weakened by hunger until He is dangerously open to any temptation.

It is prime time for Satan to make his move. Finally revealed for what he is, the epitome of evil, Satan approaches a lonely, fearful and vulnerable Jesus with three well-known temptations—physical pleasure, personal success, and political power. Mark does not record the substance of the interchange between Jesus and Satan. He gives us only the setting, which in itself has three tests for a person who is alone in the desert. One is the test of *character;* the second is the test of *creativity;* and third is the test of *communion.*

Character is tested when a person is all alone. Each of us wears public masks—a serious mask for our daily work, a smiling mask for our moments with friends, and a pious mask when we enter the House of God. When we are all alone, these masks come off and our true character is the face we see in the mirror of our privacy. Stripped down to our root desires and our raw motives, we are most vulnerable to a Devil who prowls in the wilderness and consorts with our solitude.

Put yourself in Jesus' place. Satan whispers into His ear, "If You turn the stones into bread, who but You and I will ever know?" "If You throw Yourself down from the Temple, who but angels will ever be the witnesses?" "If You accept the kingdoms of the world, who but wild animals will ever share our secret?"

For most people, the threat of being alone with their true character is more than they can bear. They echo T. S. Eliot's words, "To be alone is hell."[3] Why? Because the core of their character is corrupt. The dread of loneliness is a direct result of sin.

Creativity is also tested when we are all alone. Strip away all of the intellectual, social and spiritual supports that prop us up and what resources do we have to stand alone?

One of the aboriginal tribes in the South Seas has a rite of passage from boyhood to manhood called a "walkabout." A boy coming to puberty is sent into the jungle for six weeks without food, shelter or weapons. During this time, he must test all of the survival skills he has learned during childhood. He must also be creative when he meets the unexpected. Talk about a final examination! One mistake and he is dead. If, however, he survives to walk out of the jungle, he returns to a celebration that honors him as a man, a hunter and a warrior.

Jesus' experience in the wilderness qualifies as a spiritual walkabout. His inner resources for survival and creativity are tested when He is all alone and tempted by the Devil. What resources does He have? Of course, He has the physical conditioning to survive a forty-day fast under the desert conditions of a blast furnace by day and a deep freeze by night. Yet, we know the critical test is spiritual, not physical. For His spiritual test of survival, Jesus has one resource— the Word of God. It is not a coincidence that Jesus answers Satan's tempting offers with only verbatim quotations from the Word of God. This fits the circumstances in which He finds Himself. Vulnerable to suggestion because of His weakened condition, Jesus knows that He cannot debate the Devil. A similar scene might be a Vietnam prisoner of war whose mind is dulled by starvation and beatings. Round-the-clock interrogation is used to get him to confess spying

41

or to strike a deal for a piece of bread. Instead, all that his captor can get from him is his name, rank, and serial number. So it is with Jesus. Physically weakened and psychologically beaten, He only answers, "It is written. . . . It is written. . . . It is written" (Luke 4:4–12). Jesus has a creative reservoir in the Word of God from which He can draw when all alone and tempted. He illustrates the Truth which we take so lightly, "Thy word have I hid in mine heart, that I might not sin against Thee" (Ps. 119:11, KJV).

Communion is the third test of being alone in the wilderness. Words are a weapon that we use to control people and situations. Most of us overtalk, interrupt, gossip, joke and shout as evidence of our insecurity. But all alone in the desert, you can shout to the winds and no one answers. Is that why we fear to be alone? In silence, it is God who speaks and God who controls. We do not want to hear what God has to say to us.

Jesus has neither a need to be talking all of the time nor a dread of being alone with God. For Him, the desert is a place where He enjoys unbroken communion with His Father. For Him, to use some Quaker thoughts, silence becomes the setting for "centering in" on the will of God and getting the "green light" for His public words and actions.

Thus, Jesus passes the tests of being alone—the tests of character, creativity, and communion—but not without a price. Mark concludes his brief description of the temptation experience by noting that angels minister to Jesus. Only one other time in Jesus' life does He need angels. After He has sweat drops of blood in the agony of the Garden, angels arrive to strengthen Him. Never let it be said that the experience of being all alone, hungry, threatened, vulnerable and tempted in the desert was easy because Jesus is the Son of God. He is also the Son of Man suffering under all of the fears that we have when we are all alone. Yet, through His suffering and His triumph in the desert, Jesus redeems our loneliness. No longer is it *loneliness,* the dread of the unbeliever; it is *solitude,* the desire of the Christian. Satan must retreat as the loser of the first round in his cosmic struggle with Jesus, the Son of God.

Announced by man, affirmed by God, and acknowledged by Satan, Jesus has His credentials in order for the opening of His public ministry. No one can dispute His qualifications or His references as Christ, the Son of God. The next question is whether or not His service will equal His credentials.

NOTES

1. Charles Dickens, *A Tale of Two Cities* (New York: Macmillan, 1918), p. 3.

2. Ernest Hemingway, *The Old Man and the Sea* (New York: Scribner's, 1952), p. 5.

3. T. S. Eliot, "A Cocktail Party," in Ralph L. Woods, *World Treasury of Religious Quotations*, p. 431.

CHAPTER TWO

Outlining His Mission

Mark 1:14–39

His Message

14 Now after John was put in prison, Jesus came
to Galilee, preaching the gospel of the kingdom of
God,

15 and saying, "The time is fulfilled, and the
kingdom of God is at hand. Repent and believe in
the gospel."

Mark 1:14–15

A clean, surgical cut needs to be made between John the Baptist
and Jesus in order to avoid confusion over their identities, their time,
their place and their message. John the Baptist came as the prophetic
voice in the wilderness of Judea, preceding the Christ, and preaching
the message of repentance. Jesus comes as the anointed servant of
God into Galilee, preaching and personifying the Good News of the
Kingdom of God.

Mark sounds the note of joy every time he mentions the Good
News of the Gospel. It is Jesus, however, who writes the music in
a four-note theme. The Good News is *timely, available, decisive,* and
assuring.

The Good News is timely. Time is one of the most important resources
of God and man. The difference is that God effectively uses time
to fulfill His purpose while man struggles with the tendency to waste
time by "killing it," "delaying it," "polluting it," or "ignoring it."
Jesus gives us insight into God's use of time by announcing, "The

44

time is fulfilled." His words put the resource of time into an eternal, historical and present perspective. Eternity echoes through His words as He reaches back into God's original purpose for His creation and catches on to His role as the Lamb who is slain from the foundations of the world. Time speeds on, then, through Biblical history as we hear again the prophets announce the appearance of John the Baptist and the coming of the Messiah. Eternity and history converge once more when John is put into prison and Jesus appears in Galilee.

Urgency is built into the phrase, "The time is fulfilled." If the appearance of Jesus echoes the timelessness of eternity, vibrates with the continuity of history, and peaks with the finality of judgment, no one can afford to dally. There is a *radical now,* not with the secular meaning which squeezes all time into the urgent gratification of the senses, but with the Biblical meaning that gives urgency to our response to the coming of Christ. When I was young, evangelists petrified me with horror stories about people who had crossed the "deadline" when they did not respond to the call of salvation. Even though those evangelists perverted their ministerial prerogative by taking God's time into their own hands, they had an urgency that has been lost today in the preaching of the gospel. Today, we presume upon God's time and patience by acting as if the timing for salvation belongs to us and the urgency belongs in the past to hellfire and brimstone preachers. Not so. The timing is God's and the urgency is Biblical. Every sermon that is preached and every witness that is given must carry the tone of an urgent call. Our life and God's patience are short when it comes to the decision about His Son.

How do the weightier matters of God's timing, so sober and so judgmental, get transformed into Good News? For the Jewish people who have waited three hundred years for a prophet and thousands of years for a Messiah, the answer is obvious. Wait no longer, your Messiah has come. The desire of all nations is fulfilled and the longing of all men is satisfied. Jesus puts Himself at the peak of history and gives us our ever-present hope.

The Good News is available. As the second note of His theme, Jesus tells us that the Good News comes in near-space as well as present-time when He says, *"the kingdom of God is at hand"* (v. 15). Counterbalancing the awesome and urgent impact of His announcement, *"The time is fulfilled,"* He now brings the distant Kingdom of God close and tempers the judgmental power of God with the personal grace of His Son. At one time, I heard a scholar say that an accurate paraphrase of Jesus' words would be "the Kingdom of God is within your reach." How contrary to the teaching of the Pharisees who made the Kingdom of God so distant and so impersonal. Each of us has a bit of the Pharisee in us. Even though we know that a person who reaches out to Christ in simple faith is immediately welcomed into the Kingdom of God, we still set up many hurdles over which new believers must jump. A follow-up study of the persons who made decisions for Christ in a Billy Graham Crusade condemns those of us who want to keep the Kingdom of God out of the reach of sinners. The report shows that the decisions for Christ were genuine, and yet, a very small percentage of new believers became members of a local church after their conversion. Why? A sad conclusion follows. The churches had no provision for bringing someone else's converts into their fellowship of faith.

They are not alone. If you were to take a poll of the average man on the street, he would probably say that Christians are not conveying the message that "the Kingdom of God is at hand, reach out and take it." Instead, he would probably report the impression that Christians are saying, "The Kingdom of God is distant, and you must jump over many hurdles to get in."

The Good News is decisive. "Repent" (v. 15) is the third note of the Good News. Echoing and affirming the message of John the Baptist, Jesus does not shrink from the confession of sin. People expect that preaching will lead to a call for a decision. In this case, Jesus calls people to turn 180 degrees from the direction in which they are going and begin to walk back toward God.

"Repent" has been reduced to a whisper in popular preaching. A prominent preacher walked out on a sermon in which a colleague insisted that the Gospel included repentance that cut through to the quick of the sinner's heart. Explaining his one-man protest march, he said that contemporary man needs a message of hope, not fear. He spoke only half the truth. Surely, the people to whom Jesus speaks need hope more than fear. Ground under the heel of Roman might, they have lost the political freedom that we enjoy today. Cowed by the legalistic whip of Pharisaical religion, they do not know the spiritual liberty that the Gospel gives to us. Beaten down by the poverty of the land and by a corrupted system of taxes and usury, they are aliens to the affluence which gauges our standard of living. If anyone deserves a message of hope, they do. Yet, Jesus preaches repentance which calls out the recognition of guilt and the hatred of sin. Is Jesus cruel? Not at all. Sin is the universal human condition and until our sin is acknowledged and confessed, there is no hope. Strange as it may seem, a prominent psychiatrist walks in where a prominent preacher walks out. Karl Menninger, in his book *Whatever Became of Sin?*, sums up his years of counseling experience by challenging preachers,

> What shall we cry?
> Cry comfort, cry repentance, cry hope.
> Because recognition of our part in the
>   world's transgression is the only
>   remaining hope.[1]

Is Jesus' message to contemporary Christians any different? Of course not. Repentance is still the prelude to the hope and the prior condition for the Good News. Because we are politically free, economically fat, and spiritually flourishing, Jesus would probably begin His public ministry among us by calling "Repent" more than once, just for the sake of accent.

The Good News is assuring. "Believe in the gospel" (v. 15) is the fourth and final note of the Good News theme. It is an act that complements repentance. To repent is to reverse the direction in which we are going; to believe is to move with full speed and reckless abandon in the new direction. Elton Trueblood puts it in terms of an eternal gamble when he writes, "To be a Christian is to bet your life that Christ is right."[2]

"Belief" also carries with it the assurance of rest. Rather than perpetually fighting with the jots and tittles of legalistic religion, Jesus makes simple trust the basis for spiritual relief. With that assurance, all of the unlimited resources of grace become available to the believer. What started out as the Good News has now become the Better News and Best News. Jesus is the superlative message.

Rotarians agree to abide by a Four-Way Test as the standard for their business and personal relationships: (1) Is it the truth?; (2) Is it fair to all concerned?; (3) Will it build good will and better friendship?; and (4) Will it be beneficial to all concerned?[3] At the opening of His public ministry, Jesus also proposes a four-way test—not a human ethic to be achieved by human effort, but a divine word of hope given by the grace of God. Jesus asks of the Gospel, "Is it timely?" "Is it available?" "Is it decisive?" and "Is it promising?" If it is, we have the Good News. If it is not, we have something less than the Gospel of Jesus Christ; something short of the message that Jesus will now put into practice.

HIS MEN

> 16 Now as He walked by the Sea of Galilee, He saw Simon and Andrew his brother casting a net into the sea; for they were fishermen.
> 17 And Jesus said to them, "Come after Me, and I will make you become fishers of men."
> 18 And immediately they left their nets and followed Him.
> 19 And when He had gone a little farther from there, He saw James the son of Zebedee, and John his brother, who also were in the boat mending their nets.
> 20 And immediately He called them, and they left their father Zebedee in the boat with the hired servants, and went after Him.
>
> *Mark 1:16–20*

Jesus cannot accomplish His mission alone. He needs friends whom He can trust, disciples whom He can teach, and co-workers who will share His task. So, after publicly announcing the Good News, He starts selecting good men.

What are the qualifications that He seeks in Simon, Andrew, James and John as He walks among the fishing boats along the Sea of Galilee? Jesus calls, *"Come after Me, and I will make you become fishers of men"* (v. 17), as the basis for selecting His staff. Those who answer are asked to be trustworthy, teachable and task-oriented.

"Come after Me" is a test of *trust.* Along the line of trust flows loyalty, confidence and openness. If that line is cut or frayed, all other relationships deteriorate. Over a period of twenty-five years in college administration, I have worked with four executive secretaries—Bonnie, Gladys, Bernie, and Cec. Our work is always demanding and my style borders on chaos. Bernie is the one who said, "At least our office is never dull." But underneath the heavy work and the high pressure are sensitive and classified matters requiring full confidence—personal contracts, hate mail, legal briefs, morals charges, private memos, and the untold story behind executive decisions. Never once has our mutual trust been violated. We respect each other as colleagues and we love each other as friends. Without that strong line of trust, we could not survive the work and the pressure of the president's office.

Jesus needs the same trust in the men whom He chooses. Ironically, He calls Peter first, and it is Peter who will break the line of loyalty when He denies His Lord. In that tragic moment, Jesus will look at him as if to say, "Peter, I trusted you." One look speaks a thousand words. Peter goes out and weeps bitterly. Loyalty is the first qualification for discipleship.

Jesus also chooses *teachable* men. When He calls, "Come after Me, and *I will make you become* fishers of men," He promises a lifelong learning and growth process. Not by accident, He chooses unschooled and unsophisticated fishermen. What a miserable start for world evangelization. We must never forget that Jesus knows what He is doing. He wants teachable men without intellectual preconceptions or cultural mindsets that will be insurmountable barriers to Truth.

I am a self-made tennis player, modestly successful in a game built upon bad habits. A tennis lesson destroys me because I begin trading confidence in bad strokes for hesitation with good strokes. Of all the students of tennis, I am the worst kind because I must unlearn bad habits before I can stamp in the good ones. My twelve-year-old son is just the opposite. With nothing to unlearn, he strokes the ball better after three lessons than I do after thirty years. Without a doubt, he will be the first of my sons to beat me.

The learning principle is obvious. *It is easier to learn than it is to unlearn.* Jesus chooses men who have little to unlearn. Like hungry fledglings with their mouths wide open, they have nothing to hinder the process of becoming "fishers of men." Teachability is second only to trust.

Jesus also wants *task-oriented* men. "I will make you become fishers of men," speaks volumes about the task to which the disciples are called and the results that can be expected. Jesus knows the skills that are required to catch fish, and He does not hesitate to liken them to the skills of catching men. Fishing of both kinds is a science and an art. Without the discipline of learned skills and the intuition of natural gifts, the net will come up empty. For His disciples, Jesus wants men who have learned the science and sensed the art of fishing. Why? He needs men who are ready to live with the consequences of their work. To invoke the language of today, Jesus needs men who live by the "bottom line." Fishermen fit the definition. If they don't get a catch, they starve; but if they exercise the discipline of scientists and the sensitivity of artists, their nets come up full.

A leader never calls followers to a one-way commitment. The leader-follower relationship is a covenant. When Jesus calls, *"Come after Me"* (v. 17), He does not presume that He is the Master with the expectations all on the side of the disciples. With equal force, He is saying, "If I can trust you to follow, you can trust me to lead." He makes a commitment to be their *model.*

Jesus also agrees to be the *mentor* of teachable men. He commits Himself to all of the pains and all of the pleasures of being a teacher, watching men who are sometimes sharp and sometimes dull, sometimes growing by leaps and sometimes regressing by bounds, sometimes succeeding, but more often than not, failing in order to try again.

By choosing task-oriented men, Jesus commits Himself to be the *manager* of their tasks. A manager is like the conductor of an orchestra, he must know the limits and the potential of his players. If he pushes them beyond their limits, they will falter in frustration. If he fails to stretch them to their potential, they will fail to grow. Someplace in between is the delicate balance where the leader makes the difference. Jesus has uncanny skill at reading the readiness of His disciples for service. On their first field trip as "fishers of men," they return with eyes as big as saucers to report, *". . . even the unclean spirits . . . obey Him"* (1:27). The next time out, they slink back to Him asking, *"Why could we not cast him out?"* (9:28). Jesus makes a commitment to bring along those whom He calls at a pace equal to their skills until they will qualify as "fishers of men."

What is the "flair factor" that separates Simon, Andrew, James and John from all of the other fishermen who hear Jesus call? It is the ability to make a clean and firm decision. In each case, Mark invokes his favorite word, "immediately," to describe the fishermen's response to Jesus' call. *"Immediately they left their nets"* (v. 18), *"and immediately . . . they left their father"* (v. 20), assures us that the men whom Jesus chooses for his disciples are men who can make decisions.

Jesus still calls for trustworthy, teachable and task-oriented persons to be His disciples. In turn, He promises to be our model, our mentor, and our manager. The covenant is the secret for winning the world.

His Authority

21 And they went into Capernaum, and immediately on the Sabbath He entered the synagogue and taught.

22 And they were astonished at His teaching, for He taught them as one having authority, and not as the scribes.

23 And there was a man in their synagogue with an unclean spirit. And he cried out,

24 saying, "Let us alone! What have we to do with You, Jesus of Nazareth? Have You come to destroy us? I know who You are—the Holy One of God!"

25 And Jesus rebuked him, saying, "Be quiet, and come out of him!"

26 And when the unclean spirit had convulsed him and cried out with a loud voice, he came out of him.

27 And they were all amazed, so that they questioned among themselves, saying, "What is this? What new doctrine is this? For with authority He commands even the unclean spirits, and they obey Him."

28 And immediately His fame spread throughout all the region around Galilee.

29 And as soon as they had come out of the synagogue, they entered the house of Simon and Andrew, with James and John.

30 But Simon's wife's mother lay sick with a fever, and right away they told Him about her.

31 And He came and took her by the hand and lifted her up, and immediately the fever left her. And she served them.

32 And at evening, when the sun had set, they brought to Him all who were sick and those who were demon-possessed.

33 And the whole city was gathered together at the door.

34 And He healed many who were sick with various diseases, and cast out many demons; and He did not allow the demons to speak, because they knew Him.

Mark 1:21–34

Mark invites us into a day with Jesus. Having chosen Capernaum as His home base for the Galilean ministry, Jesus immediately goes to the synagogue as the logical starting place for His teaching. To their credit, the congregation at Capernaum listens to Jesus' teaching, responds with astonishment and acknowledges His superior authority. Students of organizational theory define "authority" according to its source. A king, for instance, has "inherited authority" by virtue of having been born into a royal line. The president of a corporation exercises "delegated authority" which comes from the board of directors. A professor in a university has "achieved authority" based upon years of academic preparation, research and experience. In each case, the source of authority is outside the person who holds the power to rule a kingdom, run a business, or teach a class.

When the people at Capernaum acknowledge that Jesus teaches with an authority that is distinct from the authority of the scribes, their insight does not necessarily demean the function of the scribes. According to Hebrew tradition, scribes are scholars of the Law who interpret it to the people and decide the cases in dispute. Attorneys-at-law are their contemporary counterparts, and neither ancient scribes nor today's attorneys find the source of law within themselves. They are at their best when they interpret the law accurately and impartially. Their authority is not their own, it is ascribed from the law itself.

Jesus' authority, which astonished the people, differed from the authority of the scribes in kind, not by degree. When He taught in the synagogue, He referred to no source of authority beyond Himself. *He is the source of authority.* Without saying it, Jesus lays claim to be the Christ, the Son of God. No person on earth has had or ever will have the "inherent authority" of Jesus. Is it any wonder that the people in the synagogue at Capernaum were astonished?

Two other reactions follow the recognition of Jesus' divine authority. One comes from the demons within a man who interrupts the orderly service of the synagogue with cries of confrontation. In this case, the demons scream their acknowledgement that Jesus has the power to destroy them. What a confession of the Christ! What a telling point for Mark's case to prove that Jesus is the Christ, the Son of God! Even a demon bows in the confession, *"I know who You are—the Holy One of God!"* (v. 24). Whenever the authority of Jesus Christ, the Son of God, is invoked in teaching or preaching, there is a violent, convulsive confrontation with the demons who possess our souls and rule our lives. The Good News of the Gospel does not exclude a confrontation with demons. In fact, it may be a test of the authority which we invoke. Is it Christ or us?

Once the news of Jesus' matchless authority begins to spread, more than demons respond. Hope begins to stir in needy people *"who were sick with various diseases"* (v. 34). Strange, isn't it? The same authority that aggravates demons awakens hope in the helpless.

Mark uses Peter's mother-in-law as a specific example of Jesus translating His authority for teaching into the power to heal. She lies in bed with fever until Jesus takes her by the hand, lifts her up, and immediately the fever leaves her. As proof of her healing, she serves them their meal.

Late into evening, Jesus pays the price for revealing his authority in the synagogue. Out of the darkness come the sick and the demon-possessed, one to be graciously lifted up, the other to be convulsively cleansed. Jesus' authority for cleansing and healing is as much the Good News as His message that the time has come and the Kingdom is near, *". . . Repent and believe in the Gospel"* (1:15).

His Field

35 And in the morning, having risen a long while before daylight, He went out and departed to a solitary place; and there He prayed.
36 And Simon and those who were with Him searched for Him.
37 And when they had found Him, they said to Him, "Everyone is looking for You."
38 And He said to them, "Let us go into the next towns, that I may preach there also, because for this purpose I have come forth."
39 And He was preaching in their synagogues throughout all Galilee, and casting out demons.

Mark 1:35–39

Temptation continues to buffet Jesus from many sides. After a successful day in which He casts out demons and heals the sick, He runs the risk of exhausting His energies and losing His perspective.

53

Jesus needs solitude. So, long before daylight on the morning after His day of success, He goes alone and prays.

When His disciples find Him, they bring the news that everyone is looking for Him. Except for the hours of solitude in the presence of His Father, Jesus might have succumbed to the seductive appeal of instant success and unbounded popularity by staying in Capernaum. But wisdom tells Him that today's ticker-tape can become tomorrow's brickbats. Answering Simon and the disciples, He says, *"Let us go into the next towns, that I may preach there also, because for this purpose I have come forth"* (v. 38). Security is always a temptation that stands off against risk. Yet, in the purpose of God, the movement is always forward through open doors and into wider horizons. Christians who have stopped going and growing are the most miserable of creatures. They clog up churches with undue caution and infect the Body of Christ with their own frustration. They are inventors of paralysis by analysis and the creators of strangulation by regulation. Thank God, Jesus chooses risk over security. He has no idea whether He will meet the rejection of Nazareth or the fame of Capernaum in the next town down the road, but to fulfill the purpose for which He came, He goes on.

A few years ago, I invited Billy Graham to be the commencement speaker at Seattle Pacific University. Commencement is a grand occasion of celebration for us, held in the exquisite Seattle Opera House with a capacity crowd. Pulling out all stops, I glamorized the invitation for Dr. Graham. He listened patiently, mused a moment and then answered, "David, I am flattered by your invitation, but I must say 'No.' You see, God has called me to be an evangelist, preaching the Gospel to sinners. I would find it a joy to be with you, knowing that I would be among Christian friends, but if I said 'Yes,' I would have to turn down an invitation to preach where other men have not preached." Graciously and humbly, Billy Graham shared the motive of Jesus when He said, *"Let us go into the next towns"* (v. 38). If all Christians followed Jesus in taking their witness to the next person, the next neighborhood, the next town, and the next nation, The Great Commission would soon be fulfilled.

The credentials of Jesus are confirmed and His mission is clear. He has been announced by man, affirmed by God and acknowledged by the Devil. His message is Good News, His men are potential leaders, His authority is all-powerful and His field of ministry is, step by step and town by town, the whole world.

NOTES

1. Karl Menninger, *Whatever Became of Sin?* (New York: Hawthorn Books, 1973).

2. Elton Trueblood, *A Place to Stand* (New York: Harper & Row, 1969), p. 60.

3. Rotary 4-Way Test of the Things We Say or Do (copyright 1946, Rotary International).

CHAPTER THREE

Introducing His Kingdom

Mark 1:40—3:6

MINISTRY OF COMPASSION

40 And a leper came to Him, imploring Him, kneeling down to Him and saying to Him, "If You are willing, You can make me clean."

41 Then Jesus, moved with compassion, put out His hand and touched him, and said to him, "I am willing; be cleansed."

42 And as soon as He had spoken, immediately the leprosy left him, and he was cleansed.

43 And He strictly warned him and sent him away at once.

44 And He said to him, "See that you say nothing to anyone; but go your way, show yourself to the priest, and offer for your cleansing those things which Moses commanded, as a testimony to them."

45 But he went out and began to proclaim it freely, and to spread the matter, so that Jesus could no longer openly enter the city, but was outside in deserted places; and they came to Him from every quarter.

Mark 1:40–45

Legalistic religion stalks the steps of Jesus as He preaches in the synagogues of the cities of Galilee. Like two large ships on a crash course with no time for turning, a collision is inevitable. His Good News challenges the drudgery of the Law; His authority threatens the legitimacy of the scribes; and His concern for human need tears at the traditions of the established church. It happens so naturally and so innocently. When Jesus takes compassion upon a leper and touches him, He is propelled into an era of contending for the Truth against a dead orthodoxy and deadly opponents.

Relive the scene with Jesus when the leper comes to Him, violating the taboos by begging, kneeling and speaking to Him, *"If you are willing, You can make me clean"* (v. 40). These are the words of a person with one last desperate hope. Even then, with a life history of disappointment, he qualifies his pleading with the contingency, ***"If You are willing,*** *You can make me clean."*

Here is the early and yet ultimate test of the feelings of Jesus. During His ministry, He will meet the full range of physical needs— blindness, blood disease, epilepsy, palsy, paralysis, and even insanity. But of all these diseases, leprosy is the symbol of hopelessness. A leper is not only considered physically incurable, but he also suffers under social rejection and spiritual condemnation. Never forget, Jesus hears the scum of the earth cry out, "If You are willing, You can make me clean."

Philip Yancey, in his helpful book *Where Is God When It Hurts,* singles out leprosy as the most hopeless of all diseases. Physically, leprosy seems incurable because it reverses the pain process. Most diseases have pain as an early warning system that helps in healing. Leprosy is just the opposite. The disease destroys the signal system for pain, leaving the body without its natural protection against self-destruction. A leper is burned, cut and broken without the warning of pain. Skin falls off, fingers, arms, toes, and legs die and drop away in defiance of the normal process of the body to heal itself. In the absence of pain, the leper loses the hope of healing.

Leprosy is also a hopeless social disease. Because lepers are so grotesque, respectable society labels them contagious and sends them into exile. It is one thing to be condemned to die, but it is quite another thing to die in isolation. Lepers are to cry out, "Unclean, Unclean," wherever they walk. Decent people avoid the contamination of even their shadows.

Here is the test. Before Jesus' ministry has gained full momentum, He meets a leper who cries out from the outer edge of human need, "If you are willing, You can make me clean." What will Jesus do? If He can love, touch and heal a leper, everyone else has hope. What will Jesus do?

Mark leaves no doubt about Jesus' response. As Peter remembers it: "Then Jesus, moved with compassion, put out His hand and touched him, and said to him, 'I am willing; be cleansed'" (Mark 1:41).

To match the most difficult of human needs, Jesus responds with the deepest of human feelings. As with us, Jesus knows the full range of human emotion. He knows cheer, anger, disappointment, laughter, sighing, displeasure, surprise, impatience, exhilaration, and depression. Among all of these feelings, compassion stands out as the deepest of all human emotions and as the truest expression of the heart of Jesus. The word "compassion" derives from the same Greek word that means "viscera, bowels, intestines," or in our vernacular, "guts." When we read that Jesus is moved with compassion, it means that He feels Himself so deeply into the sufferings of the leper that it is just as if He Himself is suffering as a leper. Jesus is not moved with pity—that is too condescending; not with sympathy—that is too superficial; not with empathy—that is too distant. Not just mind for mind, hand for hand, or even heart for heart, but stomach for stomach, blood for blood, gut for gut, Jesus feels His way into the leper's needs.

To feel with compassion is not enough. Jesus reaches out and touches the leper! Violating every medical warning and risking every social taboo, Jesus lets the leper know that He will take his place—not just in the risk of physical contagion, but in social contamination as well. How little we know of true compassion!

My wife and I edged up to the meaning of compassion when we got a midnight telephone call from our son-in-law in the Midwest. He told us that our daughter, his wife, was two months pregnant, but as children are wont to do, she had kept it a secret until she could tell us personally. They hadn't counted on a Saturday night miscarriage. Our son-in-law informed us that Debi had been rushed into emergency surgery in order to save her life. The surgery was predicted to last for about two hours and he would call us as soon as she came out.

We learned long distance what it means to have compassion. If time had permitted, no airplane would have flown across the country without us on it. Instead, we had to wait, suffer, and pray. No sleep came to my wife or me. Quite the opposite, we became physically sick, particularly after one hour edged into two, and two crawled through eternity into three hours without a word. Stomach for stomach, blood for blood, we were in an emergency room in Lansing, Michigan, with our daughter until word came that all was well.

In this case, the life of our beautiful daughter, whom we love so deeply, was at stake, and we were moved with compassion. Transfer that same love and those same feelings to Jesus, who reaches out and touches a leper who is just one among many of the wretched of the earth. Again, I say, how little we know about compassion. Why? Because compassion is so costly.

Jesus has a choice to make. Will He respond to the leper at the risk of limiting His ministry and prematurely provoking the opposition of the established church? Or will He reject the leper at the risk of losing the purpose for which He has come, "Not . . . to be served, but to serve, and to give His life a ransom for many" (10:45)? Jesus chooses the leper, but not without a price. Instead of presenting himself to the priest and entering the ritual for cleansing, the leper becomes a one-man whirlwind telling the story of his cleansing wherever he goes.

What a cost for compassion! Jesus has to give up His ministry in that city for the sake of a single soul. From now on, the people will have to come to Him in out-of-the-way, desert places. More than that, the leper's lips set the edge of legal opposition to Jesus. Conflict now becomes His never-ending and ever-escalating fact of life.

MINISTRY OF FORGIVENESS

1 And again He entered Capernaum after some days, and it was heard that He was in the house.

2 And immediately many gathered together, so that there was no longer room to receive them, not even near the door. And He preached the word to them.

3 And they came to Him, bringing a paralytic who was carried by four men.

4 And when they could not come near Him because of the crowd, they uncovered the roof where He was. And when they had broken through, they let down the bed on which the paralytic was lying.

5 When Jesus saw their faith, He said to the paralytic, "Son, your sins are forgiven you."

6 But some of the scribes were sitting there and reasoning in their hearts,

7 "Why does this Man speak blasphemies like this? Who can forgive sins but God alone?"

8 And immediately, when Jesus perceived in His spirit that they reasoned thus within themselves, He said to them, "Why do you reason about these things in your hearts?

9 "Which is easier, to say to the paralytic, 'Your sins are forgiven you,' or to say, 'Arise, take up your bed and walk'?

10 "But that you may know that the Son of Man has power on earth to forgive sins"—He said to the paralytic,

11 "I say to you, arise, take up your bed, and go your way to your house."

12 And immediately he arose, took up the bed, and went out in the presence of them all, so that all were amazed and glorified God, saying, "We never saw anything like this!"

Mark 2:1–12

Mark, as we have learned, is the master of time gaps. Rather than getting bogged down in the details of Jesus' restricted ministry in the wilderness, he skips forward to the re-entry into Capernaum. Jesus left in triumph, He returns under suspicion. Evidently, the word of the cleansed leper who disobeyed orders precedes Jesus to Capernaum. When He heals the leper, He hopes that He can still serve the needs of man and stay within the system. That hope has vanished. All around Him are critical eyes squinting to find fault with every action and skeptical tongues wagging at the implications of every utterance. Jesus has no choice but to confront the system and challenge its dead orthodoxy. The situation opens up a new facet of His personality. While still responding tenderly to people in need, Jesus reveals His ability to take the intellectual initiative, exercise irrefutable logic, and leave his opponents feeling as if they had entered a battle of wits unarmed. In the contest over Jesus' authority to forgive sins, Mark gives us intriguing insights into the mind of Jesus.

The meaning of "mind" is like a diamond with many facets as you turn it over in the light. One facet is to interpret the word to mean, "frame of mind," or to use a popular word, "mindset." Each of us has a certain "mindset" of preconceptions built out of our beliefs, our values and our experiences. What is the mindset of Jesus?

Another facet of meaning for the word "mind" is "inclinations or leanings of the mind." There is a difference between the "frame" of mind and the "leanings" of the mind. The "frame of mind" tends to be static and thus reactive to new ideas and experiences. "Leanings of the mind" are dynamic and proactive, neither fixed nor fickle, but clearly moving in a given direction. Psychologists label these leanings of the mind as "predispositions." Can we paraphrase Paul's admonition (Phil. 2:5) by saying, "Let the leanings of mind be in you which were also in Christ Jesus"?

Turn the diamond word "mind" into the light one more time. Behind the other definitions of "mind" is the root word "diaphragm." Greeks linked mental and emotional functions with parts of the physical body. When they thought about "mind," they chose the diaphragm, the membrane that operates involuntarily to control the life-giving process of breathing. To them, the mental processes were as natural as breathing. Dare we pray, "Let this mind be in me which was also in Christ Jesus, moment by moment, as natural as breathing"?

Mark's account of the healing of the paralytic man illustrates the mind of Jesus at work (vv. 1–12). While He is preaching in a crowded house in Capernaum, Jesus is startled by the debris falling on His head as a hole is being opened in the ceiling. Certainly, His preaching is interrupted by the sight of a stretcher being lowered through the hole by four pairs of willing hands and guided by four pairs of mischievous eyes. In response, Jesus speaks to the helpless creature, *"Son, your sins are forgiven you"* (v. 5).

Spontaneity is a quality of Jesus' mind. As natural as breathing, He speaks forgiveness. At first, the response seems inappropriate. Unless sin is the cause of paralysis, the poor man needs healing. Is Jesus playing into the hands of the legalists in the Law who contend that a man cannot be forgiven until he is healed of his sickness? By making sin the cause of sickness, they can justify neglect for millions of sick people throughout their land. On other occasions, Jesus categorically rejects the idea that sin is synonymous with sickness. Yet, in this moment of surprise, when a bed comes down through the roof, He responds as if the healing and forgiveness are inseparable. They are, but not in a linkage of cause and effect. Jesus' startled response reveals the natural breathing of His mind. It is to see men as whole beings needing forgiveness. *Forgiveness* is the set of His mind. Forgiveness is the leaning of His thoughts. Forgiveness is the breathing of His Spirit.

The scribes in this story show us another mindset. When they hear Jesus speak the words of forgiveness, they too are surprised and respond as naturally as their breathing. But what a difference. As scholars with an orthodox mindset, theological leanings and the natural breathings of inquiry, they spontaneously begin to argue, *"Why does this Man speak blasphemies like this? Who can forgive sins but God alone?"* (v. 7). Their questions expose the essential nature of their minds. God has to be re-created in the image of their orthodoxy. At the center of their minds is a God so small that forgiveness can only flow through the rut of their own ritual. Taken by surprise, they show how far they have strayed from the mind of God.

The mumbled questions of the scribes bring out the *sensitivity* of Jesus' mind. *"And immediately, when Jesus perceived in His Spirit that they reasoned thus within themselves, He said to them, 'Why do you reason about these things in your hearts?'"* (v. 8). His sensitivity to what the scribes are saying becomes an example for us. Jesus is fully present in any situation in which He finds Himself and, therefore, tuned to all of the cues from the people around Him. When He is in Capernaum, He is not mentally halfway to the next town. When He is introduced to a person, He is not shaking hands and looking over his or her shoulder to the next one in line. When He is preaching a sermon, He is not rethinking His last debate. A mind that is fully present in a given setting becomes keenly alert to a stir in the audience, a change in facial expression, or a mumbling word. A public speaker, for instance, who is the prisoner of his notes, cannot perceive and respond to the restlessness of his audience during a flat spot in his speech. A true master of speech, however, will be constantly in interaction with his audience. Jesus has learned to listen as well as to speak; to feel as well as to act; to see as well as to look.

Jesus' answer to the questions of the scribes adds the quality of *sharpness* to His mind—reason for reason, logic for logic, question for question. His counter tactic is to ask, *"Which is easier, to say to the paralytic, 'Your sins are forgiven you,' or to say, 'Arise, take up your bed and walk'?"* (v. 9). Jesus asks a rhetorical question. It is infinitely easier to heal the body than it is to forgive sins. The scribes are confounded. They have no answer.

Even though Jesus seems to relish intellectual combat, He does not let it become an end in itself. Along with His sharpness of mind,

He also shows us His *sureness of mind*. After raising the rhetorical ques
tion, *"Which is easier, to say to the paralytic, 'Your sins are forgiven you' or
to say, 'Arise, take up your bed and walk'?"* He goes on to say, *"But that
you may know that the Son of Man has power on earth to forgive sins . . . I
say to you, 'Arise, take up your bed, and go your way to your house'"* (vv. 9–
11). Such a statement can only come from a man whose mind is
settled. Jesus knows Himself, His mission, and His authority. For
the first time in the Gospel of Mark, Jesus declares Himself to be
the Son of Man with power on earth to forgive sins. His opponents
fall silent before the indisputable logic and the authentic ring of a
sure mind.

A mind that is spontaneous, sensitive, sharp and sure could be
the mind of a spoiled prodigy or an arrogant genius. Jesus is saved
from both of these mental malfunctions by the *submission* of His mind
to the will of God. The conclusion of Mark's story about the healing
of the paralytic man attests submission as the crowning quality of
the mind of Jesus: *"And immediately he arose, took up the bed, and went out
in the presence of them all, so that all were amazed and* **glorified God,** *saying,
'We never saw anything like this!'"* (v. 12).

The proof of Jesus' submission of mind is the fact that they *"glorified
God"* (v. 12). Rerun the story of the paralytic man once again. Jesus
forgives sins, confounds scholars, and heals sickness. One would expect a "Jesus cult" to be formed immediately. Instead, the glory is
given to God. Mark has shown us the mind as well as the heart of
Jesus. Both are so submitted to the will of God that whenever He
feels or thinks, He communicates the presence and the power of
God. Recipients give glory to God and antagonists have no choice
but to fall silent. By exercising His power to forgive sins and declaring
Himself to be the Son of Man, Jesus has won a multitude of grateful
friends and alienated a handful of deadly enemies.

MINISTRY OF HOPE

13 And He went out again by the sea; and all the
multitude came to Him, and He taught them.

14 And as He passed by, He saw Levi the son of
Alphaeus sitting at the tax office, and said to him,
"Follow Me." And he arose and followed Him.

15 And it came to pass, as He was dining in Levi's
house, that many tax collectors and sinners also sat

together with Jesus and His disciples; for there were
many, and they followed Him.

16 And when the scribes and Pharisees saw Him
eating with the tax collectors and sinners, they said
to His disciples, "How is it that He eats and drinks
with tax collectors and sinners?"

17 When Jesus heard it, He said to them, "Those
who are well have no need of a physician, but those
who are sick. I did not come to call the righteous,
but sinners, to repentance."

Mark 2:13–17

Jesus shook the taproot of Jewish theology when He proved that
He had the power to forgive the sins of the paralytic man. Authority
confronted authority. Every word and action of Jesus will now be
scrutinized as the scribes try to build a countercase against this pretender to power who has put them on the defensive. Jesus does not
shrink from the obvious threat. Instead, He proceeds to serve the
people, this time with a ministry of hope to a hated man and a
hopeless class.

If Galileans ever held a contest to choose the most hated man,
Levi, the tax collector, would win hands down. Sitting at the toll
gate in Capernaum, where he can bleed all of the people who pass
through that intersecting city between North and South, East and
West, Levi amasses a fortune by selling his soul. Spiritually, he stands
condemned as a sinner because he makes his profit by cheating, intimi-
dation, and bribery. Poor and powerless people suffer as his prime
victims. Socially, Levi fares no better. Even though his money gives
him luxury, his circle of friends extends no farther than his own
kind. To everyone else, Levi has fallen off the bottom of the social
scale because he functions as a hireling of the despised Roman government for which he collects taxes. Neither Jews nor Romans want
anything to do with him.

Why would Jesus call Levi to be a disciple? The truth is that Jesus
specializes in rejects. Whether in Levi, or Peter, or Mary Magdalene,
or John Mark, He sees the potential for spiritual growth and greatness.
To see Michelangelo's *Pietà*—the sculpture depicting Mary holding
her son, Jesus, after He was taken down from the cross—is an overwhelming experience. Yet, the legend behind the stone is an inspiration in itself. Early in his career, Michelangelo was too poor to buy
the marble for his sculpting. He had to pick his way through the

rejected or ruined stones of other sculptors. As he eyed the marble, he said that he could see the figure inside waiting to be released by his chisel. Dragging it home, he freed the figures of Mary and Jesus that he envisioned and thus produced one of the miracles of artistic creation—from a reject.

Seeing something of great value in a rejected man, Jesus puts him to the test by saying, "Follow me." Without hesitation, Levi, the son of Alphaeus, walks away from his tax tables forever. Simon, Andrew, James and John have the family fishing business to which they can return, but once Levi breaks his contract with the Romans, his career is finished.

Or is it just beginning? Jesus needs an accountant's mind to complement Mark, the journalist, and Luke, the physician, for the writing of the Synoptic Gospels. Levi's strange alliance between his Jewish background and his Roman contract gives him a perspective of Jesus, the King, and the Kingdom of God that neither Mark nor Luke can contribute. Jesus sees that prospect when He calls Levi.

After Levi leaves his tax office to follow Jesus, he invites publicans and sinners, the only friends he has, to celebrate his decision at a dinner. Jesus' ministry of hope moves from a hated man to a hopeless class of people. The double designation *"tax collectors and sinners"* (v. 16) bespeaks their double rejection as social and spiritual outcasts. Like Levi, they have sold out to the Romans as tax collectors and fail to follow the exacting exercises of orthodox religion. No one protests when Jesus calls Levi to follow Him. A token sinner in the company of the disciples is not a threat. To bring the ministry of hope, however, to a class of hated people spotlights the failure of established religion. This is where the Pharisees come in. Earlier criticism came from scribes, the scholars of the Law. Now, the criticism shifts from theory to practice, and from authority to influence. Always subtle, the Pharisees do not come directly to Jesus with their criticism. They get His disciples aside, hoping to plant a seed of doubt in their minds, and ask, *"How is it that He eats and drinks with tax collectors and sinners?"* (v. 16). Perhaps the sensitive ears of Jesus hear their hoarse whispers or perhaps the disciples bring the question to Him in order to see how He will answer. Someone once said that it takes two persons to destroy you—an enemy to slander you and a friend to tell you about it. Friends and enemies get together to put Jesus on the spot. But He is more than a match for their question. Citing an old proverb that is universally accepted among the Jews, He speaks once again of His servant role, *"Those who are well have no need of a physician, but those who are sick. I did not come to call the righteous, but sinners, to repentance"* (v. 17).

A conciliatory mood still echoes through Jesus' response. Giving the Pharisees credit for their righteousness, He simply states that He has come to bring a ministry of hope to a class of hated and hopeless people. What retort is open to the Pharisees? They have been complimented for their righteousness and they cannot contest a word of hope for needy people. At best, they must lie back like Satan after the wilderness temptation and bide their time. Meanwhile, Jesus is ministering to tax collectors and sinners.

Who are the hated and hopeless classes to whom Jesus wants to bring a ministry of hope in our generation? Ironically, studies of mental, physical and dental health clinics show that the people who come for help are more healthy than those who do not. Is it the same with the church? The least needy sop up the resources; the most needy never appear? When Jesus shifts the ministry of hope to the point of need, the Pharisees bristle in reaction. Do we?

In this lesson, Jesus throws down the gauntlet of defiance against a ministry of hope that is limited to the security of one's own kind. The Good News is that all men and classes find hope in Christ. Another principle of the Kingdom has been established, namely that true righteousness is willing to take a risk. Separation from sin does not mean separation from sinners. As proof that Jesus is the Christ, all men have hope.

MINISTRY OF JOY

18 And the disciples of John and of the Pharisees were fasting. And they came and said to Him, "Why do the disciples of John and of the Pharisees fast, but Your disciples do not fast?"

19 And Jesus said to them, "Can the friends of the bridegroom fast while the bridegroom is with them? As long as they have the bridegroom with them they cannot fast.

20 "But the days will come when the bridegroom will be taken away from them, and then they will fast in those days.

21 "And no one sews a piece of unshrunk cloth
on an old garment; or else the new piece pulls away
from the old, and the tear is made worse.

22 "And no one puts new wine into old wineskins;
or else the new wine bursts the wineskins, the wine
is spilled, and the wineskins will be ruined. But new
wine must be put into new wineskins."

Mark 2:18–22

Once the pot of controversy begins to boil, every meeting between
Jesus and the Pharisees turns up the heat. Fasting, for instance, is a
legitimate spiritual discipline. According to Biblical Law, the Jews
are required to fast only one time a year, on the Day of Atonement.
Pharisees, however, overextend and overexercise the Law until they
demand that the people fast two days a week. To lead the ritual,
they whiten their faces into a mask of death and shred their robes
as proof of their penance. Fasting loses its meaning and their religion
loses its joy.

Fasting is the issue when the clever Pharisees concoct a scheme
to trap Jesus. John's disciples are observing the Pharisees' fast days,
perhaps in mourning for their leader or perhaps because John the
Baptist's ministry has tied them so closely to repentance. Whatever
the reason, the Pharisees seize the opportunity to draw them into a
strange coalition against Jesus. Their attack comes in the form of a
relatively innocent question, *"Why do the disciples of John and of the Pharisees
fast, but Your disciples do not fast?"* (v. 18). The strategy is obvious. They
want to split the infant movement into factions that they can control.

By this time, the Pharisees should know better. Jesus answers with
another of His skilled counterquestions. He poses the question, however, in the testimony of John the Baptist himself. Just before John
went to prison, his disciples had come to him with a green-eyed
report, "Rabbi, He who was with you beyond the Jordan, to whom
you bore witness—behold, He is baptizing, and all are coming to
Him!" (John 3:26). Rather than gritting his teeth and vowing to get
even, John the Baptist rebukes them with the reminder that he is
not the Christ. In fact, he is glad, not sad, to hear about Jesus' success.
To illustrate, John uses the analogy: "He who has the bride is the
bridegroom; but the friend of the bridegroom, who stands and hears
him, rejoices greatly because of the bridegroom's voice. Therefore
this joy of mine is fulfilled. He must increase, but I must decrease"
(3:29–30).

To refresh the memories of John's disciples, Jesus brings back the analogy of the bridegroom in order to confirm the ministry of joy as a keynote of the Kingdom of God.

After a Jewish wedding, the bride and the bridegroom do not make a fast exit for a honeymoon. They wait a week so that they can celebrate the joy of their marriage with family and friends. During this week of feasting, all of the rules for fasting are lifted. Joy reigns supreme.

John the Baptist pictures himself as a friend of Christ, the bridegroom, during His wedding week. By his own words, his joy is fulfilled. Thus, to put on masks of death and garments of mourning for fasting in the presence of Jesus, the bridegroom, is totally out of place. Although Mark does not record what happens after Jesus quotes John, I can imagine that John's disciples hear their master's voice once again. The crowd splits, but not as the Pharisees had hoped. John's disciples wipe their faces, let their rags fall to the ground and move with a smile toward Jesus' side. The Pharisees stand all alone as victims of their own backlash.

Jesus turns His enemies' criticism into an opportunity to announce that joy is a quality of the Kingdom of God that the Pharisees have lost. Let it be said again and again. A sense of joy is the grace note in the musical score of the Good News symphony. At the start of my second college presidency, a distinguished scholar of American higher education visited our campus as a consultant on long-range planning. In his first meeting with us, he declared himself to be a "secular humanist." Caution crept into our expectations about his conclusions. How could an avowed secular humanist help create a vision for the future of an evangelical Christian university? His concluding statement changed our minds. After making all of his recommendations, he summarized his thoughts this way, "I have been with you a week now. Frankly, I am still not sure what you mean by an 'evangelical Christian university.' But of this, I am sure. If you are what you say you are, this campus will be characterized by *a note of joy.*" Whether he knew it or not, a secular humanist had matched heartbeats with Jesus' final prayer for His disciples, "These things I have spoken to you that My joy may remain in you, and that your joy may be full" (John 15:11).

Contrary to some opinions, Jesus does not destroy the discipline of fasting. After quoting John's words that speak of joy, He extends the wedding analogy to remind His hearers that the time will come when the bridegroom is taken away. Fasting is appropriate then. Some scholars believe that Jesus is making an early announcement of His death. Perhaps so. He is also trying to tell the Pharisees that their religion has lost its *sense of timing.* There is a time for joy; there is a time for sorrow. There is a time for feasting; there is a time for fasting. They take themselves too seriously. No longer can they laugh at their ludicrous rites, admit an error in judgment, or respond to a time of joy. In psychiatric terms, they are spiritually neurotic. Their expectations have been built so high that they can never meet them. The more they try, the farther they fall from perfection. So, with an ever-widening gap between their spiritual expectations and their religious performance, they go round and round in a vicious cycle of guilt. Jesus comes to break that vicious cycle, but their defenses are too high and too much of their egos are at stake. The common people hear Him gladly, but the Pharisees need shock treatment.

The electrodes are put into place and the charge is administered when Jesus goes on with two advanced analogies, but with one common point. The Good News of the Gospel, which is the ministry of joy, cannot be contained within the old forms of religion.

In the analogy of sewing new cloth on an old garment, Jesus rejects a patchwork approach to the Kingdom of God. By depicting the problem of new wine in old wineskins, He faces the reality that the ferment of His Gospel will burst through old structures. Neither patchwork on old systems nor new content in old structures is possible. The Gospel of the Kingdom of God is a new joy that stretches old systems beyond the breaking point and builds pressure in old structures until they burst. Decisively and deliberately, Jesus makes a decision. If He is to serve and to save all people, He must either abandon the old order in favor of the new or accept the fact that both the old and new concepts of the Kingdom of God will destroy each other. Once again, Jesus passes through a point of no return in His ministry. If He is to sound the note of joy for His ministry, He must leave behind the dead weight of old religious systems and old religious forms.

His decision is not without risk. Many new social movements are like skyrockets. They soar skyward on tails of fire toward a brief display of glory and then sputter to the earth, burned out. They lack the substance to sustain their momentum. The ministry of joy that Jesus introduces as a keynote for the Kingdom is different. It has substance as well as spirit. Jesus tests the concept for Himself in His service and His suffering. Hebrews 12:2 records the result: "looking to Jesus, the author and finisher of our faith, who for the joy that was set before Him endured the cross, despising the shame, and has sat down at the right hand of the throne of God."

A note of joy characterizes the spirit of Jesus in His service and a vision of joy sustains Him in His suffering. As a part of Mark's case for the Good News of Jesus Christ, the Son of God, let joy be added as authoritative proof.

MINISTRY OF GRACE

23 And it came to pass that He went through the grainfields on the Sabbath. And as they went His disciples began to pluck the heads of grain.

24 And the Pharisees said to Him, "Look, why do they do what is not lawful on the Sabbath?"

25 And He said to them, "Have you never read what David did when he was in need and hungry, he and those who were with him:

26 "how he went into the house of God in the days of Abiathar the high priest, and ate the showbread, which is not lawful to eat, except for the priests, and also gave some to those who were with him?"

27 And He said to them, "The Sabbath was made for man, and not man for the Sabbath.

28 "Therefore the Son of Man is also Lord of the Sabbath."

Mark 2:23–28

The plot thickens and controversy rages. Again, what starts out as a natural and innocent act by Jesus' disciples ends up escalating to a summit-level confrontation between the authority of Jesus and the authority of the Pharisees. Walking through the grainfields on the Sabbath day, the hungry disciples pick the ripened grain, shuck the skins, blow them to the wind and eat the kernels. Nothing is wrong with their act, except that they are working on the Sabbath day. Among the thousands of rules of the Pharisees are four which dictate against reaping, threshing, winnowing, and preparing a meal on the Sabbath day. Strictly interpreted, the disciples are lawbreakers. The Pharisees, who have taken to lurking behind every grainstalk, spring out with the question to Jesus, *"Look, why do they do what is not lawful on the Sabbath?"* (v. 24).

Jesus does not contest the fact that His disciples are breaking the letter of the Law. He does contest a view of the Sabbath that kills the spirit of the Law. From His fully stocked arsenal of rhetorical weapons, He draws on Scripture which the Pharisees accept as authoritative for His counterquestion. With a hint of sarcasm, Jesus says: "Have you never read what David did when he was in need and hungry, he and those who were with him: how he went into the house of God in the days of Abiathar the high priest, and ate the showbread, which is not lawful to eat, except for the priests, and also gave some to those who were with him?" (vv. 25, 26). In one question, He establishes the fact that the sacredness of the Sabbath is built upon the moral principle of Grace rather than the religious regulation of the Law.

Moral development is a concern of contemporary psychology and education. After decades of benign neglect, when psychologists avoided moral development like the plague, the new interest is refreshing. Kohlberg of Harvard is one of the fathers of the field. Out of his research, he has produced a six-stage scale of moral development. At the lowest level, a person does what is right because of the fear of punishment. At the highest level, a person chooses what is right—not because of fear or reward, but because of belief in a moral principle.

Two principles guide the Sabbath. Jesus quotes a decision from a rabbinical hearing to establish the first principle. He says, *"The Sabbath was made for man, and not man for the Sabbath"* (v. 27). Contrary to some opinions, Jesus does not give license for men to do what they please on the Sabbath day. Rather, He reaffirms the moral principle that the Sabbath is made for man—a day of physical restoration and spiritual renewal. Before we condemn the Pharisees for their petty rules on the Sabbath day, we must remember that our rules for the Sabbath have also tended to swing from petty rigidity to permissive license. When my wife and I first met, we had a hard time deciding what we could do on Sunday afternoon between church services. In my family, games were forbidden, but homework was permitted. In her family, the Sabbath rules worked in reverse. She could play games, but could not do homework. Young hearts in love have ingenious ways to solve such problems, but today our children laugh at such antiquated rules. Most of the things that their mother and father

were forbidden to do, they do along with many glamorous entice-
ments from a secular, mobile, entertainment world that we never
knew. Most families would have to confess that the Pharisees have
lost, but Jesus has not won the struggle to interpret the Biblical principle of the Sabbath which God intended.

The other principle of the Sabbath that Jesus establishes as part
of His Kingdom ministry is that *"the Son of Man is also Lord of the
Sabbath"* (v. 28). Boldly now, Jesus is declaring His authority as the
Son of Man. It is by His Spirit—the Spirit of Grace—that the Law
of the Sabbath is fulfilled.

Bells of reformation are ringing through this passage of Scripture.
When David hungered and ate the showbread intended only for
priests, he prefigured the priesthood of believers. When Jesus needles
the scholars of the Law with their own Scriptures, all of the people are freed from legalistic chains. And when Jesus calls out His prerogative as Lord of the Sabbath, Grace takes over where Law has
failed.

MINISTRY OF MERCY

1 And He entered the synagogue again, and a man
was there who had a withered hand.

2 And they watched Him closely whether He
would heal him on the Sabbath, so that they might
accuse Him.

3 And He said to the man who had the withered
hand, "Step forward."

4 And He said to them, "Is it lawful to do good
on the Sabbath or to do evil, to save life or to kill?"
But they kept silent.

5 And when He had looked around at them with
anger, being grieved by the hardness of their hearts,
He said to the man, "Stretch out your hand." And
he stretched it out, and his hand was restored as whole
as the other.

6 And the Pharisees went out and immediately
took counsel with the Herodians against Him, how
they might destroy Him.

Mark 3:1–6

Four conflicts with the scribes and Pharisees have absorbed Jesus' time and energy since the leper disobeyed His strict command and began to noise the miracle of his cleansing. Effectively using counter-questions against their criticisms, Jesus has put the scribes and Pharisees to silence on such issues as forgiveness, eating with sinners, fasting and Sabbath rules. While winning the debates, Jesus cannot win his opponents. Reluctantly, He realizes that He must take the offensive and settle the issue if He is to get on with His ministry of service to needy, waiting and responsive people.

Jesus throws down the gauntlet when He returns to the synagogue on the Sabbath day. There, the Pharisees wait to try and trap Him once again. This time, either by chance or Pharisaical plot, Jesus meets a man with a withered hand. It is not a birth defect, but the result of a disease that has robbed him of gainful employment. According to the rulings of the elders, if he wants to be healed, he must wait for a weekday because it is not a matter of life and death. Such a ruling is as absurd as the story that John Dewey, the educator, tells in spoofing the artificiality of lock-step learning. During a class in biology, when the students are dissecting frogs, a colorful bird flies through the open window, flits around the room, and escapes back out the window. Excitedly, the students ask the teacher, "Oh, tell us, what kind of bird is it?" Gruffly, the teacher raps them back to attention, saying, "Ornithology is next week." Dewey's point is that learning must take place when the students sense the need to learn and are ready to learn.

Healing, like learning, cannot be rigidly scheduled. The man with the withered hand sits in Jesus' path, needy and ready for healing, even though it is the Sabbath day. All eyes rivet on Jesus, particularly those with the skeptical squint of the members of the Sanhedrin who sit on the front row like a jury in judgment. The Son of Man has come to His Rubicon. Later in church history, Martin Luther will come to a similar kind of decision. Given one more chance to recant before the Diet of Worms, Luther speaks with reluctance, but resolution: "Here I stand; I can do no other. God help me. Amen."[1]

Jesus can do no other. The man with the withered hand comes first, even though the healing is destined to provoke a showdown. Taking the initiative, Jesus asks the man to step forward into full public view. Standing with him front and center in the synogogue, He turns to the Pharisees with one final appeal from His message

73

of Good News. Surely, they will hear His plea for mercy, *"Is it lawful to do good on the Sabbath or to do evil, to save life or to kill?"* (v. 4). Two separate questions are contained in one. The first asks that mercy take precedence over their Sabbath Law. By implication, Jesus is saying, "Here is a man in need. If I fail to heal him, even though it is the Sabbath, am I not doing evil?" Mercy shatters the logic of rabbinical Law.

There is another question. Jesus asks, *"Is it lawful . . . [on the Sabbath] . . . to save life or to kill?"* (v. 4). It is a double-edged question. If the Pharisees have no mercy for saving life, they indict themselves as killers on the Sabbath day. One by one, eyeball to eyeball, Mark tells us that Jesus makes the rounds by looking into the soul of each man among the Pharisees. As He looks, He reacts. His own eyes ignite with anger at the same time that His heart breaks. The Good News has bounced off calloused hearts and minds without the slightest effect. Israel has rejected its Savior. If He had continued looking, He might have started to weep as He would later weep over Jerusalem: "O Jerusalem, Jerusalem . . . ! How often I wanted to gather your children together, as a hen gathers her brood under her wings, and you were not willing!" (Luke 13:34).

It is not yet the time for weeping. A man with a withered hand stands at His side needing to be healed. Turning back to him, Jesus asks him to stretch out his hand as a show of faith. The man obeys and his hand is made whole. Ironically, this healing adds insult to injury for the beaten-down Pharisees. By simply asking the man to stretch out his hand, Jesus breaks none of the labor laws relating to the Sabbath. The man remains equally innocent. There is no Law against obedience. Jesus has beaten the system. The Law of the Pharisees stands intact, but their power with the people has been dealt a fatal blow.

For the Pharisees, only one alternative remains. Violating every tenet of their Law and every principle of their faith, they flee the synagogue to find their Roman enemies, the leaders of the Herodian party, and grovel at their feet seeking counsel on how they might work together to destroy Jesus. Think of it. God's specialists in human salvation counseling with Caesar's specialists in human slaughter. Will we ever learn the lesson? Throughout Christian history, we have repeated examples of entangling alliances between the church and the state. Every time it happens, both the church and the state forsake their God-given functions and become tyrants bent on the destruction of both faith and freedom. The temptation comes whenever religious authority is powerful or powerless. In the case of the Pharisees, they have lost their power. In other cases relevant to the contemporary scene, spiritual revival puts power and popularity into the hands of Christians. In either case, the temptation is to become aligned with the power of political forces, either to punish enemies or legislate morality. Although the alliance may achieve its short-term goals, the long-term truth is that the people of God have sold their souls.

From here on, the shadow will hover over the ministry of Jesus. He will continue as the Servant Lord, but always with a price on His head. The only winner coming out of this confrontation is the man with the withered hand. He goes home healed because Jesus places the quality of mercy above the value of His own life.

Jesus has entered into His ministry, not with the acceptance that He expected, but with a mix of opportunity and opposition. If we were to ask Him how He feels about His Galilean sojourn, He would probably point first to the people whom He has healed and helped. Then, He would ask us to remember the keynotes of the Good News that He has introduced—compassion, forgiveness, hope, joy, grace, and mercy. Last, and with sorrow, He would point to the company of the Pharisees who are so spiritually bankrupt that they have not only rejected the spirit of their own Scriptures, but have joined with enemies in a power plot to kill their Savior.

NOTE

1. Martin Luther, Speech at the Diet of Worms, in *Bartlett's Familiar Quotations*, p. 155, #13.

CHAPTER FOUR

Defining His Relationships

Mark 3:7–35

HERO OF THE MASSES

7 But Jesus withdrew with His disciples to the sea. And a great multitude from Galilee followed Him, and from Judea

8 and Jerusalem and Idumea and beyond the Jordan; and those from Tyre and Sidon, a great multitude, when they heard what great things He did, came to Him.

9 And He told His disciples that a small boat should be kept ready for Him because of the multitude, lest they should crush Him.

10 For He had healed many, so that as many as had afflictions pressed about Him to touch Him.

11 And the unclean spirits, whenever they saw Him, fell down before Him and cried out, saying, "You are the Son of God."

12 And He sternly warned them that they should not make Him known.

Mark 3:7–12

After the Pharisees conspire with the Herodians to kill Jesus, He has a decision to make. Will He force them to act immediately, with the risk of short-circuiting His ministry? Or will He leave the scene, not just to bide His time, but to prepare for a major move that will bring His ministry of servanthood to full maturity? An uncanny sense of the rhythm of life and a full commitment to the will of God leads Him to leave the scene.

The rhythm of life. Jesus knows the value of a rhythm of life that balances work and rest, worship and play. Without this rhythm, He will either burn out early or accomplish very little. His withdrawal to the sea is not cowardice, it is a credit to His intuitive sense that the time has come for rest and play.

Work is an activity of high intensity and high production. But as God set the example, even creative work must be balanced by a period of "rest," when physical energies are restored in order to work again. Worship and play, then, must be added to the work/rest cycle in order to fulfill the finer hungers of persons who are created in the image of God. Unlike work and rest, worship and play are not means to an end. A person does not worship or play with productivity in mind. Value is contained in the experience itself. Thus, worship and play serve as the balance wheel for work and rest in the rhythm of life. Worship regains our spiritual perspective and play restores our creative energies.

Modern society has upset the rhythm of life. Work has been de- valued and play has been invaded by the purpose of work. With so much leisure and so many options, play has been subjected to a time-clock schedule with its demand for successful production. In many instances, worship has been eliminated from the rhythm of life and rest has become a dreaded experience on a "crash pad." The result is that *work* is a necessary evil, *play* is work, *worship* is idolatry and *rest* is a short course in death.

Jesus withdraws to the sea with His disciples in order to regain His balance in the rhythm of life. During His ministry in Galilee, the rhythm has been reduced to constant work with little rest, and even less opportunity for worship and play. In fact, when He goes to the synagogues for worship, He meets either human need that requires work or spiritual hardness that requires contest. Worship and work may have become so intermingled that Jesus senses the potential loss of the effective edge in His work and the fine-tuning of His communion with God. In modern terms, He might have been on the borderline of "executive burn-out." He needs the seaside.

The renewal of the sea. Living on the shores of Puget Sound helps one understand the renewing nature of the sea. Whether in sun or fog, calm or storm, the sea has a message in its ever-changing waters.

I never stand on the shore watching the endless procession of the waves without recalling the comment of a Greek professor in a seminary who explained the phrase in John's Gospel, ". . . grace for grace" (John 1:16). Grace, he said, is God's free gift of love to us, and "grace for grace" is like the waves of the sea, love unending washing over our lives. Once we have experienced the renewing nature of the sea, there is no substitute for the rhythm of its waves as a symbol of grace.

Jesus expects renewal as He withdraws to the seaside with His disciples. Instead, He finds people—hordes and hordes of demanding people. He also finds demons, as vicious as those in the city, who try to abort His ministry by calling out His name. Mark makes it a point to emphasize the size of the crowds and the widespread region from which they came. Which is worse, Jesus' enemies in the synagogue or His friends at the seaside? His only relief is a boat. Mark takes the trouble to inform his readers that Jesus has a boat always ready to take Him out to sea.

A couple of summers ago, I learned the value of sailing in a small boat. After reading some elementary texts on sailing and listening to lore of experienced sailors, I set out to sail alone. Capricious winds swept down from the hillside, snagged my sail, then threw me into the water. After learning to work with the wind rather than against it, I also had to develop the skill of turning into the wind. More than once, I found myself dead in the water with an empty sail, "locked in the irons," as the sailors say. One day, all of the developing skills and intuitions came together. As I sprinted on the wings of the wind with white water churning in my wake, I began to shout to the fish and the gulls my praise to God. It so happened that this first experience with the joy of sailing coincided with a troubling time in my life. Pressures were on, a career change was pending, and personal attacks were mounting. In the middle of the lake, I found my freedom in a spontaneous song that I sang at the top of my voice:

> Green pastures are before me,
> Which I have never seen.
> Bright skies will soon be o'er me,
> Where dark the clouds have been.
> My peace it has not measure,
> My path to life is free.
> My shepherd has my treasure,
> And He will walk with me.

I think I know why Jesus asks that a little boat always be ready for Him. When He needs to renew His creative energies, He casts off from the shore and, in sailing, finds solitude.

The value of solitude. Solitude is not just the privilege of mystics; it has practical value for "doers" as well. A research study of teenagers, usually considered the most active of all generations, shows that they spend 25 percent of their time alone. When asked to rank the value of their time alone or in the company of people, they place the highest value upon their solitude because it gives them, as they say, a chance to "get their heads together."

Mark understands this value by making Jesus' withdrawal to the sea a transition point in the Gospel narrative.

Immediately after regaining His perspective, Jesus begins selecting His disciples and setting forth the keynotes for His ministry of servanthood.

LEADER OF THE DISCIPLES

13 And He went up on the mountain and called to Him those He Himself wanted. And they came to Him.

14 And He appointed twelve, that they might be with Him, and that He might send them out to preach,

15 and to have power to heal sicknesses and to cast out demons:

16 Simon, to whom He gave the name Peter;

17 James the son of Zebedee and John the brother of James, to whom He gave the name Boanerges, that is, "Sons of Thunder";

18 Andrew, Philip, Bartholomew, Matthew, Thomas, James the son of Alphaeus, Thaddaeus, Simon the Canaanite;

19 and Judas Iscariot, who also betrayed Him. And they went into a house.

Mark 3:13–19

Seas are for solitude and renewal, mountains are for planning and decision-making. Jesus has announced His message of Good News, chosen His method of preaching, communicated His motive for serving human need, established His authority as the Son of Man, and won public acclaim. In so doing, He has become a man marked for extinction. If His time is limited, how can the Good News be preached to as many people as possible? If He is destined to die, how will His message be continued? Jesus chooses to select men whom He can teach, test, and to whom He can transfer His power.

By the standards of leadership selection, the twelve disciples are a motley crew. At best, they were modest of means, limited in schooling, and obscure in identity. Pray tell me, someone might ask, what do they have to offer? The answer goes back to their original call from Jesus, "Follow me." The disciples qualify as trustworthy, teachable and task-oriented men. These qualifications add up to the leadership potential of the disciples upon which Jesus is willing to risk the future of His message and His ministry. Carl F. H. Henry puts it so succinctly, "God is the greatest gambler in human history. He bet the future of our redemption upon a carpenter and His small band of fishermen."

Anyone who chooses people for their potential rather than their achievement makes a personal commitment to their growth and maturity. Jesus makes that commitment in a curriculum for discipleship. He will *teach* them in person, *test* them by experience, and *graduate* them with authority.

Teaching in person. The ideal teaching-learning process has been described as Mark Hopkins on one end of the log with the student on the other end. Current educational research, however, suggests that the relationship between effective teaching and class size depends upon the subject matter and the learning goals. In cases where the teaching goal is simply a matter of transferring information from one mind to another, one teacher on television with eight hundred students may be as effective as the teacher and student alone. Someplace in between, a class of twelve to fifteen students permits the teacher to give personal attention to the students and allows the students to interact and learn from each other. Jesus chooses twelve disciples, not just as a symbolic number, but as the best size for accomplishing His teaching goals. His purpose is to teach the disciples the content of the Good News, which includes Biblical history and prophecy as well as new Kingdom principles. His method is to instruct them by parables in public with interpretation in private. His teaching goal is equally specific. Jesus expects His disciples to know Him as the Son of God who serves, the Son of Man who saves, and the Lord who reigns. They will know that He is the Messiah.

Testing by experience. As a university administrator whose first love is teaching, I admire Jesus' lesson plan that includes testing by experience as well as teaching by words. Mark will tell us later about the details of Jesus' plan to send out the disciples two by two as a test of their ability to preach the Gospel. At the time of the appointments, however, Jesus sets His objective for testing and informs His students about the test, all part of good teaching.

Graduating with authority. Assuming that the personalized teaching of Jesus is effective and the disciples pass the experience test, they are ready for graduation. Jesus confers upon them His power to heal sicknesses and to cast out demons. Can you imagine a commencement ceremony on a hillside? As a university president who has presided over more than twenty commencements, I can. Jesus gathers His twelve disciples around Him and solemnly says: "According to the authority vested in Me by God the Father, I hereby confer upon you the power to heal sickness and to cast out demons with all of the rights and privileges pertaining thereto."

The end of an education is the transfer of authority. Jesus foresees the day when it will happen—a day of sadness because He will be taken from them, but a day of gladness because His message will now be preached and His power will be exercised by disciples who have been tested to speak His Truth, convey His Spirit and exercise His authority. At the time when Jesus appoints His disciples, the dignified sounds of the commencement march can be heard in the distance.

Choosing for diversity. Mark's listing of the twelve disciples divides them into three groups. Simon is mentioned first and in a category all his own. James and John then join Peter in the inner circle of leaders and friends who are sorted out for special names.

With his typical depth of insight, Paul Tournier has written a book entitled *The Meaning of Persons.* Our names have meaning, he tells us, far beyond their sources and sounds. Family names, for instance, speak volumes about our ethnic ancestry and popular identity. According to Tournier, nicknames also play a special role in our personal development. They set us apart with individual identity, even when they are derisive. "Fatso," "Four-Eyes," "Metal Mouth," and "Bean-Pole" may not be flattering, but they are forms of identity and acceptance, far better than "Hey, you" or rejection.

Jesus gives nicknames to those who are the closest to Him. "Peter" and "Boanerges" reflect personality traits that give Simon, James, and John a charismatic presence and make them leaders of men. Eight more disciples are named, only one with a family reference and one with his place of origin. They represent a strong and perhaps silent majority among the disciples. Finally, standing alone, Mark names Judas Iscariot, who betrays Jesus.

There are other ways of looking at the three or four groups of disciples. From an organizational standpoint, Simon Peter appears to be heir apparent to Jesus' leadership role, with James and John as members of the executive committee. Andrew, Philip, Bartholomew, Matthew, Thomas, James the Son of Alphaeus, Thaddaeus, and Simon the Canaanite, constitute middle management. And Judas? Every organization seems to have its rebel and its loser.

Perhaps the most meaningful way to understand the reason for grouping the disciples is to think about the diversity that they bring to Jesus' company. In one of the books on our coffee table, *The Chosen Twelve Plus One,* written by Edward Macartney and illustrated by Harry A. Hollett, each disciple, including Matthias, who replaces Judas, is described by portrait and personality sketch. Philosophers, practitioners, introducers, skeptics, lovers, fighters—their diversity stands out.

Jesus neither chooses persons who are carbon copies of His own background nor appoints disciples who are easy to teach and manage. He prefers a team of wild horses to a bunch of worn-out plugs. Three years after He appoints them, they are still tugging at the bit. But under His personalized teaching, through His supervised testing, and by His endowed power, they will be ready to help make His message permanent in the history of man and pervasive among all nations of the world.

SON OF MAN

20 And the multitude came together again, so that they could not so much as eat bread.

21 And when His own people heard about this, they went out to lay hold of Him, for they said, "He is out of His mind."

22 And the scribes who came down from Jerusalem said, "He has Beelzebub, and by the ruler of the demons He casts out demons."

23 And He called them to Him and said to them in parables: "How can Satan cast out Satan?

24 "And if a kingdom is divided against itself, that kingdom cannot stand.

25 "And if a house is divided against itself, that house cannot stand.

26 "And if Satan has risen up against himself, and is divided, he cannot stand, but has an end.

27 "No one can enter a strong man's house and plunder his goods, unless he first binds the strong man, and then he will plunder his house.

28 "Assuredly, I say to you, all sins will be forgiven the sons of men, and whatever blasphemies they may utter;

29 "but he who blasphemes against the Holy Spirit never has forgiveness, but is subject to eternal condemnation"—

30 because they said, "He has an unclean spirit."

31 Then His brothers and His mother came, and standing outside they sent to Him, calling Him.

32 And a multitude was sitting around Him; and they said to Him, "Look, Your mother and Your brothers are outside seeking You."

33 And He answered them, saying, "Who is My mother, or My brothers?"

34 And He looked around in a circle at those who sat about Him, and said, "Here are My mother and My brothers!

35 "For whoever does the will of God is My brother and My sister and mother."

Mark 3:20–35

All of the preliminaries for Jesus' ministry are behind Him. He has chosen His message, His method, and His men. His power is recognized by both friend and foe. So now, refreshed in spirit by His sojourn at the seaside and renewed in purpose by His view from the mountain, it is time to make His move into the full-orbed ministry of servanthood. Where shall it begin? Mark tells us that Jesus comes home, either to His native town of Nazareth, where He has been rejected, or more likely to Capernaum, His adopted home, where He meets a conspiracy against His life. Whichever it is, Jesus returns to the scene where He began His ministry motivated to serve and energized to work. He is mobbed by the crowd.

The unforgettable moment. For those who do not understand, Jesus is so absorbed by His task that food loses its importance. A call to eat is neglected, a plate put at His feet goes untouched, and a final desperate demand is answered by a wave of the hand. Friends begin to panic. In a culture where meals are rituals and food is scarce, anyone who refuses to eat must be "out of his mind." Well-meaning friends of Jesus call His family, thinking that they can bring Him to His senses. Evidently, none of them has ever seen a genius at work.

Thomas Edison worked in his laboratory hours upon end without food or sleep. As he approached the discovery of the incandescent light, trays of food went untouched and his family feared that he would collapse from the lack of sleep. To the contrary, when a person is creatively engaged in work that is loved and on the verge of the discovery of a lifetime, all other values fall into second place or off the scale of priorities. Psychologists describe the moment of discovery as the "Aha!" experience. Jesus is not "out of His mind" or "beside Himself," He is fully "within Himself," enjoying the "Aha!" experience of seeing all His preparation come into focus in a ministry of service. Contrary to the fears of His friends, neither madness nor exhaustion threatens Him. When a person is fully and creatively serving others, energy is strangely, but wonderfully, self-renewing.

The unpardonable sin. Pharisees, as we expect by now, try to capitalize on the frenzy of Jesus' friends. In a devilish turn of mind, the Pharisees twist the charge of madness into deliberate perversion. According to them, Jesus is not demented, but demon-possessed. They accuse Him of being in league with the devil, having sold His soul, like J. W. von Goethe's Faust. All of their other charges against His authority, His message, His values and His deity, slip into insignificance. The confrontation peaks. To the Pharisees, Jesus is not the Son of God, He is the Son of Satan!

Although He has no trouble exposing the absurdity of their accusation, Jesus treats the perverted nature of the charge far more seriously than the faulty logic of the accusation. To accuse Him of being in league with Satan, He says, is not just a sin of the flesh or even the sin of blasphemy, both of which can be forgiven; *it is the sin for which there is no forgiveness.*

In their previous confrontations with Jesus, the Pharisees made choices that led them toward their fatal error. It began when they *denied the authority* of Jesus to forgive sins, stepped up when they *rejected the Good News* of hope and joy in His message, accelerated when they *inverted the values* of human need by putting their oral law on top, and leaped into a cardinal sin when they *conspired to destroy* Him. Rare though it is, their choice results in a perversion of Truth in which Jesus is accused of being the Son of Satan rather than being accepted as the Son of God.

The unequalled bond. Enemies react to Jesus' all-consuming passion for His ministry of servanthood by aligning Him with the devil. Friends send out an urgent call for His family. Perhaps they can calm Him down and get Him to eat. When the family arrives, they stand on the edge of the crowd and call for Him. Probably one of the disciples intercepts their message and conveys it to Jesus, saying, *"Look, Your mother and Your brothers are outside seeking You"* (v. 32). As a son, husband, father and grandfather who finds his greatest joy in his family, I struggle with Jesus' answer, *"Who is My mother or My brothers?"* (v. 33). At first, His words seem to be unloving and unloyal. Does Jesus have to deny His family in order to love the whole world? Of course not. His answer is appropriate to the situation. Enemies with malicious intent have already accused Him of a Satanic alliance in order to destroy His ministry; now, friends with good intent are using His family to divert Him from His ministry. Strange as it seems, the result will be the same—an end to His ministry of servanthood. In the cooing of the dove, Jesus hears the roar of the lion.

Christians must be "pro-family," not by making its structure sacred, but by assuring the sacredness of its personal bonds. In our century, the structure has already changed radically. The "extended family" of father, mother, children, grandparents and other relatives who lived together and worked the farm or family business has all but disappeared. In its place came the "nuclear family" with father, mother and children living at home, but being employed, schooled, socialized and entertained elsewhere. Grandmother and grandfather live alone in their own home or in a retirement center and often at a distance. The "typical" family in the last quarter of the twentieth century is radically different from the "typical" family in the first quarter of the century. Today, with social change accelerating at the speed of a downhill racer, we can only anticipate equally radical alterations in the structure of the family and equally radical pressures on our sense of the sacredness of the family. In the church, for instance, we may be headed toward the "communal family," a spiritual form of the extended family that includes the nuclear family in a love bond with adopted grandmothers and grandfathers, single parents, unmarried and widowed people, and cousins by the dozens. The "family of God," as defined by church relationships, may be the Christian's challenge for the future to counter the threat of secular values. If so, Jesus advances the idea long before its time. When He raises the question, *"Who is My mother or My brothers?"* He is not denying His human family, but affirming the family of God.

Jesus does not leave His question hanging in the air. He goes on to teach two principles for the family of God. Stretching out His arms and sweeping them over the crowd, he says, *"Here are My mother and My brothers!"* (v. 34). As the Son of Man and Son of God, He identifies His family with all whom He is called to serve. Have you ever heard people who minister to a wide range of people refer to them as "my family?" As a college president who has served thousands of students over more than twenty years, I meet members of "my family" all over the world. While driving through Monte Carlo after the International Congress on World Evangelization in Lausanne, Switzerland, for instance, I stopped at a red light on a busy corner. A missionary alumnus with TransWorld Radio who was standing on the opposite corner caught a glimpse of me just as I drove on. Startled with disbelief at the thought of seeing me thousands of miles from home, she called hotel after hotel until she found my name registered at the Holiday Inn. A telephone call, a squeal of delight, an animated conversation, a luncheon engagement—we had an unforgettable "family" reunion on a veranda overlooking the Mediterranean Sea. Isn't Jesus saying the same thing? A ministry of servanthood produces offspring for the "family of God" far beyond the number of our blood relatives.

A second principle for the "family of God" which Jesus sets forth is, *"whoever does the will of God is My brother and My sister and mother"* (v. 35). Blood relatives are very close, but spiritual relatives can be even closer. Christians who go back to family reunions often find themselves growing farther and farther apart from relatives whose name they share, but with whom they have little in common. Small talk soon evaporates and memories take over. Although memories are precious, the bond they create is limited in depth and range.

The "family of God" has so much more to offer. A network of relationships created by common obedience to the will of God, melted together by love at each intersection, and motivated to a ministry of service, is Jesus' idea of His family. Is this not also the "typical" Christian family upon which the future will be built?

Jesus has established His relationships as the hero of the masses, leader of the disciples, enemy of Satan, and member of the family of God. Each identity adds credence to Mark's argument that He is Jesus Christ, the Son of God. The masses acclaim Him, the disciples follow Him, Satan abhors Him, and all who obey Him become His sisters and brothers. Mark is ready to introduce us to the teaching of Jesus.

CHAPTER FIVE

Developing His Teaching

Mark 4:1–34

THE UNIVERSAL MESSAGE

1 And again He began to teach by the seaside. And a great multitude was gathered to Him, so that He got into a boat and sat in it on the sea, and the whole multitude was on the land facing the sea.

2 And He taught them many things by parables, and said to them in His teaching:

3 "Listen! Behold, a sower went out to sow.

4 "And it happened, as he sowed, that some seed fell by the wayside; and the birds of the air came and devoured it.

5 "And some fell on stony ground, where it did not have much earth; and immediately it sprang up because it had no depth of earth.

6 "But when the sun was up it was scorched, and because it had no root it withered away.

7 "And some seed fell among thorns; and the thorns grew up and choked it, and it yielded no crop.

8 "And other seed fell on good ground and yielded a crop that sprang up, increased, and produced: some thirtyfold, some sixty, and some a hundred."

9 And He said to them, "He who has ears to hear, let him hear!"

Mark 4:1–9

Jesus' credibility as a teacher is a vital part of Mark's case. If a common carpenter without formal schooling qualifies as the Teacher without peer, surely His knowledge of the Truth and His ability to communicate that Truth must have a supernatural origin.

Jesus' teaching follows a process that is well-known to master teachers. He: (1) *presents universal principles* in dramatic form (4:1–9); (2) *relates the principles* to His purpose in teaching (4:10–12); (3) *explains the principles* in detail (4:13–20); (4) *advances the principles* individually and in depth (4:21–32); and (5) *personalizes the principles* for the individual learner (4:33–34).

As the vehicle for His teaching, Jesus chooses the parable. A parable is a comparison; in this case, a comparison drawn between a simple, earthly picture and a singular, spiritual Truth. Although scholars delve deeply into the hidden meanings of the parables, Jesus tells them for an intuitive response, not rational analysis. They are also intended for hearing, not reading. So, the best way to understand the parable as a teaching device is to speak it aloud and then ask, "What is the simple, single Truth that Jesus is teaching?"

Teaching by parable in open fields is an alternative with several advantages. To *attract the interest* of His hearers, Jesus can use word pictures from the natural setting to illustrate simply and singularly a Kingdom principle. At the same time, He *avoids the controversy* with the scribes and Pharisees because the same story can have many meanings. Best of all, the parable serves to *awaken the minds* of those who are ready to begin a "search and discovery" mission after Truth.

Three principles of growth for the Kingdom of God are implied in the Parable of the Sower: (1) *sowing is universal;* (2) *growing is individual;* and (3) *reaping is selective.* Scholars debate the relative emphasis of these points in the parable. Some see the central Truth related to sowing the seed or disclosing the Gospel. Others prefer to call the story "The Parable of the Soils" because they feel as if Jesus is reflecting upon the differences He has encountered in the reception of His message. Still others put weight upon the harvest with its eschatological meaning for judgment and deliverance. If forced to make a choice, I choose to emphasize the readiness of the soils to receive the seed, grow the plants and produce a bounteous crop as a picture of the hearers of the Word whom Jesus encounters. But I must quickly add, the quality of the soil cannot be isolated from the sowing of the seed and the reaping of the harvest. Whether in preaching or teaching, Jesus always keeps a grasp upon whole Truth, and so must we.

Sowing is universal. The image of the sower scattering seed far and wide over all different kinds of soil prefigures the conclusion of Mark's Gospel when Jesus speaks The Great Commission, "Go into all the world and preach the gospel to every creature" (16:15). This is a principle of growth for the Kingdom of God that shocks the sensibilities of our efficiency-minded age. Economy dictates selective sowing of the seed. Particularly as we learn more about the readiness of certain cultures and certain people to respond to the Gospel, the temptation is to give our energies to people from whom we will get the greatest response. If so, we will have to rewrite the Parable of the Sower to limit the sowing of the seed to the fertile soil. But if we take seriously Jesus' teaching that the sowing of the seed of the Gospel is to be universal, we will have to take another look at the language and the location of our ministries. John Stott speaks Biblical Truth when he says that our only responsibility is to preach and teach the Gospel to all nations; responsibility for results belongs to the Holy Spirit. In every city and in every nation, there are "unreached peoples" for whom we are responsible. Intellectuals, for instance, may be hard soil, entertainers may be shallow soil, and leaders may have the thorns of wealth and power that compete with the Gospel. Should any of them be neglected because they are tough, shallow, or divided? Of course not. Our only obligation is to sow the seed universally and leave the harvest to God.

Growing is individual. The response to the Gospel is not to be stereotyped or prejudged. Different people respond differently, depending upon their readiness to receive the Gospel. Even though Jesus Christ is sovereign as the Son of God, He does not usurp the freedom of man to make a choice; nor does He brush over individual differences within that choice. On the beaten path of their tradition, Pharisees show a hardness of heart that the seed of the Gospel cannot penetrate. Sensation-seeking crowds, stony soil to be sure, see no deeper into faith than the miracles of Jesus. Wealthy and powerful people represent the thorny ground, never quite able to free themselves from their riches and their cares in order to give the Gospel its full growth.

At the start of His ministry, Jesus must have expected widespread acceptance. After all, who could turn down the Good News? His reference to the different soils in the parable tells us that He has made an adjustment to reality. Only the patience of a master teacher makes room for resistant, shallow and divided minds as well as those who are eager, ready and able to learn. On the surface, it is sometimes hard to tell the difference.

Reaping is selective. Each kind of soil, representative of different hearers of the Word, carries its own judgment within its nature. On the hardened soil, the seed lies on the surface, ready for picking by scavenging birds. Paul uses the same analogy in Athens when he accuses the Greeks of being "seedpickers" of ideas who miss the essence of the Gospel.

Both the stony and thorny soils can be mistaken for fertile and productive ground. A layer of rock just beneath the surface, or latent thorns germinating for competitive growth, are not revealed until the crop is tested by circumstances. Scorching sun and choking thorns bring judgment upon the shallow roots and mixed shoots. The seed is sown, the plants grow, but the harvest is lost. In striking contrast, the fertile soil produces crops that astound the imagination. A hundredfold harvest is such a rarity in the natural cycle of earthly production that it speaks volumes about the glorious potential of those who respond to the Word of God. Thus, we find ourselves confronted once again with the Truth that Jesus, the Messiah, comes with judgment and redemption. For those in whom the seed of the Gospel takes no root and produces no crop, He is their grim Judge; but for those in whom the Word is received and grown, He is their glad Redeemer.

At the end of His teaching, Jesus reinforces the fact that His listeners have heard eternal Truth, *"He who has ears to hear, let him hear!"* (v. 9). The exclamation echoes from His seaside classroom down through the centuries and reaches our ears with a clarity and force that we cannot deny.

The Divine Purpose

10 And when He was alone, those who were around Him with the twelve asked Him about the parable.

11 And He said to them, "To you it has been given to know the mystery of the kingdom of God; but to those who are outsiders, all things come in parables,

12 "that
'Seeing they may see and not perceive,
And hearing they may hear and not understand;
Lest they should turn again,
And their sins be forgiven them.' "

Mark 4:10–12

After teaching the masses by parable, Jesus gathers His disciples into a seminar session. His purpose is to *identify* the point of the story, *explain* it in detail and *expand* upon its content.

To His disciples, the parable is intended to unveil the Truth; but to the Pharisees, the parable drops a curtain of mystery over their eyes. Jesus quotes Isaiah the prophet in condemnation of those who refuse His message:

> *"Seeing they may see and not perceive,*
> *And hearing they may hear and not understand;*
> *Lest they should turn again,*
> *And their sins be forgiven them."*
>
> (Mark 4:12; Isa. 6:9, 10)

Despite its outward innocence, a parable is a teaching tool that divides believers and unbelievers. To believers, it unveils the mystery of the Kingdom of God; to unbelievers, a parable drops an opaque curtain upon their understanding. The more important point, however, is the fact that the mystery of the Kingdom of God has been revealed. Mystery, in this sense, is not a puzzle that can be solved by human reasoning; it is a lifting of the curtain by divine revelation. Like a great drama played before the audience of mankind, John the Baptist conducts the overture, God raises the curtain and Jesus stands on center stage. He, and He alone, is the Way, the Truth and the Life. Some of the audience, however, hoot and howl while others applaud and receive Him. Consequently, God drops back down a translucent screen in the form of a parable which confuses the hooters with an aura of mystery, but focuses the vision of those who applaud the Truth.

A parable, then, is a teaching method which serves specific aims of Jesus, the Master Teacher. *First,* it is a familiar story which finds people where they live and *gets their attention. Second,* a parable has enough mystery to *attract earnest seekers* after Truth. *Third,* the same sense of mystery confounds the enemies of Truth and thus *avoids controversies* which could detract from Jesus' ministry of servanthood. *Fourth,* a parable *awakens self-discovery* of Truth as a basis for independent learning.

So, as Jesus explains to His disciples, He decides to teach in parables as another means of announcing His coming, unveiling the mystery of the Kingdom of God, separating honest seekers from hardened skeptics, and preparing His disciples for advanced and independent learning.

THE INDIVIDUAL RESPONSE

13 And He said to them, "Do you not understand this parable? How then will you understand all the parables?

14 "The sower sows the word.

15 "And these are the ones by the wayside where the word is sown. And when they hear, Satan comes immediately and takes away the word that was sown in their hearts.

16 "And these likewise are the ones sown on stony ground who, when they hear the word, immediately receive it with gladness;

17 "and they have no root in themselves, and so endure only for a time. Afterward, when tribulation or persecution arises for the word's sake, immediately they stumble.

18 "And these are the ones sown among thorns; they are the ones who hear the word,

19 "and the cares of this world, the deceitfulness of riches, and the desires for other things entering in choke the word, and it becomes unfruitful.

20 "And these are the ones sown on good ground, those who hear the word, accept it, and bear fruit: some thirtyfold, some sixty, and some a hundred."

Mark 4:13–20

When Jesus tells His disciples that He teaches in parables so that the mystery of the Kingdom of God will be unveiled to them, He sees another mystery in their eyes. They do not understand the parable.

A master teacher is a skilled reader of unspoken cues which students convey by a look in their eyes, an inflection in their voices, a twist of the hands, or a wrinkling of the brow. In Scottish universities, students use their feet to let the professor know how they feel. If the professor fails to make a point clear in a lecture, students interrupt by shuffling their feet on the floor until the teacher goes back and clarifies the point.

Some unspoken cues from the disciples prompt Jesus to inquire,

"Do you not understand this parable?" (v. 13). Either blank stares or shaking heads let Him know that they fail to grasp the simple and singular point of the story. Expecting more from them, Jesus chides, *"How then will you understand all the parables?"* (v. 13). More parables with deeper meaning are yet to come. But before they can be taught, Jesus must stop, take His class by the hand, and patiently lead them step by step through the meaning of the Parable of the Sower. Great teachers never hesitate to repeat themselves.

Jesus' explanation of the Parable of the Sower reinforces His simple point that the *growth of the Kingdom of God is directly related to the quality of the individual response.* For the disciples' understanding, He builds a four-point scale of spiritual growth: (1) no-growth; (2) shallow-growth; (3) stunted-growth; and (4) full-growth.

No-growth people. At the lowest level of response are persons who *listen,* but do not *hear* the Gospel. Spiritually, they are case-hardened against any response to the Word of God. Jesus compares them to beaten paths bordering the fertile fields, suggesting the hardening of minds from the constant tramp of life-long habits. A hardened shell of emotional and intellectual defenses will not let the Word of God penetrate through to the point where they consciously change their minds, turn around and go the other way. In other words, their wills are formidably set against repentance.

A severe warning is implied in the analogy of "no-growth" soil. Some psychologists hold that personality patterns are fixed as early in life as the age of eleven or twelve. Others have developed a theory which states that the habits we form eventually become the motives that drive us. Still others have described various stages of moral development at which a person can fixate at an immature level and stop developing. Spiritual parallels are relevant. People tend to develop religious personalities made up of habits that have become spiritual drives and choices that make up their moral character. If the drives and character are God-ward, the seed of the Gospel takes root; if not, the threat of total change may be greater than the personality can absorb.

Is there a way to penetrate the case-hardened defenses of the person who seems spiritually destined for no-growth? To say the least, standard techniques for spiritual plowing will not work. John Alexander, former President of InterVarsity, once mentioned the technique that he used to read the Bible to university scholars who had blocked it out of their lives. As a university professor himself, he knew that scholars prize academic freedom and their claim to view objectively all viewpoints. When a colleague informed Dr. Alexander that he rejected the Bible as a source of knowledge, Dr. Alexander would remind him of his scholarly obligation to consider all viewpoints before coming to a conclusion. On the horns of a dilemma, more often than not, the scholar would have to consider reading the Bible or admitting his bias. Such breakthroughs are rare, but not unknown.

Shallow-growth. At the next level, the growth of the Gospel begins. People who have the potential for growth in the Kingdom of God must not only hear the Gospel, they must receive it and repent of their sins. In other words, it is to captivate their wills. But there is more. The Word of God must also take deep root in the emotions and intellect of the individual if growth to maturity takes place. Shallow-growth is the result of a spiritual experience that is emotionally exhilarating, but intellectually rootless.

Loving critics of the resurgence of evangelical Christianity in the last quarter of the twentieth century see the movement as volitionally sound because of the emphasis upon the "born-again" experience, emotionally high because of the return to love and joy in Christian expression, but intellectually shallow because of the failure to relate sound Biblical principles to spiritual understanding and contemporary life. According to the parable that Jesus taught, the maturity of growth for the "Born-Again" Movement will be tested under social pressure, if not under persecution. Like the scorching sun which tests the rootage of tender plants, social pressure and spiritual persecution will determine whether or not the "Born-Again" Movement has the intellectual substance to sustain it as well as a fervent spirit to drive it. Michael Novak, the syndicated columnist, is doubtful. He fears that easy faith, cheap grace, and shallow piety may be the undoing of spiritual revival in our generation. If so, evangelicals will qualify as persons in whom the Kingdom of God grows, but the growth is shallow and the plants will wither and die long before maturity.

Stunted-growth. When the Word of God is received and rooted in a divided mind, the result is a full-size plant that is stunted at the final stage of producing fruit.

In describing the hearer of the Gospel with a divided mind, Jesus specifies *"the cares of this world, the deceitfulness of riches, and the desires for other things"* (v. 19) as competing forces for the Kingdom of God. The "cares of the world" coincide with the word that Jesus chooses for the Sermon on the Mount when He admonishes, "Therefore do not worry about tomorrow . . ." (Matt. 6:34). Jesus is talking about the primary interest or the "preoccupation" of the mind. If you ask a person, "Where is your heart?," you will get a variety of answers. I went to a medical doctor for a checkup. All the while he was punching and poking me, he kept up a running commentary on the stock market. Even though he is a superb doctor, his heart was in another business. Disciples of Jesus Christ do not have the luxury of preoccupation with "other business" in their commitment, unless they are willing to forfeit the fruits of spiritual growth.

Following closely upon the *"cares of this world"* is the *"deceitfulness of riches."* Wealth can be a divider of the disciple's mind, but it is also an example of the larger question, "Where are your values?" A value, according to experts, is an assessment of worth and priority placed upon an idea that guides attitudes and actions personally, consistently, and permanently. When Jesus said, ". . . seek first the kingdom of God . . ." (Matt. 6:33), He made a statement about the priority of spiritual and material values. The Kingdom of God must be first as the highest value guiding our attitudes and our actions—personally, consistently, and permanently. Material values are not ignored, they are put into second place where anxiety is reduced and faith is exercised. In the Parable of the Sower, Jesus warns against the subtleties of secondary material values growing like weeds to compete with primary spiritual values and eventually to choke them out. All the satisfactions of bearing fruit are lost to the divided mind. Like the fig tree which Jesus curses, there is no sadder sight than a person whose spiritual growth stops just short of finding bountiful delight in the will of God.

Joining the *"cares of this world"* and the *"deceitfulness of riches"* in competition with the Word of God is the *"desire for other things."* Jesus is probing deeply into hidden motives and coming up with a person's vision for the future. "What is your dream?" is the key question. Does it compete with your vision for the Kingdom of God? If it does, the two dreams cannot grow side by side without conflict. Sooner or later, the "desire for other things" will become an entangling alliance that dulls the dream for the Kingdom of God. Over the years, I have watched one denomination develop. It began as an agitator in a revival tent with a small group of people who shouted praise to God and believed that they could change the world. They were labeled a "sect." As the movement grew, the fires of revival had to be contained within an organizational structure and the vision for changing the world had to be accommodated to reality. A sect had become a "church." Growth continued until the churches had to be organized into a denomination with leadership to remind them of their mission, administrators to run efficient programs, and standards of polity to guide the thought and life of the members. Looking back, everyone longs for the original vision. In fact, new agitative groups have broken away from the church trying to recapture the clarity and the excitement of the original vision. The subtleties of organizational development have outgrown the spiritual motive that brought the movement into existence. Is this what Jesus means when He cautions against the competing *"desires for other things"* that choke off the fruit of the Kingdom of God?

Full-growth. By the process of elimination, Jesus infers the qualities of a hearer in whom the Word of God bears a multiple harvest. Like fertile soil, the person gladly receives the seed of the Word of God, accepts its substance and its spirit for growing roots as well as shoots, keeps the soil clear of rival growth, and thus bears a multiple harvest that stands in striking contrast to the wasted seed, the withered shoots, and the thorn-choked plants.

As a Master Teacher, Jesus brings His disciples a step at a time to understand the full cycle of growth for the Kingdom of God. He gives them an analytical tool for understanding four different responses from the people to whom they will minister. His teaching includes a three-step scale of spiritual growth: (1) hearing the Word, (2) accepting it, and (3) bearing fruit which the disciples can use to evaluate their own preaching and teaching. Finally, as all master teachers, Jesus finishes with the promise of a satisfying reward far beyond expectations for students of spiritual growth who run the cycle and come to maturity.

The Manifest Truth

21 And He said to them, "Is a lamp brought to be put under a basket or under a bed? Is it not to be set on a lampstand?

22 "For there is nothing hidden which will not be revealed, nor has anything been kept secret but that it should come to light.

23 "If anyone has ears to hear, let him hear."

24 And He said to them, "Take heed what you hear. With the same measure you use, it will be measured to you; and to you who hear, more will be given.

25 "For he who has, to him will be given; and he who does not have, from him will be taken even what he has."

Mark 4:21–25

Mark continues to unfold the teaching-learning process of Jesus, the Master Teacher. The advanced course now begins. Focusing upon the singular Truth about the growth of the Kingdom of God, Jesus tells His disciples three other parables that add meaning to the universal principles of the Kingdom of God that He presents in the Parable of the Sower. His emphasis shifts from the response of the hearer to the work of God. In the Parable of the Lamp (4:21–25), we are taught that *truth is manifest;* in the Parable of the Growing Seed (4:26–29), we learn that *growth is mysterious;* in the Parable of the Mustard Seed (4:30–32), we are reminded once again that the *results are multiple.*

The Parable of the Lamp. The Parable of the Lamp contains the conundrum that the *hidden is open.* Most of us readily accept the universal principle that Truth is manifest in the Person of Jesus Christ. Few of us understand the meaning behind the principle; it is that the hidden has become open. God has chosen to lift the veil on the mystery of redemption through His Son so that all might see and be saved. In the Parable of the Lamp, Jesus teaches the fact that He, the Light, has come. Like the lamp which is the center of the Galilean home, it illuminates every corner only when it is placed on the lampstand that occupies the central place. No one would think of putting the lamp under a basket or under the bed; its function is to be at the center, casting light into the darkness so everything can be seen, and protecting the household from intruders who need darkness for their work.

Jesus is teaching His disciples three foundational Truths about Himself in this parable. *First,* He identifies Himself as *the Light of Lights.* By choosing the analogy of the lamp which is at the center of the Palestinian household and upon which the family depends, His disciples know that He is referring to the essential light. The Truth to be taught is that all other lights which shine upon Truth—natural revelation, reason, intuition, experience—are dim reflections from the brilliance of the Son of God. Thus, a standard is set for judging all other lights. Cults, for instance, can be exposed by searching for their position on the centrality of Jesus Christ. If He is not the Light of Lights, the cult has no claim to being Christian.

Second, Jesus identifies Himself as *the Light of Revelation.* When Jesus says, *"For there is nothing hidden which will not be revealed"* (v. 22), He makes it clear that the veil of mystery over God's redemptive purpose will be lifted by Him so that nothing remains hidden. Again, the Light serves as a standard for true Christian faith. If any religion places another revelation equal with the Revelation of Jesus Christ, that religion is not Christian. Even now, some borderline sects are debating whether or not the revelation that came to their founders is necessary for interpreting the Scriptures and therefore equal, if not superior, to the Word of God. Jesus, the final Light of Revelation, condemns their debate.

Third, Jesus identifies Himself as *the Light of Judgment.* As the counterpart to the Light of Revelation that leaves nothing hidden from its beams, the Light of Judgment exposes all secrets. In Matthew, Jesus warns about the workers of evil deeds who prefer darkness to the light. The assumption of evil doers is that their sin is secret. Like criminals, they do not expect to be caught. But as the light of justice shines through to expose the criminal, the Light of Christ puts sinners into the lineup under hot and blinding beams. When Jonathan Edwards preached that memorable sermon, "Sinners in the Hands of an Angry God," the Light of Christ in judgment so exposed the hearts of his congregation that unbelievers took white-knuckled grips on the backs of the pews to keep from falling into Hell. The same beam that shows the way of salvation also exposes the secrets of sin.

Jesus concludes the Parable of the Lamp with the conundrums that *some is more* and *little is none.* As in the Parable of the Sower, those who receive the Seed under conditions that bring it to full growth reap the benefits of a multiple harvest, but those who reject the Seed or lack the qualities to bring it to maturity lose all the value of the Truth.

In the natural world, all energy is subject to Entropy, The Second Law of Thermodynamics, which states that the physical universe is running down and that its material resources deteriorate with use. Oil, for instance, is a limited resource in the earth and to use it is to lose it. Oil's value may be enhanced by recycling, but even then the quality of the oil deteriorates with each cycle until its value is exhausted.

Jesus reverses the Law of Entropy when He speaks about receiving and using the Truth of Revelation. God's Word does not run down or deteriorate with use; it operates according to the Law of Syntropy, which states that spiritual resources expand with use and are lost with disuse. Personal Bible study is an example. No one can prayerfully and systematically study the Word of God without entering into an expanding world of Truth. One insight leads to another; a small phrase expands into an eternal verity; and every thought connects with other thoughts in an inexhaustible universe of Truth. On the other hand, if study of the Word is ignored, Truth tends to drain away, sin flows into the vacuum, and the Truth is lost.

The Law of Syntropy applied to spiritual Truth is a law that we must obey as any other law. When Jesus teaches, *"He who has, to him will be given; and he who does not have, from him will be taken even what he has"* (v. 25), He speaks a conundrum for deaf ears. But for those who will listen, He presents Himself as the Manifest Truth—Light of Lights, Light of Revelation, and Light of Judgment. The *hidden is open.*

THE MYSTERIOUS GROWTH

26 And He said, "The kingdom of God is as if a man should scatter seed on the ground,

27 "and should sleep by night and rise by day, and the seed should sprout and grow, he himself does not know how.

28 "For the earth yields crops by itself: first the blade, then the head, after that the full grain in the head.

29 "But when the grain ripens, immediately he puts in the sickle, because the harvest has come."

Mark 4:26–29

In the Parable of the Sower, Jesus emphasizes the part of the hearer in receiving the seed of the Gospel. If the Truth stopped here, a heresy could develop. During early church history, Pelagius contended that a man could be saved by his own spiritual decision and his own good works. Others have argued with equal force that God *selectively* plants the seed, grows the crop, and reaps the harvest in passive people who have no choice. Either extreme is wrong. The

Parable of the Sower sets out a check-and-balance in which God and man interact in the growth of the Kingdom. Lest man should assume, however, that he is the moving force behind spiritual growth, Jesus adds the Parable of the Growing Seed with a conundrum that man cannot answer: *natural is supernatural.* Man may be the hearer whose response to the Gospel bears upon its growth and results, but the growth itself is God's supernatural work. Two mysteries of the Kingdom of God follow: One is that *Truth grows beyond man's knowledge;* the other is that *Truth grows beyond man's control.*

The mystery of knowledge. Forces of life and growth continue to elude man's knowledge. Who can explain the life in a seed that grows and multiplies? How could the essence of life lay dormant for 4000 years in the seeds found in an Egyptian tomb and still spring to full growth when planted? The mystery of life is the issue of the centuries. Scientific advancement only adds to the questions. Where life forces are involved, the adage holds, "We are learning more and more about less and less, and soon we will know everything about nothing." For example, a personal and legal position on genetic engineering and abortion depends upon the answer to the question, "When does human life begin?" If human life is inherent in the genes, can we tamper with human cells without violating the sacredness of life? If it is in the fertilized egg from the moment of conception, is abortion for any reason murder? When Jesus says of the sower, *"He himself does not know how"* (v. 27), He puts the mystery of life outside the knowledge of man. Does the analogy apply only to natural life? I think not. The same life forces that operate in the process of physical and spiritual growth are supernatural in origin and therefore beyond the understanding of the natural mind.

The mystery of control. A second mysterious and miraculous principle of growth for the Kingdom of God follows logically. If the nature of life is beyond man's knowledge, *he cannot control its growth, "For the earth yields crops by itself"* (v. 28).

The ultimate aim of human knowledge is control. In the field of psychology, for instance, the declared purpose of the field is the prediction and control of human behavior. B. F. Skinner developed the theory of classical conditioning to explain the development of personality and the motives for action. He took his theory one more step in his novel, *Walden Two,* in which he imagines a perfect society in which human behavior is not only explained, but controlled, by his theory. Skinner is not wrong in searching for the facts to explain human behavior, but he enters the world of fiction when he assumes that he can close the circle of psychological knowledge to predict and control human behavior. The control of life remains a mystery, whether in dictating human behavior, growing a crop of grain, or directing the development of the Kingdom of God.

Our egos also want to control the *speed of growth* for the Kingdom of God. Impatience takes over as we try to shortcircuit the process by expecting an instant harvest. Perhaps we are victims of a culture where everything is fast foods and instant relief. Jesus slows us down when He describes a process that takes time and cannot be either speeded up or shortcircuited: *"first the blade, then the head, after that the full grain in the head"* (v. 28). Because we cannot control God's timing for the growth of the Kingdom of God, we must trade in our stopwatches for calendars. Thomas Albin, a scholar of the Wesleyan revival, reports an average of more than two years between "conviction" and "conversion" for Wesley's converts. During this time, they were testing the Truth of Scripture and the consistency of Christians' lives.

Our egos also get us into trouble because we want to *control the harvest* of the Kingdom of God. As products of a goal-oriented society, we count success in the Kingdom of God on the "bottom line." Listen to a group of pastors discuss their ministries. Attention is given to membership, dollars, and buildings. Success is measured by results as if the pastor controlled the harvest. We who are parishioners share the blame because we lay the burden of success-by-numbers upon our pastors and evangelists. In the Parable of the Growing Seed, Jesus dispels such a notion. As John Stott once preached, "God has only commissioned us to preach the Gospel to all nations; the results belong to Him."[1]

As a part of His advanced teaching by parable, Jesus makes it clear that the sprouting, growing and ripening of the Gospel is a supernatural process beyond the prediction and control of man. Our task is to scatter the seed, nourish the plants and reap the harvest.

THE MULTIPLE RESULTS

30 And He said, "To what shall we liken the kingdom of God? Or with what parable shall we picture it?

31 "It is like a mustard seed which, when it is sown
on the ground, is smaller than all the seeds on earth;
32 "but when it is sown, it grows up, becomes
greater than all herbs, and shoots out large branches,
so that the birds of the air may nest under its shade."
Mark 4:30–32

In the final example of Jesus' teaching, Mark records the Parable of the Mustard Seed. Here, the conundrum is that *small is great*. Taking a mustard seed, which symbolizes insignificance in the minds of the people, Jesus reminds them that it grows to the greatest of bushes, so large that its branches become the favorite nesting and shading place for the birds of the air. In this case, the "birds of the air" are not the agents of Satan, but all of the nations of the world, including Gentiles and heathen.

A mustard seed is all risk. It is so insignificant that it is embarrassing. Yet, Jesus makes risk and insignificance the essential ingredients for starting projects in the Kingdom of God. After I had sent out a questionnaire for my doctoral research, I began to receive criticism and sarcasm from the respondents. Discouraged, I went to my graduate advisor, who had national prominence in survey research. When I told him of my plight, he answered, "Take heart. We have learned from experience that if our questionnaires are not criticized, we are doing nothing significant." Contrary to all of our secular standards for success, the seed of the Gospel also begins with a risk in which the insigificant becomes significant.

On the success side of the Gospel, we are equally uncomfortable with the idea that the purpose of the Kingdom is to grow in service rather than power. Although it is dangerous to overwork the parable, a mustard seed is not a symbol of powerful empires; it is an herb, noted for its service rather than its domination. Christians are always tempted to align the Kingdom of God with earthly power. Whenever it happens, a principle of the Kingdom is perverted and a parable of Jesus is misread. We must be constantly drawn back to the Truth that the Kingdom of God begins small in significance and grows great in service.

Do the disciples understand these advanced parables? Probably not, because we still do not understand them today. Nevertheless, the principles are known. In the Kingdom of God, the *hidden is open*,

103

natural is supernatural, and *small is great.* By reversing all of the expectations of traditional religion and human inclination, Jesus teaches that the growth of His Kingdom is not of this world.

THE PERSONAL APPLICATION

33 And with many such parables He spoke the word to them as they were able to hear it.
34 But without a parable He did not speak to them. And when they were alone, He explained all things to His disciples.

Mark 4:33–34

Mark has shown us the full scope of Jesus' method of teaching: (1) a parable is told; (2) its purpose is stated; (3) its meaning is explained; and (4) its principles are advanced. One element is missing. Mark tells us that Jesus taught by parables and spoke the word to the people, *"as they were able to hear it"* (v. 33).

A master teacher is always sensitive to the level of the learner. Inexperienced teachers tend to be just the opposite. They expect all students to rise to the level of their learning. When I started teaching psychology for college freshmen, the class turned out to be a show of my knowledge, rather than a learning experience for the students. I prided myself on a technical vocabulary, complex theories, and impossible examinations. The students were frustrated and so was I. My first remedial step was to develop a pre-test of psychological knowledge to find out where the students were. Even though the results disappointed me, I threw away all of my lecture notes that were carbon copies of my graduate school classes and started over. My teaching then took on personal dimensions and great satisfactions. Masters of public speaking need the same sensitivity to the level of their audience. A friend who offered criticism of my speaking helped me the most. Just before I spoke to a group of prominent businessmen one day, he whispered, "Shoot low, we're riding short ponies." All of my assumptions about their sophisticated knowledge had to be reworked to make sure that I was speaking on the subject of higher education at the level of their understanding. As a rule of thumb, it is always better to start a little low and lead the audience to higher levels than to start high and miss most of the people.

Jesus had to have *patience* to adjust His teaching to the level of

His hearers. Imagine a mind filled with Revealed Truth that needs to be shared with mankind. Add to the volume of Truth the knowledge that His time is limited. Urgency would seem to dictate a spilling out of high-level Truth with the expectation that the disciples would catch up after He is gone. Jesus rejects that option. Beginning at the level of His students, He patiently takes them a step at a time, and when alone with His disciples, He continues to explain the parables in detail. Following His own principles, He lets Truth mature like the Parable of the Growing Seed: *". . . first the blade, then the head, after that the full grain . . ."* (v. 28). As Saint Augustine said, "Patience is the companion of wisdom."[2]

To patience, Jesus adds *pacing* in His teaching. Students come to a "golden moment" when they are ready to learn. As a young father, I expected that my son could ride a two-wheeled bicycle before he was physically and psychologically ready. Driven by the pride of my parental ego, I took the training wheels off his small bicycle and pushed him up and down the street, becoming more and more impatient as he failed to ride off alone. Finally, our mutual frustrations surfaced in my hot words and his hot tears. He had failed me, so I put the training wheels back on the bike and sulked. A few days later, the sight from the kitchen window destroyed the remaining bits of my shattered ego. Astride a full-sized bicycle, held up by a neighbor boy to get his balance, my son was given a quick push, and sailed down the street in triumph. He was ready to ride!

Jesus knows when His students are ready to learn. Several times, His impatience gets ahead of Him as He exclaims, "O faithless generation, how long shall I be with you . . . ?" (9:19), but He always recovers the patience to go back over the lesson until they come to the "golden moment" when all their learning converges in a moment of truth. Mark uses the words *"as they were able to hear it"* (v. 33) to denote the readiness of the disciples for learning. "Hear" is the same word that Jesus has used several times in the parables. In each case, it means to receive the seed of the Gospel so that it might take root, sprout, grow and produce a harvest. Jesus, the Master Teacher, paces His lessons to the rhythm of readiness in His disciples. When they are ready to learn, He sows the seed and then gives it time to grow and harvest before starting another season of teaching and learning.

Mark's case for Jesus, the Master Teacher, is now complete. With his typical precision of argument, he has recorded the "Who?"

"What?" "When?" "Where?" "How?" and "Why?" of Jesus' teaching. *"Who?"* is Jesus; *"What?"* is the principle of growth for the Kingdom of God; *"Where?"* is the seaside; *"When?"* is the disciples' readiness to learn; *"How?"* is teaching by parables; and *"Why?"* is the preparation of the disciples for their continuing ministry. Only Jesus Christ, the Son of God, can master and teach such Truth.

NOTE

1. John R. W. Stott, *Christian Mission* (Downers Grove, IL: Inter-Varsity Press, 1975), p. 38.

2. Saint Augustine, "On Patience," 425, in Ralph L. Woods, *World Treasury of Religious Quotations,* p. 719.

CHAPTER SIX

Exercising His Authority

Mark 4:35—5:43

OVER NATURE

35 And the same day, when evening had come, He said to them, "Let us cross over to the other side."

36 And when they had sent away the multitude, they took Him along in the boat as He was. And other little boats were also with Him.

37 And a great windstorm arose, and the waves beat into the boat, so that it was already filling.

38 And He was in the stern, asleep on a pillow. And they awoke Him and said to Him, "Teacher, do You not care that we are perishing?"

39 And He arose and rebuked the wind, and said to the sea, "Peace, be still!" And the wind ceased and there was a great calm.

40 And He said to them, "Why are you so fearful? How is it that you have no faith?"

41 And they feared exceedingly, and said to one another, "What kind of Man is this, that even the wind and the sea obey Him!"

Mark 4:35–41

Mark loves striking contrasts. After the violent confrontation with the Pharisees which produced a plot against Jesus' life, Mark slows down the action by an elaborate explanation of the teaching of Jesus. But lest his readers think that Jesus is limited to theory rather than practice, he throws Him into conflict against forces that are considered

107

the most formidable of all: wild nature (4:35–41); rampant demons (5:1–20); incurable illnesses (5:25–34); and certain death (5:21–24; 35–43). In a contest of wills with the ravages of natural forces, Jesus will show whether or not He is the Christ, the Son of God.

An ominous setting serves as the backdrop for the test of Jesus' authority over the forces of nature. He has just completed a full day of teaching—sensitive to every learning cue, careful to explain every detail and patient with every question. A weary and empty Jesus—so expressive of His full humanity—needs freedom from the crowd and solitude for His soul. Asking for the boat that has been put at His command, He proposes that they sail to the eastern side of the lake for refuge from the masses. Mark even includes the fact that Jesus is given the honored place in the stern of the boat with a pillow upon which to rest. Once out at sea, however, nature turns loose all of the forces of violence with a storm that not even the seasoned fishermen—Simon, James, and John—have seen. How can Jesus sleep through a life-threatening storm? Is it His exhaustion or His peace? In panic, the sailors cry out, *"Teacher, do You not care that we are perishing?"* (v. 38).

Nature is God's creation. God created the heavens, earth, sun, moon, stars, seas, land, plants, animals, and man. Viewing His work, God pronounced it "good." David sang, "The heavens declare the glory of God; and the firmament sheweth his handywork" (Psalm 19:1, kjv).

Original nature was good because it had unity and balance that worked together in the harmony that made the morning stars sing together. We still see the traces of that harmony. Astronauts rocket into space, assured that orderly laws of the universe will not be canceled during their flight. Naturalists see the beauty of the earth in the delicate and interlocking balance of plant life. Ecologists remind us that everything in the universe is so connected with everything else that when a person stubs a toe on earth, it is felt in Mars. No one can watch a sunset spreading in varicolored splendor across the Western sky without wanting to exclaim, "It is good." Thomas Higgins said it for us, "Creation is an overwhelming outpouring, the overflow of infinite good news."[1]

At the same time, we recognize that *nature is sin's victim.* Man's fall from grace is so pervasive that even innocent nature is affected. As Paul writes to the Romans, physical nature joins human nature in the eager wait for redemption: ". . . the creation itself also will be delivered from the bondage of corruption into the glorious liberty of the children of God" (Rom. 8:21).

While nature awaits redemption, man has the responsibility to *conserve and control its balance wherever possible.* God makes man the steward of the earth and its resources when He blesses Adam and Eve in the Garden: "Be fruitful, and multiply, and replenish the earth, and subdue it: and have dominion over the fish of the sea, and over the fowl of the air, and over every living thing that moveth upon the earth" (Gen. 1:28, KJV).

Man's responsibility did not cease with his sin. He is still the steward of the earth.

Some environmentalists have accused Christians of a theology that spoils the earth. They are referring to a misguided interpretation of the Protestant ethic rather than a contemporary interpretation of the Biblical ethic. Rene Dubos, in his book *Only One Earth: The Care and Maintenance of a Small Planet,* acknowledges the difference when he cites Genesis 1:28 as the keystone for the stewardship of the earth and its resources.

Christians should have been primary advocates for the control and conservation of natural resources all along. Ecology is a scientific term describing balance and the harmony of God's original creation. Environmentalism is another way of reminding us that God instructed Adam and Eve in the Garden to replenish the earth as well as subdue it. Now that the politicized, isolated, and temporary wave of environmental interest has passed, Christians have the opportunity to teach the Biblical, holistic and eternal principles about conserving and controlling our natural resources as an integral part of Biblical theology.

Our best efforts to be the stewards of the earth will always fall short because *nature has wild and unpredictable tendencies that only God can tame.* The storm on the Sea of Galilee hit Jesus' boat and His small fleet with unpredictable and unprecedented force. After standing on the shore of that sea and noting the contour of the surrounding hills, I can understand how capricious winds create violent storms. Our favorite vacation spot in the summer is at a lake in a Galilean setting. Between the barren hills are gullies that become funnels for blasts of wind that crisscross the water and endanger small boats. More than once, I have started across the lake in a favorable breeze, only to be caught by a gale before returning home. Every skill of sailing is tested as winds shift and waves wash over the bow. Fear still strikes at my heart as I remember the wind that broke my lines, tore the sail, and capsized the boat. By the time I swam the boat to shore and collapsed on the beach, the wind was down and the sea was calm. Like Jesus' disciples, I learned what Goethe meant when he wrote in *Faust*: "Nature . . . is a great organ, on which our Lord God plays, and the Devil blows the bellows."[2]

God is at home with His nature, even when it goes wild. The contrast between the disciples' panic and Jesus' peace attests the deity of the man asleep on a pillow at the stern of the boat. He who is the Word by which all things were made has no reason to fear a storm. He who foresees the making of a new heaven and a new earth sleeps in the knowledge that nature's peevish outburst can be controlled by its Maker.

Fear wipes out faith. If the disciples had not been paralyzed by the fear of death, they might have remembered Who it was that slept in the stern of the boat. Instead, they shook Him awake with anger and accusation, *"Teacher, do You not care that we are perishing?"* (v. 38). I wish that I could have compared their look of paralyzed panic with the eyes of Jesus as He blinks Himself awake, looks around to survey the situation, and with a calmness of spirit that puts the worst fears of men and the wildest winds of the seas to rest, He speaks, *"Peace, be still!"* (v. 39). The wind stops blowing and the sea settles into resolute calm. God has put His creation at rest.

Turning to the disciples, Jesus asks. *"Why are you so fearful? How is it that you have no faith?"* (v. 40). Rather than relieving the disciples' fears, He multiplies them. With an awe that only comes when fearful men stand in the presence of a peaceful God, the disciples buzz to each other, *"What kind of Man is this, that even the wind and the sea obey Him!"* (v. 41).

Awe is our only response to the God who controls the wildest whims of nature. Photographs of Mount St. Helens' volcanic eruption have now become still-life posters that convey a sense of unbelievable force to the viewer. But the awe of the mountain cannot begin to approach the awe of the God who can speak winds and seas, mountains and volcanoes to calm. Jesus speaks with that awesome power, proving that He who rules the wind, controls the sea, and stills the tempest is the Christ, the Son of God.

OVER DEMONS

1 And they came to the other side of the sea, to the country of the Gadarenes.

2 And when He had come out of the boat,

immediately there met Him out of the tombs a man with an unclean spirit,

3 who had his dwelling among the tombs; and no one could bind him, not even with chains,

4 because he had often been bound with shackles and chains. And the chains had been pulled apart by him, and the shackles broken to pieces; neither could anyone tame him.

5 And always, night and day, he was in the mountains and in the tombs, crying out and cutting himself with stones.

6 But when he saw Jesus from afar, he ran and worshiped Him.

7 And he cried out with a loud voice and said, "What have I to do with You, Jesus, Son of the Most High God? I implore You by God that You do not torment me."

8 For He said to him, "Come out of the man, unclean spirit!"

9 And He asked him, "What is your name?" And he answered, saying, "My name is Legion; for we are many."

10 And he begged Him earnestly that He would not send them out of the country.

11 Now a large herd of swine was feeding there near the mountains.

12 And all the demons begged Him, saying, "Send us to the swine, that we may enter them!"

13 And at once Jesus gave them permission. And the unclean spirits went out and entered the swine (there were about two thousand); and the herd ran violently down the steep place into the sea, and drowned in the sea.

14 And those who fed the swine fled, and they told it in the city and in the country. And they went out to see what it was that had happened.

15 And they came to Jesus, and saw the one who had been demon-possessed and had the legion, sitting and clothed and in his right mind. And they were afraid.

16 And those who saw it told them how it happened to him who had been demon-possessed, and about the swine.

17 And they began to plead with Him to depart from their region.

18 And when He got into the boat, he who had been demon-possessed begged Him that he might be with Him.

19 However, Jesus did not permit him, but said to him, "Go home to your friends, and tell them what great things the Lord has done for you, and how He has had compassion on you."

20 And he departed and began to proclaim in Decapolis what great things Jesus had done for him; and all marveled.

Mark 5:1–20

Jesus and His disciples start out across the Sea of Galilee for respite from the pressure of the crowds. On the way, they encounter a wild storm that threatens their lives and calls out the authority of Jesus over the forces of nature. After Jesus rebukes the winds and calms the waters, their voyage continues toward the Eastern shore of Galilee, a relatively remote area inhabited by Gentiles. No sooner do they land on the shore in the country of Gadarenes, than Jesus is challenged again. This time, it is the wildest of human nature, a demon-wracked man. Like the storm, nature has spun out of control so that the creature who meets Him is more monster than man. Mark tells in picturesque detail that the devils "on the other side" are the worst kind and only God can cast them out.

Devils "on the other side." Jesus needs to escape and relax. Instead, He sails in the wildest seas of physical and human nature. Like us, He learns that there is no escape from reality. The "other side" may be as literal as the eastern shore of the Galilean Sea, or it may be as symbolic as our desire to retreat into the past, seek an alternative for the present, or assume that the future will be better. How many times have you heard people express the wish for the "good, old days?" The truth is that those days are peopled with the demons of the past. Senility frequently uncovers those demons. After a series of little strokes in the brain, the elderly person may blank out current events one minute after they happen, but assume astonishing clarity for events in the distant past that everyone else has lost. Yet, those memories have their demons. A senile person not only sees an instant replay of the glory of the past, but also recalls with equal clarity the traumas and the fears. On a recent visit to an aged and senile friend, we witnessed the glow in her eyes as she spoke of her child-hood home and then, without warning, the glow turned to pitiful weeping as she relived her mother's funeral. The mother had died fifty years ago.

Other people long for the "other side" by wishing for alternatives to present circumstances. "If only I could do something different" is their motto. They fail to realize that any alternative has its trade-offs. At one time, I survived a process that brought me to a finalist role for a Cabinet position in the Reagan administration. Enticing thoughts about the glamour of being close to the center of world power swept through me. Then, a friend sent me an article entitled, "So You Want To Be a Cabinet Officer?" The trade-offs paraded before me like demons "on the other side." My healthy margins of independence, privacy, and leadership would be substantially nar-rowed by politics, public life, and governmental bureaucracy. Jesus speaks with profound wisdom when He asks, "For which of you, intending to build a tower, does not sit down first and count the cost, whether he has enough to finish it—?" (Luke 14:28). Half-fin-ished towers are monuments to the demons "on the other side."

An eye forever fixed on the future also fails to see the special kind of demons "on the other side" of time. To anticipate the future is a gift of the image of God given to man. If the gift is lost, the loser sinks in hopeless despair. Young corporation presidents who reach the top of their profession at an early age are sometimes subject to a loss of future vision. Having achieved every goal that they have sought in life and with no more worlds to conquer, they start looking back and there they find demons. Ulcers, alcohol, sex, divorce and even suicide become symptoms of their frustration. Therapeutic ses-sions for these executives are aimed at turning them away from the past and toward the future once again. They are then helped to de-velop a philosophy of life that says, "The older you get, the longer your view of the future." If the advice is sound, Christians who have the hope of eternal life as an ever-lengthening view of the future should get younger with age.

During my internship experience as a chaplain in the mental health wing of a hospital, I was introduced to a man whose faith had been twisted into the fantasy that he was living out the Book of Revelation. One day, he went berserk and tried to kill several people. When asked why, he said that he was doing the Lord's will. While reading his Bible, he came to the passage in Revelation that speaks of the

113

last days when ". . . blood came out of the winepress, up to the horses' bridles . . ." (Rev. 14:20) and decided that he could speed the day of redemption if he started the blood flowing now. Mercy made it necessary to take his Bible from him.

There is a sense in which Jesus brings out the worst as well as the best in a person. Immediately upon beaching the boat and stepping out, He hears the most ungodly shriek and sees a naked, bleeding, and half-shackled wild man running toward Him, falling down in a posture of worship, and screaming, *"What have I to do with You, Jesus, Son of the Most High God? I implore You by God that You not torment me"* (v. 7). One of the most pitiful sights in all the world is a person whose mind is so torn that he or she worships while cursing, and confesses while blaspheming. If ever a picture of Satan's ultimate motive in possessing a person has been painted, this is it. The Devil is never content until he has destroyed the last vestige of the image of God in the human personality.

Mark leads us to the inevitable conclusion that *the worst of demons "on the other side" can only be controlled by God Himself.* Jesus has His choice of responding either to the worshiping posture or the cursing questions of the madman of Gadarenes. Thank God, He takes hold of the smallest thread of hope and responds to the worshiping posture. *"Come out of the man, unclean spirit!"* (v. 8), He calls. There is a pause. Nothing happens, or perhaps some demons leave while others remain. Jesus' past experience with demon-possessed people is not adequate. He must control them to expel them. *"What is your name?"* (v. 9), He asks. From the very beginning of time, when God gave Adam the responsibility to name the animals, it is acknowledged that he who knows the name also knows the nature and can therefore control either persons or demons.

Jesus' authority has won out. The answer comes back, *"My name is Legion; for we are many"* (v. 9). Roman legions which occupy the land of Gadarenes are made up of six hundred armed men. In its extended meaning, Legion means "thousands." Whatever the number, demon-possession is so complete and so multiplied that Jesus has to resort to extraordinary means to save a man. The demons themselves give Him a choice. He can wipe them out of existence by expelling them from the country or He can send unclean spirits into unclean animals, the two thousand swine which rooted nearby. Jesus chooses the swine. Why? Critics complain that He disregards the property of the swine-owners or exposes His Jewishness by penalizing

Gentiles who traffic in unclean meat. A more consistent view is that Jesus knows that the power of Satan is not yet bound so that He does not expel the demons forever. If He had, the purpose of the Incarnation would have been aborted because all evil would have been destroyed. Jesus would have won the submission of man, but not his love. So, as the alternative, He chooses to demonstrate the destructive power of Satan by sending the unclean spirits into the swine. Jesus shows that only God can dispel the worst of demons and only at a high cost. Two thousand pigs drowning in the sea is minimal cost in comparison with Jesus dying on the cross for the same reason—the redemption of a man and men.

Results of deliverance are mixed. Fear strikes the swineherders, who beg Jesus to sail back across the sea. He has ruined their business. The man who is healed, however, appears as a witness to the glory of God. Sitting rather than pacing, clothed rather than naked, and sane rather than mad, the miracle strikes fear into the hearts of those who see him.

It is time for Jesus to leave. As He gets into the boat, the madman of Gadarenes, who is now known as the miracle-man of Gadarenes, begs to go along. Jesus decisively answers "No," and urges him to *"Go home to your friends, and tell them what great things the Lord has done for you, and how He has had compassion on you"* (v. 19).

One of the toughest lessons of my life is learning to live my faith at home. After a day of making decisions and giving orders at the office, it is easy to bring the "presidential" image home, expecting everyone to bow and everyone to obey. Somehow, I failed to establish an absolute chain of command. If my wife or children think I'm wrong, they let me know it. If they disagree with my inspired decision, they will say it. One night, I came home looking forward to doing some painting. Like Old Mother Hubbard, I went to the cupboard where I kept my brushes and found it bare. "Who took my paintbrush?" echoed through the house. No one confessed, but I remembered that my oldest daughter had agreed to help her boyfriend, who was president of the student body at the university, paint his office. Yelling once more, I confronted her in the corner of the basement. She then remembered that they had taken the brush to paint the office and had left it in the Student Union Building. "Go get it," I ordered. Hereditary stubbornness met head on. "No," my daughter answered, "I'm busy." Words became shouts, shouts became tears, and tears became silence. For three days, we did not talk to each

other. I was convinced that I was right and she had no doubt about
her father being a dictator. Finally, after three days of misery, God's
Spirit put upon me the responsibility for the impasse. I was supposed
to be the strong, spiritual model for my daughter. Right or wrong
no longer made a difference. I had treated my family like chattels
on a slave farm. So, broken in spirit, I made my way to my daughter's
room and confessed that my spirit was wrong, that I loved her so
much more than a paintbrush, and that I needed her forgiveness.
Fathers never talk with daughters that way except tears begin to
flow. Weeping together and kissing away her tears, I was home again.

My imagination visualizes a similar scene for the miracle-man of
Gadarenes. Only God can tame his wild nature and only the healing
of home can bring him the peace he needs. No wonder, then, that
he becomes a one-man witness in the ten cities of the Decapolis,
telling what Jesus has done for him. No wonder that everyone marvels.
Jesus Christ, the Son of God, has tamed the wildest of human nature.

OVER SICKNESS AND DEATH

21 And when Jesus had crossed over again by boat
to the other side, a great multitude gathered to Him;
and He was by the sea.

22 And behold, one of the rulers of the synagogue
came, Jairus by name. And when he saw Him, he fell
at His feet

23 and begged Him earnestly, saying, "My little
daughter lies at the point of death. Come and lay Your
hands on her, that she may be healed, and she will
live."

24 And Jesus went with him, and a great multitude
followed Him and thronged Him.

25 And a certain woman had a flow of blood for
twelve years,

26 and had suffered many things from many
physicians. She had spent all that she had and was
no better, but rather grew worse.

27 When she had heard about Jesus, she came
behind Him in the crowd and touched His garment;

28 for she said, "If only I may touch His clothes,
I shall be made well."

29 And immediately the fountain of her blood was dried up, and she felt in her body that she was healed of the affliction.

30 And Jesus, immediately knowing in Himself that power had gone out of Him, turned around in the crowd and said, "Who touched My clothes?"

31 And His disciples said to Him, "You see the multitude thronging You, and You say, 'Who touched Me?' "

32 And He looked around to see her who had done this thing.

33 But the woman, fearing and trembling, knowing what had happened to her, came and fell down before Him and told Him the whole truth.

34 And He said to her, "Daughter, your faith has made you well. Go in peace, and be healed of your affliction."

35 While He was still speaking, some came from the ruler of the synagogue's house who said, "Your daughter is dead. Why trouble the Teacher any further?"

36 As soon as Jesus heard the word that was spoken, He said to the ruler of the synagogue, "Do not be afraid; only believe."

37 And He permitted no one to follow Him except Peter, James, and John the brother of James.

38 And He came to the house of the ruler of the synagogue, and saw the tumult and those who wept and wailed loudly.

39 And when He had come in, He said to them, "Why make this commotion and weep? The child is not dead but sleeping."

40 And they laughed Him to scorn. But when He had put them all out, He took the father and the mother of the child, and those who were with Him, and entered where the child was lying.

41 And He took the child by the hand and said to her, *"Talitha, cumi,"* which is translated, "Little girl, I say to you, arise."

42 And immediately the girl arose and walked, for she was twelve years of age. And they were overcome with great amazement.

43 And He commanded them strictly that no one

should know it, and said that something should be
given her to eat.

Mark 5:21–43

Whoever suggests that Mark is an undisciplined writer of a hodge-podge Gospel fails to understand the precision and the pattern of his writing. Having shown that Jesus has authority over the worst of physical nature and psychological demons, he advances his case to an encounter with incurable disease and tragic death. Interweaving the stories of the woman with the issue of blood and Jairus' daughter who died, Mark attests the authority of Jesus over the ravages of sin upon physical nature. As with the storm at sea and the demon-possessed man, the drama unfolds with: (1) a point of *surprise;* (2) a confession of *futility;* (3) a show of *authority;* and (4) a testimony of *peace and awe.*

A point of surprise. The storm at sea came up as a surprise and the madman of Gadarenes ran and fell at Jesus' feet as a surprise. Another surprise awaits Jesus when He crosses back over the sea to the Galilean side. Jairus, ruler of the synagogue, comes out to meet Him with the surprising act of falling at His feet. Earlier, we pondered the question, "How can the seed of the Gospel penetrate the hardened minds of the Pharisees?" We now have the answer. Jairus has a twelve-year-old daughter who means more to him than interpretations of the Law or his standing in the synagogue. For her sake, he is willing to risk religious ridicule and public embarrassment by kneeling at Jesus' feet and begging Him to come to his home and heal his daughter, who is at the point of death.

Only a father can understand the love for a twelve-year-old daughter. She is just short of becoming a woman, but still young enough to be his baby. From life experience, I know that there is nothing a father will not do for a beloved daughter. Just the word "daddy" assures that every request is granted and a tear melts the heart of a tough university president or corporation executive as if it were a snowman in a heat wave. Never before or never again will the relationship between father and daughter be quite the same. At the age of twelve, a daughter views her father as her special beau. Let the shadow of death fall over the beauty of that relationship and a father's love becomes focused like a laser beam upon survival. There is no treatment too costly, no travel too distant, no plea too humiliating. ". . . A little child shall lead them" (Is. 11:6, KJV) may have a thousand meanings, but none so personal or none so penetrating as a father trying to save the life of his daughter.

Surprise also catches Jesus as He moves through the milling masses toward Jairus' house. An equally desperate woman with an incurable blood disease develops a scheme to try and touch one of the tassels on the hem of Jesus' robe as her only hope of healing. Drawing upon the last ounces of her assertive energies, she shoulders her way to a position close to Jesus, falls into step with the crowd, and then at a well-timed moment lunges through a maze of moving legs to touch Him. Both she and Jesus feel the effect of her touch. According to Mark, *"she felt in her body that she was healed of the affliction"* (v. 29). Jesus spins on His heel and throws a question toward a blur of faces, *"Who touched My clothes?"* (v. 30). From His strong body, He has felt the transfer of healing power to the woman's diseased shell. Too much can be made of this unintended transfer of power. If Jesus loses power every time He heals a person, how much can He sacrifice without exhaustion? Or, to ask the skeptic's question, "If His power is divine and therefore, inexhaustible, how can He lose power?" Far more important is the sensitivity of Jesus which causes Him to feel the difference between an anxious tug of faith and the casual bumps of the jostling crowd. Furthermore, no one responds to desperate human need without giving something of themselves. Elevated to the level of a divine response to an incurable disease, it reminds us that our healing is only given freely to us because of the price that Jesus paid. Isaiah's prophecy, ". . . and with his stripes we are healed" (Is. 53:5, KJV), comes true in Jesus' gift to the woman and in the price for her healing.

Jesus' disciples miss the point of Jesus' surprise. Almost in derision, they scoff, *"You see the multitude thronging You, and You say, 'Who touched Me?'"* (v. 31). Logic supports their retort, but shows that they do not yet understand the nature of the Man in their midst. Later, they will talk about the episode and pray that they might be like Jesus, sensitive to human need and able to discern between true and false touches. Ananias and Sapphira put Peter's discernment to an early test after the coming of the Holy Spirit. Their ruse of trying to gain the benefits of membership in the Spirit-filled community while holding back part of the price for their property is immediately detected by Peter. By learning from Jesus and living in the Spirit, he calls their bluff (Acts 5:1–11). His discernment continues to develop as he confronts Simon, the converted sorcerer, who offers money to be filled with the Holy Spirit. Wasting no time and mincing no words, Peter cuts him off with the condemnation, "Your money perish with you, because you have thought that the gift of God may be purchased with money!" (Acts 8:20).

These experiences are readying Peter for the crucial moment in His ministry as the leader of the infant church. God puts him in a trance to show him the vision of a great sheet, bound at the four corners, descending from heaven and filled with all the species of the animals, reptiles and birds. Peter balks at the meaning of the vision, which opens up salvation to the Gentiles as well as the Jews. But as the Holy Spirit leads him to Cornelius, a Gentile of Caesarea, Peter discerns that God has spoken. Thus, when he arrives at Cornelius' house, he is ready to erase the prejudice of a lifetime, and he does when he confesses to Cornelius, ". . . God has shown me that I should not call any man common or unclean" (Acts 10:28). Spiritual discernment is a gift of the Holy Spirit.

A confession of human futility. Coupled with a point of surprise in the stories of the storm at sea, the demon-possessed man, and now in the accounts of the death of Jairus' daughter and the woman with the incurable blood disease is the *confession of human futility.* In each case, the people involved have given up. Disciples decide that they are fated to die at sea; and the Gadarenes consign the demoniac to a graveyard after shackles fail to control him. Futility with human instrumentality plagues Jairus as well. Only as a last resort will he risk his career and reputation by falling at the feet of Jesus and begging Him for help. No doubt remains in his mind about his daughter's impending death unless God Himself intervenes. Within moments, a messenger from home confirms his futility. *"Your daughter is dead. Why trouble the Teacher any further?"* (v. 35). Even the slightest hope for a miracle vanishes. In the initial shock of disbelief that always follows death, he may fail to hear Jesus' confident words, *"Do not be afraid; only believe"* (v. 36). If he does hear, the words take on a hollow ring as they approach the house and find that the professional mourners have already arrived, wailing with false tears and intoning the sounds of death on their funeral flutes. Every symbol of human futility is in place. For Jairus, it is all over except for the burial.

Mark also records the details of human futility for the woman with the issue of blood. Her disease itself marks her with a social stigma. Like a perpetual menstrual cycle, she has suffered twelve years of uncleanness. Her innocence before the ravages of disease that cannot be cured does not exempt her from social and spiritual penalties. Separated from her home, isolated from her family, and segregated in the synagogue, she uses up whatever wealth she has seeking medical help. Mark adds a gentle dig at the doctors of the day by inserting the phrase, *"and had suffered many things from many physicians"* (v. 26).

Mark's mildly caustic comment is more than an aside to his argument. As a part of his case to prove that Jesus has authority over incurable illness, he is saying the best and most expensive of medical science has joined with the woman in a confession of human futility. Almost as certain as the sound of the death knell over Jairus' daughter, the woman with an issue of blood has explored the outer reaches of human knowledge and ends up without hope.

A show of authority. To paraphrase an oft-spoken adage, "Man's futility is God's opportunity," Jesus acts with clear and decisive authority in stilling the storm, casting out demons, and now—curing the incurable and raising the dead. Taking Jairus' daughter by the hand, He speaks the words of life, *"Little girl . . . arise"* (v. 41). Peter's memory of the event is still so vivid that he slips into Aramaic, the familiar language, as he tells Mark the story. *"Talitha, cumi"* is an invitation of love that literally means, "Little lamb, arise." Jesus' authority, tough with wild winds and raging demons, becomes as tender as a shepherd lifting the littlest of lambs.

The woman with the incurable blood disease gets a similar response. Jesus' brusque inquiry, *"Who touched Me?"* (v. 31), causes her to cower with fear and trembling at His feet. Will He condemn Her for being presumptuous or cancel the healing that she feels in her body? Jesus entertains no such thought. After all, Who has called others to a reckless faith? Jesus' words echo back to Him through the ingenuity of a daring and, yes, even presumptuous woman. So, rather than rebuking her, He addresses her as a woman of mature and courageous faith. *"Daughter, your faith has made you well"* (v. 34), is a commendation of honor that Jesus reserves especially for her. As a bonus, then, He adds two blessings: *"Go in peace"* (v. 34), which puts an end to a twelve-year search for wholeness; and *"be healed of your affliction"* (v. 34), which assures her that the disease is gone forever.

Faith, by its own definition, is creative and presumptuous. I dreaded my first funeral sermon. The call came one day after a woman of cultured taste and community leadership died. For years, she had lived just outside of the community of faith, a person of the highest moral character who never made a profession of faith in Christ, but still wanted her daughters to have the spiritual values of the church to complement the cultural values of their home. Her community position meant that many people would be attending the service who did not know the familiar language that Christians use when they talk to each other. My dread bordered on panic until one of her daughters told the story of her mother's faith as she had written it in a letter sometime before incurable cancer began to spread through her body. Confessing that her desire to live a good life did not bring her the peace or the joy she sought, a simple confession of sin broke her from the futile search of the past and projected her into the future as a forgiven and whole woman. After reading the letter, the Spirit of God filled in a flowing sermon around the text, *"Daughter, your faith has made you well"* (v. 34).

Hidden behind the woman's healing and the raising of Jairus' daughter is the truth that Jesus does not exercise His authority as a mechanical response in a clinical setting. Mixed with His decisive action as the Son of God are His feelings as the Son of Man. When He cures the incurable, His authority blends the raw power of God with feelingful respect for a woman who has become a full partner in the faith. When He raises Jairus' daughter from the dead, His omnipotence carries the touch of a father's love.

A testimony of peace and awe. The interwoven stories of Jairus' daughter and the woman with the blood disease end with *a testimony of peace and awe.* As proof of her return to a full and normal life, Jesus asks that the little girl be given something to eat. For the woman made whole, He sends her away with a benediction of peace, forever cured of her illness. Peace is the common element they share, along with the victims of the storm and demon-possession. A calm sea, a relaxed man, a free woman and a hungry child are all pictures of peace that are the products of Jesus' power. In contrast, the peace that comes from human power is temporary at best. Just beneath the veneer of tranquility is a turmoil that can break out under the slightest provocation. An expert in international affairs said that he feared treaties on nuclear weapons almost as much as the arms race itself because conflict could be provoked, and presumably justified, if one party or the other violated a jot or a tittle of a negotiated agreement. The peace of Christ is not a negotiated treaty between God and man; it is a trust without reservation or qualification.

All witnesses to Jesus' exercise of authority over the ravaging forces of nature respond with a mingling of fear and wonder. As the astounded disciples felt the winds die and the seas calm, "They feared exeedingly, and said to one another, 'What kind of Man is this, that even the wind and the sea obey Him?' " (4:41). The Gadarenes who heard the swineherders' story and came out to see the demoniac sitting, clothed and in his right mind. ". . . *were afraid"* (5:15). Those who heard the man's testimony throughout the Decapolis *". . . marveled"* at the miracle (v. 20). All who saw Jairus' daughter up and walking, including those who had laughed Jesus to scorn, *"were overcome with great amazement"* (v. 42). Only in the case of the woman who touches the hem of Jesus' garment are the reactions of the witnesses missing. The reason is obvious. While Jesus is speaking to the woman (v. 35), an emergency message comes that Jairus' daughter is dead. All attention turns to the new crisis, with its own reactions of fear and wonder hushing the noisy, jostling crowd.

Mark has taken us to the outer edge of human experience where only God can make a difference. Out there, Jesus confronts the most destructive forces known to man—the sea, demons, disease and death—all out of control. Exercising His authority over these forces, in response to human futility, Jesus brings the peace that passes all understanding. Mark's case can almost be closed. Who can deny that Jesus, through His Servant ministry, is the Christ, the Son of God? At least, the burden of proof is shifting heavily toward those who will still deny Him.

NOTES

1. Thomas J. Higgins, *Perfection Is for You* (Milwaukee: Bruce Publishing Co., 1953).
2. J. W. von Goethe, *Faust* (1790), in Ralph L. Woods, *World Treasury of Religious Quotations*, p. 676.

CHAPTER SEVEN

Acknowledging His Limitations

Mark 6:1–29

OF HUMAN UNDERSTANDING

1 And He went out from there and came to His own country, and His disciples followed Him.

2 And when the Sabbath had come, He began to teach in the synagogue. And many hearing Him were astonished, saying, "Where did this Man get these things? And what wisdom is this which is given to Him, that such mighty works are performed by His hands!

3 "Is this not the carpenter, the Son of Mary, and brother of James, Joses, Judas, and Simon? And are not His sisters here with us?" And they were offended at Him.

4 But Jesus said to them, "A prophet is not without honor except in his own country, among his own relatives, and in his own house."

5 And He could do no mighty work there, except that He laid His hands on a few sick people and healed them.

6 And He marveled because of their unbelief. And He went about the villages in a circuit, teaching.

Mark 6:1–6

Jesus has just come through His shining hour. In quick succession, He has stilled a storm at sea, cast demons out of a mad man, healed a woman of an incurable disease, and raised Jairus' daughter from the dead. As a result, His fame spreads like wildfire and wherever He goes, the common people hear Him gladly. It is time to go home.

The anticipation of coming home. Deep in the heart of every man, there is a wistful desire to be welcomed home as a hero. No human event is filled with greater anticipation. Whether it is a ticker-tape parade, a family reunion, a high school homecoming, or just a return from a long business trip, there is nothing like coming home. Home is a place where love lets us be ourselves, pride shares our achievements, and understanding covers our faults.

Jesus wants the same response for His homecoming. A little more than a year earlier, He left the village of Nazareth as a nobody, but now He returns home as a person who is rumored to be the Son of God, with a message of Good News and a ministry of miracles. Earlier, before He had established His reputation, His townsfolk apologized for His supernatural claims by suggesting, "He is beside Himself"— a gentle way of protecting the reputation of the family. Jesus needs no excuses now. He comes home a second time with all the evidence that He needs to back up His claims. "Surely," He thinks, "My family and My friends will welcome Me now."

The attitude of unbelief. Loyal to His townspeoples' tradition of worship, Jesus chooses the synagogue as the place to demonstrate His authority as a teacher. Astonishment ripples through the congregation. They cannot deny the Godliness of His presence, the wisdom of His words or the power of His miracles. Still, they cannot accept the change. Familiarity has bred a contempt which spouts forth in disbelief: *"Where did this Man get these things? And what wisdom is this which is given to Him, that such mighty works are performed by His hands!"* (v. 2).

To the credit of the townsfolk, they ask the right questions. *Who is this Man? What is His wisdom? Where does He get His power?* Until these questions are asked, there is no faith. Is Jesus human or divine? Are His words human philosophy or Eternal Truth? Is His power to work miracles natural or God-given? Once these questions are asked, a decision must be made. C. S. Lewis and others have said it so well: If Jesus is not the Son of God, He is a lunatic; if His words are not the Truth, He is a liar; if His power is not given by God, He is in league with the devil.

The tragedy of the townspeople of Nazareth is that they ask the right questions with the wrong attitude. Prejudice so overrules all the evidence that they answer themselves: *"Is this not the carpenter, the*

Son of Mary, and brother of James, Joses, Judas and Simon? And are not His sisters here with us?" (v. 3).

These questions are rhetorical, self-contained with the sneer of prejudice and the sting of unbelief. At the very least, they are saying that His birth is human and therefore He cannot be the Son of God. At the very worst, they are resurrecting the scandal of Mary's pregnancy before marriage and smearing Jesus with the charge of illegitimacy.

Where does He get His wisdom? The answer of blind prejudice comes back, *"Is this not the carpenter?"* (v. 3). Again, the mildest meaning of the question is a putdown for an unschooled craftsman who now claims to be a rabbi. More likely, the barb goes deeper to twist and to turn. To be called a carpenter in Jesus' time did not necessarily mean a skilled craftsman with high position among laboring classes; it also meant a "handyman" who traveled from house to house doing small, odd jobs for a pittance. On the scale of honor, a handyman stood just above the village idiot. If this is the stereotype of Jesus that His townsfolk still hold, we can understand why they have trouble accepting the wisdom of His articulate and authoritative words. Prejudice produced a gap which was filled in with unbelief.

Where does Jesus get the power to perform mighty works? Again, the answer comes back in prejudicial terms, *"Is this not the . . . brother of James, Joses, Judas, and Simon? And are not His sisters here with us?"* (v. 3). By inference, the whole family of Jesus is maligned. Pointing to His brothers and sisters, the skeptics call attention to the fact that they are not only natural progeny of Mary and Joseph, but undistinguished in gifts or reputation. How can their brother suddenly appear with a claim on the supernatural?

Jesus has come home anticipating a welcome. Instead, He is crushed under an attitude of unbelief growing out of the familiarity and prejudice of people who try to remake Him in their own despicable and defensive self-image.

The atmosphere of unbelief. Unbelief has consequences that are tragic and sometimes eternal. For the people of Nazareth, their prejudice prohibits Jesus from doing any mighty work among them. How sad! Certainly, Nazareth needs mighty works. What about those who waited to be healed? How about those who wanted to believe? A despised town becomes the prototype of rejection.

Jesus wanted to make Nazareth His place of personal triumph. The best He can do is use the occasion to remind the disciples that they should not be surprised by the lack of honor in their country, among their own relatives and in their own houses. Can you put yourself in Jesus' place as He walks out of His hometown for the last time? He feels the wrenching hurt of His own prediction, "Foxes have holes and birds of the air have nests, but the Son of Man has nowhere to lay His head" (Luke 9:58). All of the values of home are left behind. Rejection is the cross on which He is already dying. Jesus dare not look back.

OF HUMAN PRESENCE

7 And He called the twelve to Him, and began to send them out two by two and gave them power over unclean spirits.

8 And He commanded them that they should take nothing for their journey except a staff—no bag, no bread, no copper in their money belts—

9 but to wear sandals, and not to put on two tunics.

10 And He said to them, "In whatever place you enter a house, stay there till you depart from that place.

11 "And whoever will not receive you nor hear you, when you depart from there, shake off the dust under your feet as a testimony against them. Assuredly, I say to you, it will be more tolerable for Sodom and Gomorrah in the day of judgment than for that city!"

12 And they went out and preached that people should repent.

13 And they cast out many demons, and anointed with oil many who were sick, and healed them.

Mark 6:7–13

Shock by shock, hurt by hurt, bit by bit, Jesus' hope that He will be accepted as the Messiah is being picked to pieces by jealousy, cynicism, and hatred. His rejection at home shreds whatever remains of His lofty idealism. From now on, a new reality will dictate His ministry, a reality in which the scales tip from service to suffering, a reality in which the clock of destiny ticks into fast time on an appointment with death. Jesus knows what He has to do. The mantle of His leadership has to be passed on to His disciples. No longer can they be leisurely learners at His feet, no longer can they be spectators at His miracles. At a moment's notice, the Twelve have to be ready to preach, teach, heal and cast out demons. Rejection by scholars, priests, family and friends has brought Jesus' leadership into crisis. He has to answer the questions that separate great leaders from small pretenders:

—Can the vision of the leader be grasped by others?
—Can the authority of the leader be transferred to others?
—Can the teaching of the leader be taught to others?
—Can the actions of the leader be duplicated by others?
—Can the results of the leader be multiplied by others?

After His rejection at Nazareth, Jesus entrusts His message and His mission to the band of Twelve who respond to His call, "Come after Me, and I will make you become fishers of men" (1:17). Mark tells us that *"He called the twelve to Him, and began to send them out"* (v. 7), but not without the resources that will transform them from followers to leaders in their own right.

Jesus sends out His disciples. Among the hundreds of forgettable speeches that I have given, one stands out as worthy of remembrance. For a baccalaureate address, I chose the subject, "Love Means Letting Go." Graduates, parents and grandparents made up my audience, but I was speaking to myself as well as to them. In the graduating class sat my son who would soon leave for graduate school in a large, Midwestern research university. Behind me sat my executive vice president, who was slated to leave immediately after Commencement for his new post as a Christian college president. Selfishly, I wanted to hang on to both of them because they were my best friends, competitors, and confidants. But in each case, I had counseled them in their career decisions and enthusiastically recommended them to the institutions where they were going. Loyalty might have kept them close to me, but only to stunt their growth as persons, professionals and leaders. Hard as it was, love meant letting go.

Jesus not only lets His disciples go, but *He sends them out with full confidence.* The qualities for which He had originally chosen them as trustworthy, teachable and task-oriented men are coming to maturity through His teaching and personal example. No doubt remains about their potential to lead; they just need the experience of preaching, teaching and healing on their own. Can they stand alone without the presence of their Master? Jesus fills the gap between their known qualities and their untested leadership with unconditional confidence.

Jesus also gives His disciples resources for their test. Dividing them into teams of two, Jesus extends His presence six times. Jesus has more than efficiency in mind when He divides the disciples into teams. Having just faced the sting of rejection Himself, He knows the disciples will need moral support when they too are ridiculed. More than that, they need the check-and-balance of another disciple to handle the heady success of working miracles. Leaders, in particular, live constantly with the hazards of being alone. Without someone in whom to confide, criticism can produce paranoia; without someone who speaks the truth in love, success can lead to a swelled head. One of the best bits of advice that I have ever heard for leaders who occupy lonely posts of responsibility came from a consultant who advised, "Every leader needs someone as a listening confidant and a loving critic."

Jesus confers upon His disciples the power to cast out demons. Power, in this context, is a specialized term meaning superior authority that is conferred from an external source. It is like a judge who pronounces a verdict with the words, "By the power vested in me by the people of this state, I hereby pronounce you guilty as charged." Similarly, in their encounters with demons, Jesus confers upon His disciples the authority to pronounce, "By the power vested in me by Jesus Christ, I hereby command you to come out of that person and never return."

By conferring upon His disciples the power to cast out demons, Jesus demonstrates two principles of truth in the transfer of leadership. One is the truth that we are engaged in a show of force between Good and Evil. If the disciples try to duel with the Devil, depending only upon their own resources, they will be courting disaster. Only the power of God can cast out demons.

The second truth is that Satan must continue to be bound so that the work of God can go on among men. At this point, a distinction is drawn between power and authority. Whereas power is an externally imposed force, authority tends to be an influence that must be earned and exercised. By giving His disciples power over demons, Jesus sets them free to earn the authority among the people to preach, teach and heal. The ultimate conflict belongs to Him. Their ministry is to serve human needs, not battle with demons.

Jesus sends the disciples out with instructions to operate by the principle of *functional simplicity.* He tells them to take nothing for their journey except a staff and sandals, the essentials for physical protection. They are to take no bag, no bread, no money, and no more than one tunic—earmarks of independence and evidence of complete trust in God. He wants His disciples to give the critics of the faith no easy targets for their slings and arrows.

Warnings about the trappings of affluence need to be heard again today. Reports of multiplied millions of dollars flowing into Christian ministries, and media blowups of the slightest financial indiscretion remind us that Jesus' principle of functional simplicity is still valid. The question of functional simplicity is, "What are the essentials that I need to function effectively as a witness for Christ without losing my primary dependence upon God?" If this question is honestly asked, answered, and acted out, many things will disappear from our lives and many more things will fall off our "want" list. Henry David Thoreau addressed the same principle when he proposed an equation for happiness. Divide your wants into your needs, he wrote, and the result will equal your happiness. If your wants are two and your needs are one, your happiness is one-half. But if you reduce your wants to one and your needs are one, your quotient for happiness is also one. To avoid criticism and win freedom, Jesus instructed His disciples to trust God for their needs and reduce their wants to the level of their needs.

Jesus' mood now changes. His rejection at Nazareth must still be on His mind when He proposes that His disciples take decisive action against the villages that refuse to believe their message. *"Shake off the dust under your feet"* (v. 11) is its own symbol of rejection. The picture of disciples standing at the outskirts of a village and shaking the dust of that village from their feet compares to the action of Jews crossing the border of Samaria into Judea. Every speck of dust is shaken or brushed from their sandals in order to avoid contaminating the Holy Land with the dirt of dogs. Rather than persisting in a lost cause, grousing about ungrateful people, or counterattacking them with a sanctified hatred, Jesus recommends a clean cut, a quick move, and a clear symbol that will take the disciples to the next village and leave the vengeance to God.

The principle of *progressive mobility* is worthy of contemporary consideration. Someplace along the line of historical development, the church lost its identity as a pilgrimage and became a "church-in-place." As some scholars have diagnosed the problem of American society, the frontier has been lost so that our problems coagulate within us. Has the church become a company of squatters, rather than a caravan of pilgrims? What spiritual values have we lost when we quit moving? Certainly, the spiritual needs have not diminished.

The question is whether or not we have become a "church-in-place," fighting old battles and battering against time-worn barriers. In eighteenth-century England, masses of people migrated from farms to industrial cities seeking employment. The church failed to follow them, but John Wesley did. Through his preaching in the marketplace and open fields, God moved upon the masses and changed the face of England. Revivals are born when the church moves on.

Along with His confidence, power and instruction, *Jesus gives His disciples a personal model for their ministry.* It is notable that Jesus does not confer upon them the power to preach, teach and heal. He doesn't need to. The disciples have the model; it is up to them to put it into practice and earn their own authority with the people. Great teachers are always emulated by their students. New professors confess that they use the outline of esteemed mentors when they first start teaching. Once they begin to gain confidence in their role, they build in more and more of their own personality and research until they develop a greatness of their own. The disciples honor Jesus with that distinction. When He sends them out, they follow His model—preaching repentance, casting out demons and healing the sick. The only discernible difference is the sachet of oil that they use to anoint the sick. Perhaps it is needed to establish the unique identity of their healing ministry. How well I remember the little bottle of oil that our pastor kept on the shelf under the pulpit. When he took it out, brought it to the altar, and touched the head of the sick with its balm, I expected the lame to walk, the blind to see, and the dead to be raised. With the little bottle of oil as their eminent symbol, the disciples will come into their own as leaders.

Jesus has attested His greatness once again. Others will grasp His vision, receive His authority, teach His Truths, follow His actions, and multiply His results. Acknowledging His limitations, Jesus has multiplied His presence.

OF HUMAN FREEDOM

14 And King Herod heard of Him, for His name had become well-known. And he said, "John the Baptist is risen from the dead, and therefore these powers are at work in him."
15 Others said, "It is Elijah." And others said, "It is the Prophet, or like one of the prophets."

16 But when Herod heard, he said, "This is John, whom I beheaded; he has been raised from the dead!"

17 For Herod himself had sent and laid hold of John, and bound him in prison for the sake of Herodias, his brother Philip's wife; for he had married her.

18 For John had said to Herod, "It is not lawful for you to have your brother's wife."

19 Therefore Herodias held it against him and wanted to kill him, but she could not;

20 for Herod feared John, knowing that he was a just and holy man, and he protected him. And when he heard him, he did many things, and heard him gladly.

21 And an opportune day came when Herod on his birthday gave a feast for his nobles, the high officers, and the chief men of Galilee.

22 And when Herodias' daughter herself came in and danced, and pleased Herod and those who sat with him, the king said to the girl, "Ask me whatever you want, and I will give it to you."

23 And he swore to her, "Whatever you ask me, I will give you, up to half of my kingdom."

24 And she went out and said to her mother, "What shall I ask?" And she said, "The head of John the Baptist!"

25 And immediately she came in with haste to the king and asked, saying, "I want you to give me at once the head of John the Baptist on a platter."

26 And the king was exceedingly sorry; yet, because of the oaths and because of those who sat with him, he did not want to refuse her.

27 And immediately the king sent an executioner and commanded his head to be brought. And he went and beheaded him in prison,

28 brought his head on a platter, and gave it to the girl; and the girl gave it to her mother.

29 And when his disciples heard of it, they came and took away his corpse and laid it in a tomb.

Mark 6:14–29

Mark's Gospel is filled with surprises. At first reading, it appears as if he is scattering random stories about the life of Jesus in fragmented sections across the pages. What has the rejection at Nazareth to do with sending out the Twelve disciples? Now, how does the beheading of John the Baptist relate to either of these episodes? Step back for a moment to consider once again the source of Mark's information. In some relaxed and reflective setting, Mark is listening to Peter reminisce. It is not the time nor the occasion for a disciplined chronology or a tightly woven treatise. Peter is in the mood of free association in which one memory releases another, perhaps by sequence, but also by connecting words and thoughts. Beginning with the rejection at Nazareth, Peter's mind leaps to make the connection with Jesus' decision to prepare His disciples for leadership if and when He is suddenly removed from the scene. But then, you can almost hear Peter saying to Mark, "Oh, yes, speaking about the threat of death, it was about this time that we heard about the beheading of John the Baptist. As I remember, Jesus mourned John's death and seemed to be sobered by the realization that He too will become a victim of evil men with political power."

In this context, Mark's Gospel escapes the criticism of being a disjointed and undisciplined account of the life of Jesus. Rather, it takes on the character of an artistic happening—filling the pages with the free form of Peter's memory, but joined together by the thread of inspired thought.

The beheading of John the Baptist can be read in many ways. Any one of the characters—John the Baptist, Herod Antipas, Herodias, or Salome—invites detailed study. My preference is to read the account as a moral encounter between Good and Evil in which Jesus sees the prefiguring of His own death.

The arrogance of sin. Sinners may be kings or peasants, but the sin of kings is usually more visible, if not more flagrant. Herod has all of the power, wealth and privilege of a king. Wives and women are his for the asking. Nothing is enough. Herod lusts for his brother's wife, in direct violation of the Mosaic law. All it takes is a snap of the royal fingers and she is his, but not without complications. Not only does he violate Jewish law and break the code of family trust, but he extends the limits on the ancient taboo against incest. The branches of the Herodian family tree have become so hopelessly entwined that Herod steals his sister-in-law and marries his niece!

Sin has been defined as "missing the mark" of God's will and Law. Herod's sin seems more blatant. Recklessly exercising his power and privilege, he takes dead aim upon every standard of decency and morality. His murders of his own children have already made him the subject of a common saying, "It is better to be Herod's pig than Herod's son." A pig has a chance to live longer. So, slaughtering men and flaunting God, Herod deserves a niche in the pantheon of history's villains along with Caligula, Nero, Genghis Khan, Adolph Hitler, and Idi Amin. They hold in common the arrogance that led them to commit the most heinous crimes.

Biblical history is replete with warnings about leaders who sin because they take advantage of their God-given power to challenge God Himself. David defies his kingly trust when he has Uriah killed so that he can satisfy his lust for Bathsheba. Solomon succumbs to the sensual influence of his six hundred wives and brings idolatry back into the land in direct defiance of God. Balaam rates the title as "the Mercenary Prophet" when he tries to manipulate the will of God to serve his own materialistic desires.

By contrast, the secret of Samuel's greatness may have been his mother, Hannah's, prayer of dedication for him at the time of his birth: "Talk no more so exceeding proudly, let not arrogancy come out of your mouth; for the Lord is a God of knowledge, and by him actions are weighed" (1 Sam. 2:3, KJV).

This is the prayer of dedication for all who have the potential to rise to leadership and power. The capacity to be a great saint or a great sinner rises accordingly. Like Samuel, a leader may be honored for humility before God or, like Herod, condemned because of the sin of arrogance.

The arrest of sin. No matter how arrogant the sinner may be, God is faithful to get his attention and arrest him in his sin. Herod is no exception. Conjecture has it that Herod may have invited John the Baptist, the famous wilderness preacher, for a personal audience at his fortress-castle at Macherus. Most prophets would have been flattered and avoided any hint of controversy. Not John the Baptist. Stepping into the first-century counterpart of "the Oval Office," he thrusts a bony finger at the red-faced, purple-robed monarch and denounces him for the sin of adultery. With a turn of the thumb, Herod could have killed him on the spot. Instead, at Herodias's urging, he throws John into the infamous dungeon of Macherus. From time to time, then, Herod has the Baptist brought out of the dungeon to hear his message. Mark credits Herod for recognizing John the Baptist as a just and holy man. We can also reason that he still has some traces of character and conscience that sin has not destroyed. These are the traces, even in the most evil of men, with which God chooses to work. How good He is!

Herod still has hope. If only he had responded to John's call for repentance as David did:

> Have mercy upon me, O God, according to thy lovingkindness. . . .
> Against thee, thee only, have I sinned. . . .
> Purge me with hyssop, and I shall be clean: wash me,
> and I shall be whiter than snow.
>
> (Ps. 51:1, 4, 7, KJV)

The alignments of sin. Rationalization is a part of sinning, particularly when traces of character and conscience still remain. When Herod seduced Herodias while she was still married to Philip, he must have told himself, "It doesn't matter. I am above the law." Lesser sinners need other excuses, such as "Why not? Everybody's doing it," or "Why not? I owe it to myself." Whatever the invented reason, the sinner is selfish, assuming that he or she acts alone. Other people do not count. Nothing can be further from the truth. Sin is like a spider building a web. Beginning with a single filament, thread after thread is spun and interconnected until the filmy structure forms a world of its own. Sin, like a spider's web, has personal and political alignments which trap us and the people with whom we are associated. Looking back at the consequences of Lochinvar's sin, Sir Walter Scott wrote, "Oh, what a tangled web we weave,/When first we practice to deceive!"[1]

Herod's web of sin includes entanglements with Herodias, his wife, and Salome, his stepdaughter. Herodias shares her husband's sin, but does not have his ambivalence about the existence of the prophet. She will not rest until John is dead.

The web of Herod's arrogance and Herodias' vengeance also spins out to snare their daughter and stepdaughter, Salome. Little does she know about the stakes for which she dances. But once her alcohol-crazed stepfather promises her anything up to half his kingdom and her hate-crazed mother sees her chance, Salome is pushed into being an accomplice to a senseless, helter-skelter kind of crime.

If only we would stop long enough to consider the innocents who are always drawn into our sins. Out of the atrocities of Hitler's era came the "Eichmann syndrome." As the commandant in charge of the final resolution of the Jewish question, Eichmann orders the slaughter of millions of Jews. Yet, at the trial for his life, his defense is, "I was only obeying orders." Salome has made the same defense. At the Judgment Day, when she is indicted as an accomplice in the murder of John the Baptist, she might well point a finger at Herod and Herodias, pleading, "I was only obeying orders."

Adding to the complications, Herod's sin also has political alignments. When Salome returns from her mother, asking for the head of John the Baptist, Herod instantly sobers. His word is on the line, a word that has been broken many times before. But looking around, he sees his public promise in the faces of all of his subordinates. If he backs down now, he will lose his power. Politics overrule principle and the mighty Herod slumps and cowers, a victim of runaway Evil. His sin has gone full cycle—enticing at first, enslaving at the end. Like Lady Macbeth, Herod will spend the rest of his miserable life washing his hands and crying, "Out, damned spot! Out, I say!"[2]

The agony of sin. Guilt, like sin, is contagious. It has the capacity for infecting a person physically and psychologically. Herod, despite his dictatorial power and regal wealth, suffers the same agony for his sin. When the news of Jesus' fame as a preacher of repentance and a performer of miracles reaches him, all his guilt springs to the surface in the confession, *"This is John [the Baptist], whom I beheaded; he has been raised from the dead!"* (v. 16). His agony is written in his words. Not only does he acknowledge John the Baptist as a man like Jesus, bearing Good News and doing good deeds, but he personally accepts the responsibility for the beheading, blaming neither Herodias, Salome, nor his lords. Then, with an odd mixture of Jewish theology and pagan superstition, he concludes that Jesus is John the Baptist, risen from the dead and returning to haunt him. Ghosts of sins past inhabit the world of the guilty, perhaps as a preview of hell "where 'their worm does not die and the fire is not quenched' " (9:46). John the Baptist loses his head, but Herod loses his soul. In final tribute to the two men, the saying persists, "We name our sons John, but we name our dogs Herod."

In Herod, Jesus confronts evil at its worst—possessing a man with the potential for greatness, convincing him that he is above the law, entangling him in personal and political alliances from which he cannot escape, causing him to sin far beyond his conscience, and leaving him to suffer from the haunting of guilt's hobgoblins. Jesus now knows that these same evil forces will be launched against Him, not just to soften Him up, but to destroy Him utterly.

NOTES

1. Sir Walter Scott in *Bartlett's Familiar Quotations,* p. 431, #1.
2. William Shakespeare, "The Tragedy of Lady Macbeth, Act V," in *Shakespeare Arranged for Modern Reading,* ed. Frank W. Cady and Van H. Cartmell (New York: Doubleday, 1936), p. 852.

CHAPTER EIGHT

Showing His Compassion

Mark 6:30–56

FOR HUNGRY CROWDS

30 And the apostles gathered together to Jesus and told Him all things, both what they had done and what they had taught.

31 And He said to them, "Come aside by yourselves to a deserted place and rest a while." For there were many coming and going, and they did not even have time to eat.

32 And they departed to a deserted place in the boat by themselves.

33 And the multitudes saw them departing, and many knew Him and ran there on foot from all the cities. They arrived before them and came together to Him.

34 And Jesus, when He came out, saw a great multitude and was moved with compassion for them, because they were like sheep not having a shepherd. And He began to teach them many things.

35 And when the day was now far spent, His disciples came to Him and said, "This is a deserted place, and already the hour is late.

36 "Send them away, that they may go into the surrounding country and villages and buy themselves bread; for they have nothing to eat."

37 He answered and said to them, "You give them something to eat." And they said to Him, "Shall we go and buy two hundred denarii worth of bread and give them something to eat?"

38 But He said to them, "How many loaves do you have? Go and see." And when they found out they said, "Five, and two fish."

39 And He commanded them to make them all sit down in groups on the green grass.

40 And they sat down in ranks, by hundreds and by fifties.

41 And when He had taken the five loaves and the two fish, He looked up to heaven, blessed and broke the loaves, and gave them to His disciples to set before them; and the two fish he divided among them all.

42 And they all ate and were filled.

43 And they took up twelve baskets full of the fragments and of the fish.

44 And those who had eaten the loaves were about five thousand men.

Mark 6:30–44

When His tired but exhilarated disciples return from their first preaching mission, Jesus follows His pattern of inviting them to take a boat and sail to a distant and deserted shore for reporting and resting. His plans are frustrated. Hordes of people, numbering in the thousands, run along the shore and beat the boat to its landing. Personal privacy, which Jesus cherishes for times of spiritual renewal and teaching seminars, is impossible. He now belongs to the public and crowds will dog His steps wherever He goes.

Each of us nurses a hidden desire for fame, but few of us know the frustrations of the famous. In 1976, during the Year of the Evangelical, I got just enough taste of public notoriety to know that I prefer the personal privacy which goes along with being unknown. *Time* magazine published a feature article on evangelicals which quoted me twice. I puffed when I saw my name and cut out the article for the family scrapbook. Little did I know about the negatives that would follow. At midnight, the phone rang and a woman asked me if I was the person quoted in *Time* magazine. When I naively answered "Yes," she released a torrent of tear-filled words that ended with the threat of suicide. Trying to help her, I found out that she was from Cleveland, Ohio—2500 miles away, where the time was 3:00 A.M. Then, as suddenly as she had called, she turned on me with a curse and slammed down the receiver. The next day, another telephone call came. This time, it was the San Francisco office of an international airline. Again, a voice asked me if I was the person mentioned in *Time* magazine. When I confirmed my identity, I was informed that a priest in Rome had charged the ticket for a round-the-world trip to my name and with my authority. After I denied any knowledge of the priest or the ticket, I hung up with relief and decided that I would rather be unknown and free, than famous and exploited.

Jesus' encounter with the masses is a study in itself. Compassion arises within Him as He sees the same signs in the crowd that He has often seen in a flock of sheep which has lost its shepherd—noisy bleating that borders on hysteria and aimless wandering that signals hopelessness. Jesus understands the hungers and the hazards of a crowd. With the compassion of a shepherd, He responds to them.

The hunger of the masses. Without a shepherd, sheep are directionless, dumb and defenseless animals. The comparison seems too strong for a "flock" of human beings, until you understand the psychology of the masses. Without a leader, a crowd is like a tumbleweed, twisting and turning in different directions, depending upon the gust of the wind. Mass motivation is equally whimsical. Imagine thousands of people gathering on the shore as Jesus and His disciples leave in a boat. Suddenly, someone in the crowd starts to run, others follow and soon thousands are stampeding along the shore. Mass hysteria is a phenomenon that accounts for hundreds being trampled to death at a soccer game. Investigations prove fruitless because no one really knows how the rush started. Masses have a hunger for a leader to give them direction.

Crowds are also dumb. How many times have you been in a situation where everyone is talking at once? A local television station sponsors a weekly forum on a controversial issue. Sixty people who hold different viewpoints on the issue are invited to come and speak their minds. The moderator functions as a referee of voices, interrupting the one who speaks more than a few sentences, ignoring those who are yelling with their hands in the air, and finally admitting that the forum has come to no conclusion. Everyone leaves mutually mad, disappointed, and entrenched in the bias with which each one has come. My judgment is that the forum is "dumb" and meaningless. The masses hunger for a spokesman.

People in crowds are also defenseless. They have no structure for outward protection and no division of labor for internal effectiveness. Like an army in rout, the enemy can pick them off one at a time or let them run over each other. Jesus' picture of the sheep without a shepherd is even more pitiful. Of all the animals, sheep are the most vulnerable. Senselessly, they will wander away from the flock to become easy prey for wolves. Futilely, they will pick over wastelands and starve unless the shepherd leads them into green pastures. Crowds of people are equally vulnerable. With just a word from an evil shepherd, more than nine hundred members of the Jonestown cult will drink cyanide. Or without a shepherd, thousands of decent people will turn into bloodthirsty "boo-birds" at a boxing match. The milling masses can be turned by a leader, a voice, or a protector to the uses of good or evil.

The hazards of the masses. All human history is made up of mass movements, whether revolutions or revivals. French revolutionaries stoked the hate of the masses until they stormed the streets, overthrew the king, and bloodied the pages of French history. John Wesley chose to preach the Gospel to the masses in England and was honored by a spiritual revival that changed the moral tone of the nation and, as some historians contend, saved it from bloody revolt.

The masses have never been more vulnerable to fickle and volatile movements than they are today. With electronic media that have the potential of reaching the masses of the whole world in our generation, the questions are: "Who will be their leader?" "Who will be their voice?" and "Who will be their protector?" At present, the mass media are dominated by commercial interests. With profit as the "bottom line," there is little hope that the moral responsibility of leadership, voice, and protection will get first consideration. A few years ago, I participated on a television panel with a Hollywood producer who had just released a popular, profitable, and "R"-rated film. The subject of our discussion was "The Moral Responsibility of the Arts." When I questioned the producer about the moral values that he exhibited and promoted in his new film, his answer was, "My job is not to lead or change moral values, only to reflect them at a profit." I countered with the contention that he was leading the masses by appealing to the lowest common denominator of moral values as the standard for the average citizen, and particularly the young. My fear is that the same "commercial mindset" will dominate religious mediacasts which depend upon the donations of millions of dollars to sustain the programs. The code words "success," "growth," "good," and "positive" by which we identify so many religious telecasts give us pause as we think about the commercial interests that dominate the media. ". . . Repent and believe in the Gospel" (1:15), is Good News, but is it salable?

The helper of the masses. Out of compassion, Jesus chooses to help the masses of people who crowd around Him on the shores of Galilee. Because of their plight, He could have manipulated them for His own purposes by the power of His personality. His integrity will never permit it. Not once in His ministry is there a shred of evidence that Jesus infringes upon the freedom or the dignity of persons in order to work His will. Mark informs us that Jesus helps the masses by *teaching* them, *organizing* them, *speaking for* them and *feeding* them. Thus, He becomes their leader, their voice and their protector, but as we shall see later, not without leaving them free to decide whether they believe that He is the Messiah or just a miracle-worker who serves a good meal.

Jesus *teaches* them many things. Emotions rule the masses and many leaders play upon feelings in order to retain control. Hitler, for instance, had the verbal ability to whip the Germans into a frenzy. If emotions run high enough, no one stops to ask whether what is being taught is right or wrong. Jesus, however, refuses to play the game that will make the masses shallow believers whose faith has to be constantly reinforced by emotional jags. He teaches them many things in order to build under their enthusiasm the foundations of Truth that will sustain them when feelings fall and He is not physically present. Jesus sets the example for all leaders of the masses who have true compassion and unblemished integrity.

Jesus *organizes* them. Mark gives us a unique and perceptive insight into the setting when we read, *"And He commanded them to make them all sit down in groups on the green grass. And they sat down in ranks, by hundreds and by fifties"* (vv. 39–40). Nothing can be accomplished with crowds until they are organized. Mark's language makes that organization colorful and artful. His word picture for the clusters of people sitting on the grass envisions a well-kept flower garden with the varieties arranged according to kind and color. Why does Jesus organize the crowd? Where resources are limited, organization makes the difference. Food can be distributed fairly among the groups and, within the groups, no one will be neglected.

Jesus *speaks for* the crowd. Like sheep that are dumb, the masses have no singular voice. Consequently, the disciples come to Jesus protesting the stupidity of a crowd that ran far away from home with nothing to eat. *"Send them away"* (v. 36), they recommend. But Jesus, with the same compassion that spent a day teaching the masses, answers, *"You give them something to eat"* (v. 37). He becomes the voice of the crowd.

The dialogue that follows between Jesus and the disciples is well known. An accounting shows that the disciples have only 200 denarii among them and an appeal to the crowd produces only five loaves and two fishes. Using what He has, Jesus takes the food and becomes the voice of the crowd once again, this time in a prayer of thanksgiving that the masses will never forget. He thanks God for a pittance of food that will never go around. How many times have the people in the crowd been in the same situation at home? Never again will they sit down at their humble tables without remembering that Jesus gave thanks in similar circumstances.

Jesus feeds them. The miracle of the Feeding of the Five Thousand is written in the simple sentence, *"And they all ate and were filled"* (v. 42). In seminary, I remember a debate over the manner in which the miracle took place. Conservative Biblical scholars believe that the bread and the fish were stretched to serve them all. Liberal theologians, seeking to bypass the supernatural, propose that a little boy's offering of his lunch, the social pressure of the small groups, and the thankful prayer of Jesus shames everyone else into sharing the food that they had hidden in their knapsacks. The essence of the Truth is what counts. God works a miracle through His Son and the manner is incidental or He would have revealed it to us.

Mark's report on the Feeding of the Five Thousand might also be called "The Miracle of the Masses." In it, we see the compassion of Jesus from another perspective and learn something about leading, speaking for, and protecting the masses who are always "like sheep not having a shepherd" (v. 34).

FOR HELPLESS HUMANS

45 And immediately He made His disciples get into the boat and go before Him to the other side, to Bethsaida, while He sent the multitude away.

46 And when He had sent them away, He departed to the mountain to pray.

47 And when evening had come, the boat was in the middle of the sea; and He was alone on the land.

48 And He saw them straining at rowing, for the wind was against them. And about the fourth watch of the night He came to them, walking on the sea, and would have passed them by.

49 But when they saw Him walking on the sea, they supposed it was a ghost, and cried out;

50 for they all saw Him and were troubled. And immediately He talked with them and said to them, "Be of good cheer! It is I; do not be afraid."

51 And He went up into the boat to them, and the wind ceased. And they were greatly amazed in themselves beyond measure, and marveled.

52 For they had not understood about the loaves, because their heart was hardened.

Mark 6:45–52

Reading between the lines, the Feeding of the Five Thousand was a failure. Neither the crowd nor the disciples got the message Jesus intended to convey. He hoped that the crowd, as recipients of the miracle, would join Him in thanking God, but according to John's account of the same miracle in his Gospel, they rushed to make Jesus king. He intended that His disciples, as participants in the miracle, would take a giant step toward their recognition that He is the Christ. Instead, one gets the impression that the disciples, each one with a basket of food, stood flat-footed and complained, "What do we do with all these leftovers?"

With an open show of disappointment, Jesus sends both groups away—the disciples to the other side of the lake, the crowd back to their homes. Jesus needs to regain His perspective and restore His patience all alone in the presence of His Father.

Misunderstanding miracles. God's miracles are always open to two questions of misunderstanding, "What's next?" comes from people of little faith who seek the proof of religion in the spectacular. "So what?" arises out of the hearts of believers for whom God's miracles are so familiar that they take them for granted.

Jesus deals with the attitude of "What's next?" in the parable of the rich man and Lazarus. Once the rich man feels the reality of hell and sees the bliss of Lazarus in heaven, he knows his doom is final. Peering up from the torments of hell and seeing Lazarus in the bosom of Abraham, he turns beggar and pleads for Abraham to let Lazarus cool his tongue with a drop of water from his finger. Abraham reminds him of his chances on earth and the inseparable gulf that forever divides them. Accepting his doom, the rich man begs once more, not for himself, but for his brothers who are still alive and at home. If only Lazarus will rise from the dead, return to earth and testify to them, the rich man knows that they will hear him and repent. Abraham's response is direct and final, "If they do not hear Moses and the prophets, neither will they be persuaded though one rose from the dead" (Luke 16:19–31). Through this parable, Jesus is saying that even a witness from the dead will not stop the unbeliever from the cynical question, "What's next?"

For people of faith, however, the Spirit of God can still awaken our sensitivities to the evidence of miracles in our midst. When the Holy Spirit fell upon the company of believers at Pentecost, a fear of God came upon the people, followed by ". . . wonders, and signs . . ." (Acts 2:22). The sequence cannot be reversed. If the Holy Spirit comes upon the church and all of the people are filled with Holy Awe, there will be "wonders and signs" which no one will shrug off with the question of complacency, "So what?"

A point of desperation. Sometimes God lets us come to the end of our human resources in order to get our attention. Mark's account of the miracle at sea carries the inference that Jesus sees the disciples straining against the wind, when He looks up from prayer at nightfall. His decision to go to them, however, comes during the fourth watch, or between 3:00 and 6:00 A.M. Is Jesus cruel to let the disciples row all night? Perhaps when He first sees them, they are frustrated, but not desperate. Strong fishermen who know the sea and the winds are confident that they can still make their destination. Six or more hours later, Jesus looks up again and sees that the disciples have made no progress. Their strength is gone, their nerves are raw, and their minds are filled with fear. Perhaps just one more angry wave will swamp their boat.

As long as we have a shred of our own strength or confidence upon which to rely, we hang onto that shred and hold off God. As a hospital chaplain, I watched people move from the discovery of acute illness during a routine checkup into the desperate hours of a fatal diagnosis. Those who shifted the weight of their trust from

145

gritty self-confidence to faith in God found healing in many forms. Sometimes they walked out whole, sometimes their disease went into remission while they ministered to others, sometimes they died with the "sweet amen of peace" upon their lips. God does not make miracles with a cookie-cutter. In response to desperate people who put their total trust in Him, He customizes and personalizes the supernatural to show that the will of God is "good."

The peace of Christ's Presence. The desperate disciples need a dramatic event—not just to save them from drowning, but to shock them wide-awake into the reality of the supernatural. To date, the disciples have put Jesus in the category of "almost God." For them, the boundary between the natural and the supernatural is a scribble, not a bold, black line of demarcation. Jesus decides that the time has come to draw the solid line. Stepping out on the water and walking into the wind, He moves toward them. The disciples almost miss Him because they are paralyzed by fear and preoccupied with survival. But then, one of the rowers lifts his head, blinks at the image of Jesus walking on the water, and stammers, "L-l-l-look. It's He. . . . No, it's a ghost. We are all going mad." Panic ricochets through the boat, some stand, some scream, and some start to jump into the sea when a strong and confident voice speaks through the howling wind, *"Be of good cheer! It is I; do not be afraid"* (v. 50).

Jesus comes to our most desperate moments the same way. He doesn't start by overruling the forces of nature, but by telling us to look up, see the reality of His presence, and calm down. Of all the miracles, His presence is first and foremost. If we know that He is personally present with us in the middle of the storm, the stilling of the sea and the stopping of the winds are incidental.

"Be of good cheer! . . . do not be afraid" (v. 50)—these are presumptuous words for anyone other than Jesus Christ during the middle of a storm. Sentimental bantering is a slap in the face of a person who is about to die. Only against the strength of His presence do the words make sense. Otherwise, they sound like the "Cheerio, tut-tut" of a reckless Englishman going over the top with a suicide squad. But when Jesus says, in effect, "Look up, cheer up, calm down," He has the power to back up His words with action. The disciples look up to see the shimmer of moonlight on a mirrored sea. In trying to explain this miracle, Mark can hardly contain himself. He enters into the feelings of the disciples so fully that he strains at the limits of his vocabulary, *"And they were greatly amazed in themselves beyond measure,*

146

and marveled" (v. 51). Never again can the disciples put the miracles of Jesus into a margin between the natural and the supernatural. The Man who walks on water is God Himself.

For Hurting Humans

53 And when they had crossed over, they came to the land of Gennesaret and anchored near the shore.
54 And when they had come out of the boat, immediately the people recognized Him,
55 ran through that whole surrounding region, and began to carry about on beds those who were sick to wherever they heard He was.
56 And wherever He entered, into villages, cities, or the country, they laid the sick in the marketplaces, and begged Him that they might just touch the border of His garment. And as many as touched Him were made well.

Mark 6:53-56

Almost as an afterthought, Mark tells how far off course the disciples had been blown the night before. Starting from the west side of the lake, on the west side of Galilee, they headed for Bethsaida, on the northeastern shore. The next morning, after being rescued by Jesus from their nightmare at sea, they anchored off the shore of Gennesaret, far to the south on the western side.

In further testimony to the fact that Jesus has become public property, the moment He steps ashore, He is recognized. Instantly, the primitive communications network of the marketplace, the town well, and the backyard fence begins to buzz with the electrifying news. In no time at all, the whole region knows that Jesus has come to their land. Like a magnet, then, He draws the sick to Him. What a sight it must have been. If you had been a traveler in the region at that time, you would have seen safaris of the sick being pushed, pulled, carried, and crutched along the road. Grim determination tenses the muscles of their faces as they struggle on, but only to accent the flashes of bright hope that have been foreign to their eyes for a long, long time.

Jesus' reputation for healing. Out of all the facets of Jesus' ministry— preaching, teaching, healing the sick, casting out demons, raising the dead, feeding the multitudes—the people identify Him first as a healer. At times, Jesus must have been disappointed to think that they missed the substance of the Truth, but then, again, He Himself has chosen to be known as a "servant." Therefore, rather than being insulted by the sick who are brought to Him, He feels flattered to know that the first purpose of His earthly mission is being accomplished.

What is the reputation of Christ's church today? Out of all the functions of the church, what is its primary identification? When I am stranded in a strange city for a weekend, I make it a practice to read the Saturday church ads. My intention is to scout the reputations of churches as they post their slogans and announce their sermon titles. "Social concerns" dominate the topics of the so-called "liberal" churches, and "salvation sermons" mark the "conservatives." "Fundamentalists," usually independent churches, popularize prophecy, and pageants are popular. Someplace in between are the "community" churches with a heavy emphasis upon "touchy-feely" topics and "relational" seminars. I wonder where the "servant" churches are?

Jesus' ministry of wholeness. "And as many as touched Him were made well" (v. 56). Jesus' ministry of healing is unique. *First,* "as *many* as touched Him were made well." Healing is not selective. Jesus does not sort out the easy diseases or respond to the desirable people. Egalitarians of our generation will be hard pressed to criticize Him for sexual, racial, age, or creedal bias. *Second,* "And as many as *touched him* were made well." Some show of faith and determination is required of those who are sick. God does not force healing upon people nor does He reward those who play games. The availability of His presence and the determination of their touch are complementary in the healing process. *Third,* "And as many as touched Him *were made well."* In this context, being "made well" carries two connotations. One is *freedom* from the disease that has enslaved a person. The other is the *wholeness* that comes to the person who touches Christ. These same criteria can be applied to the witness of Christians today. *Are the people who touch our lives set free and made whole?* Too often, the opposite happens. We add to their chains and increase their fragmentation. What a difference it would make if we constantly checked our Christian witness against Jesus' example of setting people *free* and making them *whole.*

Mark has shown us that Jesus' compassion overrules all of the arguments against ministering to thankless crowds, hardened disciples and selfish sicklings. These are the same people whom we block out with a wave of the hand. Have we missed the ministry of compassion? Do we wonder why the church has lost its reputation as "servant"? Mark's Gospel points to Jesus and bids us to follow.

CHAPTER NINE

Meeting His Opposition

Mark 7:1–37

OVER THE SOURCE OF SIN

1 Then the Pharisees and some of the scribes came together to Him, having come from Jerusalem.

2 And when they saw some of His disciples eat bread with defiled, that is, with unwashed hands, they found fault.

3 For the Pharisees and all the Jews do not eat unless they wash their hands in a special way, holding the tradition of the elders.

4 And when they come from the marketplace, they do not eat unless they wash. And there are many other things which they have received and hold, like the washing of cups, pitchers, copper vessels, and couches.

5 Then the Pharisees and scribes asked Him, "Why do Your disciples not walk according to the tradition of the elders, but eat bread with unwashed hands?"

6 He answered and said to them, "Well did Isaiah prophesy of you hypocrites, as it is written:

'This people honors Me with their lips,
But their heart is far from Me.

7 And in vain they worship Me,
Teaching as doctrines the commandments of men.'

8 "For laying aside the commandment of God, you hold the tradition of men—the washing of pitchers and cups, and many other such things you do."

9 And He said to them, "All too well you reject

the commandment of God, that you may keep your tradition.

10 "For Moses said, *'Honor your father and your mother'*; and, *'He who curses father or mother, let him be put to death.'*

11 "But you say, 'If a man says to his father or mother: Whatever you might be profited by me is Corban (that is, a gift), he shall be free';

12 "and you no longer let him do anything for his father or his mother,

13 "making the word of God of no effect through your tradition which you have handed down. And many such things you do."

14 And when He had called all the multitude to Him, He said to them, "Hear Me, everyone, and understand:

15 "There is nothing that enters a man from outside which can defile him; but the things which come out of him, those are the things that defile a man.

16 "If anyone has ears to hear, let him hear!"

17 And when He had entered a house away from the people, His disciples asked Him concerning the parable.

18 And He said to them, "Are you thus without understanding also? Do you not perceive that whatever enters a man from outside cannot defile him,

19 "because it does not enter his heart but his stomach, and is eliminated, thereby purifying all foods?"

20 And He said, "What comes out of a man, that defiles a man.

21 "For from within, out of the heart of men, proceed evil thoughts, adulteries, fornications, murders,

22 "thefts, covetousness, wickedness, deceit, licentiousness, an evil eye, blasphemy, pride, foolishness.

23 "All these evil things come from within and defile a man."

Mark 7:1–23

Popularity and persecution seem to be at the opposite ends of the public response to a public figure. In truth, they are more like the extreme ends of a line that may be stretched out straight at one moment and drawn up to meet at the top of a circle the next moment. On the straight line, popularity and persecution are far apart; on the encircling lines, they are very close together.

Jesus' ministry is moving on a fast-closing circle. At the same time that His popularity peaks with the miracles of walking on the water, feeding the five thousand, and healing as many as touch Him, the Pharisees in Jerusalem are commissioning a "truth squad" to pursue and discredit Him. Such contradictory circumstances are not uncommon for public figures. Highs and lows have a strange way of coming together at the same time. After the publication of an article criticizing some tendencies in the "Born-Again Movement" of the middle 1970s to fall into the traps of cheap grace, easy piety, and shallow love, my mail reflected the dilemma of public exposure. The first letter in the stack commended me for writing with the "pen of a prophet." Never before had I received such commendation for my writing. But while still basking in the warm glow of public favor, I opened the next letter. Without so much as the courtesy of a greeting, the writer began, "You are the voice of the Devil." Emotions plummeted from the highest of the high to the lowest of the low with just two slashes of a letter opener.

Jesus must have known some of the same feelings. From the exhilaration of the responsive crowds and the sight of seeing so many made whole, wouldn't His heart sink when the hawk-eyed Pharisees miss all of the truth and the beauty of those glorious moments by bringing a picayunish charge based upon hearsay evidence, *"Why do Your disciples not walk according to the tradition of the elders, but eat bread with unwashed hands?"* (v. 5).

Whatever His emotions, Jesus decides that the moment of truth has come. Confrontation is His only alternative. Carefully choosing His words, Jesus traces four steps that the Pharisees have taken to twist God's Law into an excuse for sin.

First, a spiritual truth is represented by a meaningful symbol. The ancient rite of hand-washing originated with God's instruction that priests had to wash their hands and feet before entering the tabernacle (Exod. 30:19–20, KJV). Behind the ceremonial act lay the truth in trust—clean hands and feet represented a pure heart without which no one enters the presence of God.

Second, the meaningful symbol is ritualized as a required spiritual exercise. Time extended the priestly rite of hand-washing to include all of the people of Israel and tradition weighted down a simple ceremony with burdensome, bureaucratic details that eventually encompassed the whole of life. Hand-washing had become so precisely defined that the amount of water, the posture of the hands, and even the direction of the flowing water were all strictly regulated. Cleansing and spirituality depended upon perfectionistic attention to the details.

Third, the rite itself is substituted for the spiritual experience that it originally represented. An outward symbol is no longer a sign of an inward grace. Instead, it is internalized and given a spiritual meaning so that the ritual becomes an end in itself.

Up to this point, the intentions of the interpreters of the law are good. In the first step, it is valuable to have an outward symbol as a sign of inward grace. Jesus fills His teaching with meaningful symbols. Only the misuse of symbols is condemned. In the second step, when the symbol is ritualized, the intention to relate the symbol to the whole of life is still good, although misguided. Life loses its freedom and religion loses its spirituality when ritual controls rather than enriches every part of human existence.

Now, in the third step, *good intentions are overbalanced by mixed motives and bad results.* Someplace in the process, the spirit of God's Law is replaced by a ritual that confuses the cleanness of hands with the purity of heart. Jesus takes up the Pharisees' accusation at this point. Whereas they infer that His disciples are sinners because they eat with unwashed hands, He comes back with the outright countercharge that the Pharisees are hypocrites. To support His contention, He quotes Isaiah, the prophet, with whom both parties agree:

> *"This people honors Me with their lips,*
> *But their heart is far from Me.*
> *And in vain they worship Me,*
> *Teaching as doctrines the commandments of men."*
> (Mark 7:6–7; Isa. 29:13)

Jesus indicts the Pharisees as hypocrites because they have interpreted the law to substitute lip service for heart religion and human tradition for the commandments of God. What started out as a legitimate religious symbol has become a stage for spiritual play-acting.

Jesus is on the offensive. By shifting the burden from the ceremonial

sin of His disciples to the spiritual hypocrisy of the Pharisees, He
has opened a breach over which no bridge of reconciliation can be
built. He does not stop there.

The fourth and final step in the perversion of legitimate religious
symbols is *to use ritual to justify sin.* Hypocrisy is to substitute an outward
symbol for an inward grace, but the greater sin is to pervert the
symbol from good to evil uses. Jesus again uses an illustration that
cannot be denied. "Corban" is a word-symbol anchored in the Law
of God by which a material possession can be set apart as a "gift"
for holy use. Through the process of ritualization and substitution,
the Pharisees exercised their legalistic casuistry until the interpretation
of Corban as a sacred vow conflicted with the commandment, "Honor
thy father and thy mother . . ." (Deut. 5:16, KJV). Taken to its logical
extreme, a son could justify neglect for needy parents, even though
he had the means to help them, if his money had been declared
Corban. Ironically, the same son who meticulously kept the oral tradition by neglecting his needy parents could use the same resources
to indulge his own greed without violating the Pharisees' law.
Whereas Jesus has called them hypocrites for substituting outer ritual
for inner spirituality, He now goes a step further in His denunciation
of the Pharisees by adding to His earlier indictment, *"All too well
you reject the commandment of God, that you may keep your tradition"* (v. 9);
*"making the word of God of no effect through your tradition which you have
handed down"* (v. 13). The final verdict comes down with the indictment,
"And many such things you do" (v. 13).

There is no turning back. Jesus has undercut the foundational prem-
ises upon which Pharisaical religion is built and cast its adherents
into the ranks of sinners who reject the Law of God. No response
from the Pharisees is recorded by Mark. One can guess, however, that
the "truth squad" returned to Jerusalem in triumph, carrying with
them the documentary evidence that Jesus defied the scribal tradition and the oral law. "Death" is their unanimous recommendation.

A warning independent of time is contained in Jesus' condemnation
of the Pharisees. Christian history is tragically replete with examples
of a spiritual Truth being represented by a meaningful symbol, elevated to a required ritual, substituted for the original truth and, finally,
perverted to justify an evil act. Cults are created by this process.
Rev. Jim Jones, for instance, developed the People's Temple around
the truth of Christian community. Somewhere in the process of developing community, however, the spirit of a Biblical principle lost out

to ritualistic demands upon its members. As blind loyalty and rigid obedience took control, Jim Jones substituted the law of the People's Temple for the Law of God, exemplifying in his own life the hypocrisy of pure hands and a polluted heart. From there, it was but a short, perverted step into justification of mass suicide as a spiritual good.

In keeping with His pattern, Jesus uses the confrontation with the Pharisees as an opportunity to teach another spiritual Truth to the masses by a parable and interpret that Truth in private with His disciples. For the first time, the human body is used as a parable. Everyone can understand the physical functioning of the digestive system that takes in a variety of foods, purifies the needed elements for digestion, and passes out the remainder as waste. Equally, the simplest mind can understand that the physical process is not the source of the spiritual motives which result in good or evil acts. Although the two processes are interlinked in mind, body and spirit, they are not in a cause-and-effect relationship. Thus, Jesus makes it clear that purity is an inner, spiritual quality, not an outward, physical practice.

Later, alone with His disciples, Jesus explains the parable of the body in detail. The key is the distinction between the stomach and the heart. The stomach is a purifying, pass-through organ that is not absolutely essential to life. A heart, by contrast, is indispensable to the life function, but only pumps the good or bad blood that the body supplies for it. My mother died of leukemia. The doctor told us that the bone marrow produced blood with cells that were deficient for fighting infection. Consequently, when the heart pumped the bad blood to all parts of the body, a series of symptoms and related illnesses developed that eventually led to her death. Adapting a similar analogy to the spiritual life, Jesus makes the "heart of man" the source of sin. His list of the symptoms of sin is ugly. Notably, He begins with "evil thoughts" which are the entry point for all of the sins that follow. Jesus' conclusion is to throw down the gauntlet and irretrievably separate Himself from the religious ritual and the oral tradition of the Pharisees. *"All these evil things come from within and defile a man"* (v. 23).

The heart has been made the center for a defilement that no outward ritual can cleanse. Jesus has signed His death warrant, but at the same time, positioned Himself for the redemptive act which only He can fulfill.

OVER THE SCOPE OF SALVATION

24 And from there He arose and went to the region of Tyre and Sidon. And He entered a house and wanted no one to know it, but He could not be hidden.

25 For a woman whose young daughter had an unclean spirit heard about Him, and she came and fell at His feet.

26 The woman was a Greek, a Syro-Phoenician by birth, and she kept asking Him to cast the demon out of her daughter.

27 But Jesus said to her, "Let the children be filled first, for it is not good to take the children's bread and throw it to the little dogs."

28 And she answered and said to Him, "Yes, Lord, yet even the little dogs under the table eat from the children's crumbs."

29 And He said to her, "For this saying go your way; the demon has gone out of your daughter."

30 And when she had come to her house, she found the demon gone out, and her daughter lying on the bed.

Mark 7:24–30

To the best of our knowledge, Jesus journeys beyond the borders of Israel only once. After making the pronouncement that shakes the foundations of established religion (7:23), He leaves Galilee for Tyre and Sidon, a region of ten fortress towns best known for their fierce independence and frequent battles. Three reasons probably prompt Jesus to leave Galilee. *One,* interruption after interruption stalks His steps as He searches for a place to rest. Perhaps in alien territory, He can be alone. *Two,* Jesus chooses to withdraw from the scene after denouncing the Pharisees as hypocrites and sinners. If He stays in Galilee, the "truth squad" might be succeeded by a "hit squad" carrying a subpoena for His arrest, thereby cutting short His ministry before He accomplishes the "servant" phase of His mission. Withdrawal is not always a sign of cowardice. Psychologists identify three ways to resolve a conflict: fight, flight, or compromise. Any one of these three approaches can become emotional sickness, if carried to the extreme, and no one of them can be utilized all of the time. A healthy person is one who knows when to fight, when to flee, and when to compromise. Jesus verbally fought with the Pharisees moments before, but now for the sake of the Gospel, wisdom dictates separation and distance from the conflict. *Three,* Jesus uses space to act out the meaning of His statement that all foods are clean (7:19). The issue goes far beyond a division between pure and impure foods, as prescribed by Jewish tradition and law. At stake is the scope of salvation. Is redemption limited to the Jews? Is the promise of "whosoever will" truly universal? By walking across the border into the land of the Gentiles, Jesus symbolically breaks down the barrier which keeps the Gospel from the heathen.

"Space" speaks loudly in many ways. After visiting most of the regions of the nation, I have developed my own unsophisticated theory about the way in which the nature of the place affects the nature of the culture. In New England, for instance, the "stern and rock-bound coast" so aptly described in Whittier's poetry,[1] seems to fit the personality of a hardy, proud, and tradition-tied people. Going to the opposite corner of the nation, the heat and sand of the Southwest shapes a "laid-back" population that shuns tradition and nourishes fads. In between, on the Midwestern flatlands, people huddle together in small towns where community is formed by the social pressure of face-to-face relationships and close physical proximity. Obviously, these generalizations will not stand up under the dynamics of mobility and communications which make Americans across the country more alike than different. Still, the nature of the space around us does make a difference, and the place we choose to be does speak with meaning. Jesus uses space and place to dramatize the truth that there are no clean and unclean people, any more than there are pure and impure foods. God is no respecter of persons and the Gospel is for all people.

In the land of the heathen, Jesus finds temporary freedom from His enemies, but not from His reputation. A Greek woman of Syro-Phoenicia puts Truth to the test. Desperate and dauntless, she asks Jesus if He will come to her home and heal her daughter. Whether testing His courage or her faith, He puts her down gently but firmly, *"Let the children be filled first, for it is not good to take the children's bread and throw it to the little dogs"* (v. 27). In Jesus' mind, the Jews still come first, but not to the exclusion of the Gentiles. It is all a matter of timing. But He meets His match in a Grecian woman who does what no Pharisee can do. With an impish twinkle in her eyes and a touch of genius in her words, she pushes the door of healing and salvation wide open with the retort, *"Yes, Lord, yet even the little dogs under the table eat from the children's crumbs"* (v. 28). Nowhere in Scriptures is there a better example of the creativity that is born out of a childlike faith.

Long ago, I learned that a creative child can always beat an adult system. Annie, our loquacious two-year-old granddaughter, wanted to get down from her high chair before finishing her meal. Her mother bargained, "Annie, don't you want to be a member of the Clean-Plate Club?" Annie pouted, "No." Holding up five fingers, Mother lowered the ante, "How about five bites just like your brother David did?" Annie held up five jelly-smeared fingers, pondered them for a minute, cocked her head with the devil in her eyes, and blurted out her insight, "David's five. I'm not five, I'm two . . . two bites, Mommy?" What else could Mommy do? Annie "skipped the light fantastic" as she left the table after just two bites.

The Syro-Phoenician woman caught Jesus with the same kind of creative surprise. What else could He do except chuckle at her uninhibited comeback, marvel at her prophetic insight, and send her home with the promise that healing had already come to her daughter?

My guess is that the woman also ministered to Jesus. After laboring with hard-hearted Pharisees and dull-minded disciples, the interlude with an open spirit and a lively mind must have been as good as a night's rest.

OVER THE STIGMA OF SICKNESS

31 And again, departing from the region of Tyre and Sidon, He came through the midst of the region of Decapolis to the Sea of Galilee.

32 And they brought to Him one who was deaf and had an impediment in his speech, and they begged Him to put His hand on him.

33 And He took him aside from the multitude, and put His fingers in his ears, and He spat and touched his tongue.

34 And looking up to heaven, He sighed, and said to him, *"Ephphatha,"* that is, "Be opened."

35 And immediately his ears were opened, and the impediment of his tongue was loosed, and he spoke plainly.

36 And He commanded them that they should tell
no one; but the more He commanded them, the more
widely they proclaimed it.

37 And they were astonished beyond measure,
saying, "He has done all things well. He makes both
the deaf to hear and the mute to speak."

Mark 7:31–37

Jesus' sojourn in Tyre and Sidon appears to be brief, but He takes
the long way home by circling north through Phoenicia, turning
southeast on the far side of the Sea of Galilee, and passing through
the region of the Decapolis before re-entering Galilee on the south
side of the lake. Time gets lost on this journey. Some scholars believe
that the trip may have taken as long as eight months on foot. If
so, what was Jesus' purpose? We can speculate that He needs freedom
from the crowds so that He might spend the time alone with His
disciples. In that case, the long way home is the shortest route to
the accomplishment of His purpose. During this uninterrupted period,
Jesus can intensify His teaching with the disciples in order to prepare
them for leadership after His death.

The privacy of their walking seminar ends as Jesus and His disciples
pass through the region of the Decapolis to the southeast of the
Sea of Galilee. The people of the region present a deaf man with a
speech impediment to Jesus and beg for the comfort of His touch
and blessing. From this incident, Mark unfolds a sensitive story about:
(1) a pitiful case; (2) a private healing; and (3) a public confession.

A pitiful case. Pity can be a positive part of public feelings. In fact,
there is a certain beauty in the picture of people putting aside their
own needs in favor of the most needy person in town. By inference,
the deaf man with the speech impediment provoked pity because
he was the victim of a physical accident that was aggravated by a
social trauma. If he had been deaf from birth, he would not have
known how to speak. Instead, either disease or accident had taken
away his hearing, leaving him with the memory of clear speech, but
with crippled motor skills for speaking. Mark uses a rare word to
describe the man's impediment, a word that is used only one other
time, in Isaiah 35:5, 6, KJV: ". . . and the ears of the deaf shall be
unstopped . . . and the tongue of the dumb [shall] sing. . . ."

Whatever the medical diagnosis for this rare problem might be,
the man suffers the social stigma attached to a lisping, stuttering

person. Victims of deafness and speech impediments tend to withdraw within themselves, rather than live through the stigma inflicted by a staring, impatient public who may add insult to injury by equating intelligence with the ability to speak clearly. Evidently, the deaf man with the speech impediment suffers from these social stigmas, including a public pity that assumes his case is hopeless. Rather than asking Jesus to heal the man, they only beg Him for a blessing.

A private healing. Jesus' sensitivity to people and circumstances is illustrated once again. If He responds to the pleading of the crowd, Jesus will reinforce their pity and embarrass the man by making him a public spectacle. A blessing will only add to the physical, social and psychological stigmas which have already defeated him. So, Jesus takes him away from the crowd to communicate by touch and taste as well as to heal by the spoken word.

Elton Trueblood refers to the act of taking the man away from the crowd as an example of the "courtesy of Jesus."[2] Common courtesy is a lost art in contemporary culture. Drivers refuse to wait in turn at four-way stops, children do not know how to say "Thank you," women ignore a man who holds the door open, and waiters expect tips without a smile. Jesus makes no apology for His act of common courtesy. He will not use a person for personal gain or embarrass a person for a public show. No matter what the crowd thinks, the feelings of the deaf man come first.

In the same spirit, Jesus communicates with the man before He heals him. Critics complain that Jesus resorts to techniques of black magic when He puts His fingers into the deaf man's ears and touches his stammering tongue with the taste of spit. How wrong they are. If Jesus begins to communicate with spoken words, He will bury the man in his fear and helplessness. Instead, He moves to the kinds of communication with which the man will have no struggle. Fingers in the unhearing ears and spit on the uncoordinated tongue tell the man that Jesus understands his problem and intends to do something about it. Then, with even greater nonverbal eloquence, Jesus sighs, not with the pity of the crowd, but with the compassion of the Christ. To say, then, to those ears, *"Be opened"* (v. 34), serves as the confirmation of healing for the deaf man. Immediately, he begins to speak plainly, confirming the fact that his deafness came in later life and caused his speech impediment.

Mark's Gospel serves as a working manual for the art of nonverbal communication. Jesus masters the art by His sensitivity to the cues conveyed to Him by people and from the surrounding circumstances. Rather than barging ahead with His own agenda, He reads the setting and responds accordingly. Arab leaders are always seen in dark glasses. They have learned to read the pupils of the person with whom they are negotiating. Lies, tensions, submission, and confidence can all be seen in the eyes. So dark glasses are worn to hide the nonverbal cues in the narrowing or dilating of the pupils. If we are to be equally sensitive and responsive to human need, we need to understand what is really being said by the look in the eyes, the inflection of the voice and the pressure of the hand.

A public confession. Jesus expects too much from the people who hear their townsman speak plainly. Hoping for a low-key re-entry into Galilee, He asks that they keep the miracle silent. He might as well have asked that the stones keep silence if human voices do not give praise to God (Luke 19:40). Not only do the people spread the word, but Mark says that *"they* **proclaimed** *it"* (v. 36) and dares to use the root word "kerygma" to describe their proclamation. The Gospel itself flies on the wings of their witness.

Confession also falls from the lips of the people who hear the man speak plainly. Astonished beyond measure, they blurt out, *"He has done all things well. He makes both the deaf to hear and the mute to speak"* (v. 37). Two unique elements distinguish this confession from other moments when people have been the awe-stricken witnesses of Jesus' miracles. One is the statement, "He has done all things well." Both in substance and spirit, these words connote the creative act of God when He said, "It is good." In a burst of spiritual maturity given by revelation, the people see God at work in Jesus Christ. The other unique element in this confession is the paraphrase of Isaiah's song mentioned earlier (Isa. 35:5, 6). Mark has used the same rare word as Isaiah when he identifies the problem of the "deaf" man who is brought to Jesus. Now, after the healing, the people themselves see the connection and proclaim Jesus as the Messiah. Even though they do not know the full meaning of their prophetic song, neither flesh nor blood could have revealed it to them. *"He has done all things well. He makes both the deaf to hear and the mute to speak"* (v. 37) has the rhythm and the ring of a doxology. It is the People's Confession of the Christ.

Mark has taken us through a cycle which began with the Feeding of the Five Thousand (6:31–44), led to confrontation with the Pharisees (7:1–23), advanced to the healing of the Syro-Phoenician woman (7:24–30), and finished with the People's Confession of Jesus as the

Christ (7:37). He now opens another cycle, paralleling the first one. Feeding the multitudes, confronting the Pharisees, healing the sick, and hearing the confession of Peter are just ahead for us. Like a great drama of rising and falling action, Mark is building the plot, developing the characters, and recording the events that will lead us to the grand denouement when we, with all his readers, will confess that Jesus Christ is the Son of God and His Gospel is the Good News.

NOTES

1. John Greenleaf Whittier, "The Landing of the Pilgrim Fathers," in *Bartlett's Familiar Quotations*, p. 470, #14.
2. D. Elton Trueblood, *Confronting Christ* (Waco, TX: Word Books, 1960), p. 66.

CHAPTER TEN

Dealing with Signs

Mark 8:1–26

THE SIGN OF BREAD

1 In those days, the multitude being very great and having nothing to eat, Jesus called His disciples to Him and said to them,

2 "I have compassion on the multitude, because they have now been with Me three days and have nothing to eat.

3 "And if I send them away hungry to their own houses, they will faint on the way; for some of them have come from afar."

4 And His disciples answered Him, "How can one satisfy these people with bread here in the wilderness?"

5 And He asked them, "How many loaves do you have?" And they said, "Seven."

6 And He commanded the multitude to sit down on the ground. And He took the seven loaves, gave thanks, broke them, and gave them to His disciples to set before them; and they set them before the multitude.

7 And they had a few small fish; and having blessed them, He said to set them also before them.

8 So they ate and were filled, and they took up seven large baskets of the broken pieces that were left.

9 And those who had eaten were about four thousand. And He sent them away.

Mark 8:1–9

Mark steps up the pace of his narrative in the second cycle of feeding the multitudes, confronting the Pharisees, healing the sick, and receiving Peter's confession of His deity. Critics find fault with his account of a second feeding of the multitudes. In fact, they have worked overtime to prove that Mark is reporting the same event twice and thus flawing the claim of revelation. Their argument is weak. Learning theory informs us that the use of two similar illustrations in teaching reinforce each other and help the student make discriminations in practical situations. Read, then, the Feeding of the Four Thousand as a progressive step at a higher level of insight in Mark's case to prove that Jesus is Christ, the Son of God.

The similarities between the first (6:30–44) and the second feedings (8:1–9) of the multitudes are obvious. Thousands of hungry people who come to hear Jesus are fed in a desert setting where food is scarce. In each instance, human hunger pulls at the heart of Jesus so that He invokes a miracle of thanksgiving to feed them all with a few loaves and fishes and still have plenty of food left over. Sad to say, the lack of understanding on the part of the disciples mars the meaning of both miracles.

All is not lost in the apparent failure of the disciples to comprehend the lesson that Jesus is trying to teach them by repetition. Just the shades of difference between the first and second feedings invite us, along with the disciples, to the higher level of spiritual insight which Jesus intends.

A different crowd. Continuing His homeward journey, Jesus has come to the southeastern shore of the Sea of Galilee. He has not yet left the region of Decapolis. The composition of the crowd, then, would either be Gentile or mixed with a sprinkling of Jews. By contrast, the five thousand men plus women and children who were fed earlier on the other side of the lake were exclusively Jewish. A second miracle of feeding the Gentiles makes it clear to the Roman Christians, for whom Mark writes, that the Good News of salvation extends beyond the walls of the House of Israel to include all people.

A different need. The circumstances surrounding the two feedings differ significantly. In the first case, Jesus is moved with compassion toward the thousands, not because they are hungry, but because they are leaderless, ". . . like sheep not having a shepherd . . ." (6:34). They need to be taught, not fed. The question of food comes up only after a full day of teaching, when the disciples see the need and say, "Send them away, that they may go into the surrounding country and villages and buy themselves bread; for they have nothing to eat" (6:36). The miracle follows.

Jesus' compassion for the crowds leads the way again, at the time of the second feeding. Now, however, He feels deeply their physical hunger after three days of teaching. Food supplies are depleted and weakness from hunger will overtake them before they can return to their distant homes.

Without overworking the difference in the spiritual hunger of the Jewish crowd and the physical hunger of the Gentiles, the point of Truth is that both kinds of hunger move the heart of Jesus with compassion. One of the darkest days of American Christianity in the twentieth century came when liberals and conservatives divided up the Gospel into personal and social parts. Jesus would be grieved to think that the Truth He teaches in the feedings of the multitudes still goes unheeded. There is a time and a place for both responses with equal compassion.

A different challenge. The conversation between Jesus and His disciples in the first and second feedings has a tone of difference that hints at a small, but encouraging, advancement in the disciples' learning. The interchange of words at the time of the first feeding carries the tone of challenge and counterchallenge. The disciples come to Him saying, "Send them away . . ." (6:36). Jesus retorts, ". . . You give them something to eat." They respond skeptically, "Shall we go and buy two hundred denarii worth of bread and give them something to eat?" (6:37). They have the money, but not the motive.

Jesus initiates the action at the Feeding of the Four Thousand by calling His disciples to Him and stating the problem—not with a command, but with compassion. The difference in tone carries over into the disciples' response. No longer do they urge, "Send them away." Instead, they ask the question, *"How can one satisfy these people with bread here in the wilderness?"* (v. 4). There is a world of difference between this question and the one that they asked at the first feeding. Earlier, they questioned, *"Why* should we feed them?" Now, with faith in Jesus, they ask, *"How* can we feed them?" "Why?" is the query of a skeptic; "How?" is the question of a person who wants to believe.

Jesus is so encouraged by the disciples' answer that He puts the question of faith back to them, *"How many loaves do you have?"* (v. 5). Between the lines, you can read the assumption that whatever number of loaves they have, it will be all that Jesus asks and all that He needs. The story of the widow's mite is heard once again in a new setting. "Find a need and fill it" may sound like an old saw, but God only asks that we give Him what we have so that He can show us how He works miracles with our meager resources. The situation has not changed. What we have to give can never match the size of the need. Only God can fill in the gap.

THE SIGN OF HEAVEN

> 10 And immediately He got into the boat with His disciples and came to the region of Dalmanutha.
> 11 And the Pharisees came out and began to dispute with Him, seeking from Him a sign from heaven, testing Him.
> 12 And He sighed deeply in His spirit, and said, "Why does this generation seek after a sign? Assuredly, I say to you, no sign shall be given to this generation."
> *Mark 8:10–12*

Immediately after Feeding the Four Thousand, Jesus leaves by boat for the region of Dalmanutha. Although the exact location of the region is lost from history, it is assumed to be the landing point for Jesus' return to Palestine on the western shore of the Sea of Galilee. Of course, the Pharisees are there to meet Him. Whenever Jesus performs a miracle that captures the imagination of the masses, a Pharisaical "truth squad" tries to cast doubt in the minds of the people by some kind of counterchallenge. In this case, they ask for a sign from heaven, hoping to win the people by appealing to their love for the spectacular.

Behind the Pharisees' question lurks a more serious charge. They cannot deny the proof of His power. Four thousand people will take the stand as witnesses against them. Thus, they choose to challenge the *legitimacy* of His power, the *trustworthiness* of His character and the *authority* behind His acts. Asking for a sign from heaven does not qualify as an honest question, it only serves as another way to repeat the damning questions, "Why does this Man speak blasphemies like this? Who can forgive sins but God alone?" (2:7), and to infer once again that Jesus stands in league with the devil (3:22).

Jesus has no more time to waste in futile debate with the Pharisees. Speaking volumes in a groan of disgust, He cuts short the conversation by verbally refusing to give a sign and physically walking away. As painful as it is, there comes a time when debate over spiritual issues must be cut off. An angry man called me by telephone demanding an explanation for a decision that had confidential, moral overtones. The more we talked, the more he demanded. Finally, I had to say, "I made a judgment call on the basis of what I believe is right and I accept the full responsibility for the decision. Nothing more can be said. Thank you for calling." I hung up, feeling badly, but having no other recourse.

Jesus has good reason to refuse the Pharisees a sign from heaven. If He gives them a sign, *He will deny the meaning of His miracles.* What further sign is needed beyond four thousand people with the taste of the loaves and fishes still in their mouths? If a deaf man hears and a mute man speaks, isn't that more convincing than fire and lightning? Matthew is even more pointed in his record of Jesus' response to the Pharisees' request. With just a touch of sarcasm, Jesus answers: "When it is evening you say, 'It will be fair weather, for the sky is red,' and in the morning, 'It will be foul weather today, for the sky is red and threatening.' Hypocrites! You know how to discern the face of the sky, but you cannot discern the signs of the times" (Matt. 16:2–3).

He adds, then, ". . . no sign will be given to it [this generation] except the sign of the prophet Jonah" (Matt. 16:4). In other words, if the Pharisees are not spiritually blind, they will see the signs of His miracles with all of the confirmation they need from Biblical history.

Jesus has other reasons for refusing to give the Pharisees a sign from heaven. False prophets traffic in sensational signs, and He wants no part of their company. Furthermore, the request for a sign to confirm His authority is an insult to His character. If the integrity of Jesus' life, the Truth of His words, and the hope of His acts do not convince the Pharisees that He is the Christ, nothing else will. The blind cannot see signs.

Most of all, Jesus refuses to give the Pharisees a sign because of their evil partnership with the Devil in temptation. Mark deliberately uses the Greek word for temptation when he writes that the Pharisees are *"testing Him"* (v. 11). The same word is used in the desert experience when Jesus is ". . . tempted by Satan . . ." (1:13). In each case, the intent is evil. If only they can get Jesus to give a sign from heaven, He will align Himself with false prophets, destroy the necessity of faith, and open Himself to judgment according to the scribal tradition: "If there arise among you a prophet, or a dreamer of dreams, and giveth thee a sign or a wonder, and the sign or the wonder come to pass, whereof he spake unto thee, saying, Let us go after other gods . . . that prophet . . . shall be put to death . . ." (Deut. 13:1–2, 5 KJV).

What appeared as an innocent request on the surface is actually an insidious rerun of Satan's temptation.

In their book *The Future of World Economic Development: Projections to the Year 2000 and Beyond,* Herman Kahn and Garrett Scalera predict that the future of religion will be filled with ecstatic experiences and spiritual sensationalism. One reason is that the high technology of our post-industrial civilization tends to dehumanize people. Therefore, we expect religion to superhumanize us with sensational signs. Alas, the more signs our religion requires, the less faith we have. Does He still groan and wonder, *"Why does this generation seek after a sign?"* (v. 12).

The Sign of Leaven

13 And He left them, and getting into the boat again, departed to the other side.

14 Now the disciples had forgotten to take bread, and they did not have more than one loaf with them in the boat.

15 And He charged them, saying, "Take heed, beware of the leaven of the Pharisees and the leaven of Herod."

16 And they reasoned among themselves, saying, "It is because we have no bread."

17 And Jesus, being aware of it, said to them, "Why do you reason because you have no bread? Do you not yet perceive nor understand? Is your heart still hardened?

18 "Having eyes, do you not see? And having ears, do you not hear? And do you not remember?

19 "When I broke the five loaves for the five thousand, how many baskets full of fragments did you take up?" They said to Him, "Twelve."

20 "And when I broke the seven for the four

thousand, how many large baskets full of fragments
did you take up?" And they said, "Seven."
21 And He said to them, "How is it you do not
understand?"

Mark 8:13–21

Like the quick, clean cut of a scalpel, Jesus tells the Pharisees,
". . . *Assuredly, I say to you, no sign shall be given to this generation*"
(8:12). Acting out His words, He walks away, gets into a boat with
His disciples and, once again, puts the distance of the lake between
Him and His enemies. The abrupt ending of the conversation and
the speed of the exit has an opposite effect upon Jesus and His disciples. The Master lapses into deep, reflective thought about the spiritual meaning of the confrontation. His men, however, can only think
about physical necessities—manning the boat and stocking the larder
for another campout in the desert.

How many times have you found yourself physically present with
another person, but worlds apart in thought? The situation is ripe
for misunderstanding. Just the cue of a single word can set you and
your companion running down opposite tracks. This is what happened
with Jesus and the disciples. Out of His reflection, Jesus mentions
the word "leaven." Backtracking on His line of thought, Jesus has
connected the miracle of the bread and the call for a sign from
heaven with the idea that the Pharisees' subtle perversions of truth
are like leaven in a loaf of bread. His mind takes another leap when
He thinks, "And the same thing can be said for the twisted thinking
of Herod." Jesus may have expected too much, too soon, for His
disciples. Without walking them back through the steps in His line
of thinking, He voices only His frightening conclusion, *"Take heed,
beware of the leaven of the Pharisees and the leaven of Herod"* (v. 15).

Put yourself in the place of the poor disciples who have completely
forgotten to bring bread in the rush to the boat. To them, "leaven"
can mean only one thing: their failure to bring bread. Guilt is like
a genie in a bottle; one magic word calls it out and creates a monster.
A lie detector test works on the same principle. Into a list of neutral
words, a psychologist inserts cue words that relate to the crime under
investigation. Unless the person is a psychopath with no conscience
at all, guilt will show in the emotional reactions to the loaded words.
Because we are all guilty of preoccupation with physical necessity
rather than spiritual Truth, we should understand rather than condemn the disciples' reaction to the cue word "leaven."

Jesus' thoughts about the leaven of the Pharisees and Herod are deep probes into *the nature of human systems of thought.* On the surface, the Pharisees and Herod appear to be antagonistic at every turn. The Pharisees are religious Jews who live by moral law; Herod is a secular Roman who survives by brutal force. Beneath the surface, however, are soul-shaking similarities which prompt Jesus to use "leaven" as the common element in the two systems.

In its root meaning, the "leaven" of which Jesus speaks refers to the kind of yeast that activates fermentation in the making of beer. Carried over into a spiritual context, Jesus is referring to original corruption of human nature and the pervasive influence of evil throughout the human system. Even though representing the bitter conflict between religious and secular powers on the surface, the Pharisees and Herod are more alike than different underneath. Both of them have built human systems of thought that spring from the source of corrupt human nature.

Once we understand the "leaven" of human systems, we also understand the "loaf." Pharisees and Herodians both rely upon human forces to keep them in power. The Pharisees rely upon the rigidity of their legal interpretations of the law to control the people. Herod, their secular counterpart, risks his regime upon the brutality of military might to assure his authority. Constantly having to confirm their positions, the Pharisees call for signs from heaven that fit their law, while Herod marches his legions through the streets as a sign from Rome. Although the Pharisees would vehemently deny their commonality with Herod, neither can understand Jesus' vision of a spiritual Kingdom. Evil human nature and corrupt human systems can see no further than the end of the earth.

Jesus' insight into the true nature of the institutionalized human systems of the Pharisees and Herod leads Him to a prophetic conclusion. The two systems are not only evil at their source, but totalitarian in their exercise. Thus, Jesus foresees the deadly coalition of religious rigidity and secular expediency that will kill Him. Three things can happen when religious and secular totalitarians abide side by side. *One,* the religious and secular tyrants may merge in the common cause of survival. When they do, the most shameful atrocities of human history are written. *Two,* one totalitarian system can be traded for the other. In Eastern Europe after World War II, for instance, the Communist takeover in many countries was eased because the Roman Catholic Church held absolute power over the people. With hardly a ripple, Communist dictatorship replaced Catholic dominance. *Three,* a nation where religious rigidity and secular expediency exist side by side is particularly vulnerable to what George Cabot Lodge calls "the totalitarian lurch"—a wild swing between anarchy and dictatorship. Again, much of human history can be read and predicted by "the totalitarian lurch." As strange as it may seem, when people have freedom, they want security; and when they have security, they want freedom. Democracy is a precarious balance between freedom and security, and as the French historian Alexis de Tocqueville inferred, we are never more than an election away from either extreme.

Jesus' warning to His disciples *"Take heed, beware of the leaven of the Pharisees and the leaven of Herod"* (v. 15) is one that has timeless relevance. The history of our twentieth century is being written by the coalitions of religious rigidity and secular expediency at home as well as abroad. "Open your eyes and use your mind," Jesus says to His disciples. He gives the same charge to us today.

The disciples miss the point. Fixated on their failure to bring enough bread, they reveal the other side of Jesus' problem in dealing with human nature. Moments earlier, His thoughts centered upon two institutionalized systems of sin represented by the Pharisees and Herod. Now, His attention turns to *two personal barriers to belief.* One is the hardness of heart of the Pharisees. Jesus has given up on them. Their protective religiosity has grown so thick and calloused that not even the Good News of the Gospel can penetrate the shell. The other is the dullness of heart of the disciples. After being witnesses and doers of miracles, they still are deaf, dumb and blind to spiritual truth. How patient Jesus is with them. Rather than blasting their stupidity, He couches His distress in nine questions that are designed to help them open their eyes, see the evidence, and understand the meaning of His words. Using the miracles of feeding five thousand and four thousand people, Jesus asks, *"Do you not remember?"* (v. 18). Repeating the details of the broken loaves and the unique nature of the leftover baskets, He credits the disciples by asking them questions rather than giving them answers. Slowly, their eyes will see and their ears will hear as they remember the twelve baskets left over from the first feeding and the seven large baskets that remained the second time. As the dim light begins to dawn, Jesus leaves them with a question to ponder, *"How is it you do not understand?"* (v. 21).

Memory and understanding go together in discerning spiritual Truth. God does not ask that we understand Truth without evidence.

Our problem is that we forget so quickly. Every step of faith is like learning to walk all over again. If only we would remember what God has done for us in the past, we would better understand what He is trying to do for us in the future. When I made my decision to accept the presidency of Asbury Theological Seminary, friends wondered why I would move from the broad educational base of Seattle Pacific University to a specialized graduate program in theology. They implied that I was stepping backward. God had shown me otherwise. In my throes of decision-making, He asked me to remember the other changes in career through which He had led me. With the evidence before my open eyes, He asked the rhetorical question, "How is it you do not understand?" (v. 21). Because I remembered, I understood. So did the disciples.

THE SIGN OF SEEING

22 And He came to Bethsaida; and they brought a blind man to Him, and begged Him to touch him.

23 And He took the blind man by the hand and led him out of the town. And when He had spit on his eyes and put His hands on him, He asked him if he saw anything.

24 And he looked up and said, "I see men like trees, walking."

25 After that He put His hands on his eyes again and made him look up. And he was restored and saw everyone clearly.

26 And He sent him away to his house, saying, "Neither go into the town, nor tell it to anyone in the town."

Mark 8:22–26

Mark is taking us through the second cycle of feeding the multitudes, contesting with the Pharisees, and healing the sick as the prelude for the confession of Christ. In the first cycle, the people in the region of Decapolis confess, ". . . He has done all things well. He makes both the deaf to hear and the mute to speak" (7:37). Even though their words spring from the doxology of Creation and the prophecy of Isaiah, they stop short of the full unveiling of Jesus as the Christ. This confession is reserved for Peter, speaking for the disciples, at the close of the second cycle, in Mark 8:29. Thus, we should sense that Mark's narrative in the second cycle is not just a case of parallel stories repeated on the same plane, but advanced accounts requiring a higher level of spiritual insight and taking us to the threshold of Peter's unprecedented insight.

Common elements between the healing of the deaf man with a speech impediment (7:31–37) and the restoring of sight to the blind man at Bethsaida (8:22–26) remind us again that Mark writes by inspirational design, not by impulsive whimsy. The deaf man of Decapolis and the blind man of Bethsaida both suffer because of an accident or disease which handicaps them later in life. Both men are brought to Jesus by friends or relatives, not for healing, but for the comfort of His blessing. In both cases, Jesus leads the person away from the crowd to avoid the embarrassment of a public healing. Once they are alone, the Master enters into their suffering by touching them and using spit to anoint their defective sense organs. The healings, then, complement each other in the fulfillment of Isaiah's prophetic vision of Christ's servant ministry, "Then the eyes of the blind shall be opened, and the ears of the deaf shall be unstopped" (Isa. 35:5, KJV). To conclude, Jesus warns each of them against telling about the miracle.

Of all the recorded miracles of healing that take place during Jesus' ministry, this is the only one in which the restoration is not instantaneous. Two discrete and progressive steps are reported. After Jesus' first touch, the blind man looks up and reports, *"I see men like trees, walking"* (v. 24). His sight has been restored, but he remains a victim of blurred and myopic vision. With a second touch from Jesus, the vision of the man from Bethsaida is fully restored. Now he *"saw everyone clearly"* (v. 25). Men move as men and trees stand as trees. Mark selects his words carefully in describing the results of Jesus' second touch. In combination, the Greek verb and adverb mean that the man can now see "clearly and at a distance."

Many reasons have been given for this gradual, two-step miracle. Some have conjectured that the dazzle of the bright Middle Eastern sun would be too great a physical shock upon the eyes of a man who has learned to live in darkness. Others have read into the event a lesson on the nature of miracles. Is God limited to miracles that are instantaneous rather than gradual? Of course not. When all the evidence is in, the miracle of the mustard seed will undoubtedly outnumber the wonders of the twinkling eye. Still others find theological meaning in the two steps toward total healing. Spiritual maturity is never instantaneous. Even though the person whom Christ forgives is free from sin, the growth line is just beginning. In the Acts of the Apostles, the spiritual experience of Christians is described in two steps. Following the coming of the Holy Spirit at Pentecost, the Apostles' message includes the question, "Did you receive the Holy Spirit when you believed?" (Acts 19:2). The Ephesians believe in Christ without ever having heard of the Holy Spirit, so the Apostles baptize them in Jesus' name and lay their hands upon them so that they will know their own personal Pentecost. Augustus Toplady describes that second spiritual touch in the hymn, "Rock of Ages":

> . . . Be of sin the double cure,
> Save from wrath and make me pure.[1]

Mark, I believe, has yet another meaning in mind. He has just reported Jesus' question, *"Having eyes, do you not see? . . ."* (8:18). Ever so patiently, the Lord leads His disciples back through the miracles of feeding the multitudes so that their eyes will be opened to see who He is and understand what He does. Through the partial sight given to the blind man, the disciples see themselves. Slowly, their spiritual vision is clearing, but the Message remains opaque and the Man remains a mystery. To see clearly and far, they need a second touch upon their eyes. Jesus does not choose to touch them directly. Rather, He selects a blind man with whom they can identify. With just a little imagination, we can visualize the disciples empathetically following Jesus' instructions to the man of Bethsaida—stretching to look up, blinking in the blinding sun, shaking the head to brush away the last of the blurs, and narrowing the eyes to pinpoint men who are walking in the distance. Then, with him, they proclaim, "I see! . . . I see clearly!! . . . I see afar!!!"

In all learning experiences, there is a time when the disparate pieces of listening, talking, reading, memorizing, and practicing come together. Learning a foreign language is an example. A beginning student labors to the point of discouragement with vocabulary, pronunciation, grammar, and cultural meaning. At best, the beginning student is a technician in the language—memorizing the meaning of words, mouthing alien sounds, and mechanically marching through the prose word for word. At this stage, everyone I know is ready to give up the language. But if the student persists, something happens. Suddenly, all of the pieces of learning converge into an "Aha!" experience which cannot be explained as just another logical step in learning. The student literally leaps from a plodding technician to a budding artist in the language. Words are meaningful, sounds are smooth, reading flows, and understanding builds. The student now can focus attention upon the clarity of communication and the meaning of the language.

The healing of the blind man of Bethsaida serves to bring all of the pieces of the disciples' learning into convergence. Moments before, they are forgetful and stupid. Now, they stand on the threshold of insight with their eyes wide open and ready to exclaim, "Aha! I see! . . . I see clearly! . . . I see afar!" The test of their new insight is just ahead.

NOTE

1. Augustus M. Toplady, "Rock of Ages," in *Hymns of the Living Faith* (Winona Lake, IN: Light and Life Press, 1951), p. 233.

CHAPTER ELEVEN

Revealing His Nature

Mark 8:27—9:13

As the Anointed of God

27 And Jesus and His disciples went out to the towns of Caesarea Philippi; and on the road He asked His disciples, saying to them, "Who do men say that I am?"

28 And they answered, "John the Baptist; but some say, Elijah; and others, one of the prophets."

29 And He said to them, "But who do you say that I am?" And Peter answered and said to Him, "You are the Christ."

30 And He charged them that they should tell no one about Him.

Mark 8:27–30

Mark brings the second cycle of feeding the multitudes, confronting the Pharisees, and healing the blind to closure in the call for confession. The cycle itself is part of a sequence of events that begins with the opening verse of the Gospel when Mark declares his purpose, "The beginning of the gospel of Jesus Christ, the Son of God" (1:1). The Evangelist has not been spraying his pages with scattershot events. Every word, every act, every feeling that he reports is building an inescapable demand for an answer to Jesus' question, *"But who do you say that I am?"* (8:29).

Mark has proved his skill as a journalist, an attorney, and a dramatist. As a journalist who introduces his Good News story with the crisp questions, "Who?" "What?" "When?" "Where?" "Why?" and "How?", he returns his readers to the pivotal question, "Who?" As an attorney, he rests his case with the confidence that the evidence he has presented about the Person of Jesus will speak for itself. As a dramatist, Mark has woven together the threads of content and character into fast and rising action until the tension demands resolution. Mark has brought us to the watershed of his writing. Like a raindrop falling on the Continental Divide with half a drop flowing into the Atlantic and the other half flowing into the Pacific, Peter's answer to Jesus' question divides itself between the "Who?" of the first half of the Gospel and the "How?" of the half that is yet to come.

Where are we? Jesus and His disciples are on the road to Caesarea Philippi. The setting is significant. Jesus has started down the long road that will lead Him to Jerusalem and His death. Pointing toward that goal, He begins with the challenge "Who am I?" in the land of pagan gods. Caesarea Philippi is the place where gods are born and made. In ancient history, the city gained its fame as the center for Baal worship, carrying the name Balinas in honor of the Phoenician god. Greeks, too, found their god of gods at the same site. According to Greek mythology, the birth of Pan, god of nature, took place in a cave from which sprang the waters of the Jordan River. In recognition of this god of the Hellenists, the city also became known as Panias. Today, it still carries the derivative name of its religious history. With Baal's altar and Pan's grotto vying for pilgrims of the two religions, perhaps its current name, Banias, is a commercial compromise between the gods in favor of the tourist traffic.

By Jesus' time, Banias is a province of the Roman Empire and the site of a magnificent marble temple built in honor of Caesar Augustus, the Emperor of Rome. Even though Caesarea Philippi appears to be out of the way on Jesus' journey to Jerusalem, it stands as the religious fortress of the pagan world which challenges His Godhead. Furthermore, Christians in Rome, for whom Mark writes, need to know that Jesus Christ, the God to whom they pledge allegiance, has gone before them to deny the deity of Caesar. So, in the arena of Caesarea Philippi, where gods duel to the death, Jesus asks His disciples, *"Who do you say that I am?"* (v. 29). If He is the Christ who comes, there is no alternative. The half-gods of Baal, Pan, and Caesar must go, and go forever.

What do men say? To test the disciples' power of distinction, Jesus gives them a frame of reference with His first question, *"Who do men say that I am?"* (v. 27). Even while testing His disciples, He is teaching them. Professors who want to help the student understand the integration of Christian faith and human learning will often use this method of teaching. In literature, the teacher will select authors whose writings reflect varying assumptions about the nature of man. For instance, are the author's views realistic, romantic, Utopian, existential, or nihilistic? Once the student can discriminate among these varying views of human nature, the professor can pose the critical question, "What is the Christian view of man?"

The disciples know what people are saying about Jesus. In response to His question, they answer, *"John the Baptist; but some say, Elijah; and others [say], one of the prophets"* (v. 28). The range of their answers reflects their developing power of discrimination. They remember Herod's response when he first hears of Jesus' fame: "And he said, 'John the Baptist is risen from the dead, and therefore these powers are at work in him' " (6:14).

They also recall the speculation of those who contend that the fiery Elijah or one of the other prophets has returned in the Person of Jesus (6:15). These are the half-truths of half-blind men. No one, friend or enemy, can deny that Jesus' teachings are sound, His miracles are good, and His power is great. The blur of half-sight, however, is to see Jesus as extraordinarily human, but not distinctly divine. Identified with the preaching of John the Baptist, the social reform of Elijah or the teaching of one of the prophets, Jesus is more than a common man, but still less than God.

By the very nature of their answer, the disciples position themselves for a spiritual breakthrough. They have come to the time when they have to decide whether Jesus stands apart from other men in *kind* as He has stood above them in *degree.*

What do you say? Against the background of man's opinions, Jesus puts the critical question to the disciples, *"But who do you say that I am?"* (v. 29). All of the teaching, preaching and the miracles of Jesus converge in this moment to produce one of the greatest synergisms of spiritual history. A "synergism" is a working term of science which describes a breakthrough in human knowledge when pieces of information suddenly come together in a surprising new discovery. The invention of the laser beam is an example. Forty years ago, only Buck Rogers possessed a laser beam in his ray gun. Scientists predicted that the laser would pass from fiction to fact sometime toward the close of the twentieth century. Their prediction, however, was upset by decades when accumulating knowledge and advancing technology during the 1960s synergetically converged to produce the formula for the laser beam twenty or thirty years ahead of its time. Today, the laser is a beneficial instrument for medicine and a deadly weapon for the military.

Whenever the Spirit of God touches the mind of man, there is the synergism of Revealed Truth. How else can we explain Peter's response to Jesus' question, *"But who do you say that I am?"* (v. 29). For all of the disciples, he answers, *"You are the Christ"* (v. 29). It is a wonder that the heavens did not open to let all the earth hear the angels singing, "Holy, Holy, Holy, Lord God Almighty. . . ." It is even more a wonder that the mention of Jesus' name did not bow every knee on earth and loosen every tongue in heaven, confessing that ". . . Jesus Christ is Lord, to the glory of God the Father" (Phil. 2:10–11). Why not? The answer is that Jesus' earthly mission is not yet finished and the disciples' learning is not yet complete. *"You are the Christ"* (v. 29) is proof that the disciples now clearly see "who" Jesus is, but they do not yet see afar enough to understand "how" He will fulfill His mission as the Christ. Wisely, Jesus charges them to hold the Truth in confidence until they can handle its full implications.

As The Suffering Savior

31 And He began to teach them that the Son of Man must suffer many things, and be rejected by the elders and chief priests and scribes, and be killed, and after three days rise again.

32 And He spoke this word openly. And Peter took Him aside and began to rebuke Him.

33 But when He had turned around and looked at His disciples, He rebuked Peter, saying, "Get behind Me, Satan! For you are not mindful of the things of God, but the things of men."

Mark 8:31–33

Peter's confession that Jesus is the Christ opens a new chapter of Truth in Mark's Gospel. With the very breath of the Spirit of God,

Mark turns the purpose of his writing from the evidence that Jesus is the serving Christ to the proof that He is the suffering Savior.

A second prologue to Truth. Once again, Mark introduces his subject with the precision of a journalist who has the facts and the confidence of an attorney who has the evidence. Introducing Himself as the Son of Man, Jesus details for the disciples what it means for the Christ to suffer many things. Mark 8:31b can be analyzed with the journalist's questions:

The Suffering of Jesus

Who?　*"Elders . . . chief priests and scribes"*
What?　*"be rejected"* (by trial)
How?　*"be killed"* (on a cross)
Why?　*". . . after three days rise again."*

As precisely and as boldly as Mark has anticipated Peter's confession of the Christ in Mark 1:1, he now prefigures the Truth that the outcome of Jesus' suffering, rejection, and death will be the Resurrection of the Son of Man as proof of human redemption and eternal life.

A second encounter with temptation. To human minds, the Truth is a contradiction. The Christ who serves cannot be the Son of Man who suffers. So, when Jesus voices the paradox of Truth openly and honestly, He finds Himself quite alone. The disciples slip back into their blindness and Satan goes on the offensive.

Much is said between the lines of Mark's words in verse 32. Moments earlier, Peter has been the spokesman for the disciples when he confesses the Christ. But when Jesus begins to teach them that He is the Son of Man who must suffer many things, Peter switches from confessor to counselor. Acting as a condescending friend, he takes Jesus aside and begins to set Him straight on what it means to be the Christ. Like us, Peter can accept only the immediate and positive side of Truth. The Christ whom he confesses is the God of Power, not Passion. He may serve, but He cannot suffer. Human thoughts and secular values still dominate the mind and heart of Peter.

For Jesus, the rebuke of Peter causes a flashback into the wilderness where Satan tries to get Him to give up the Way of the Cross, taking only the Way of the Christ. "If you are the Son of God," Satan says, "command that these stones become bread," or ". . . throw yourself down" from the pinnacle of the temple (Matt. 4:1–11). Satan has come back, not as a roaring lion or a cooing dove, but in the caring love of His closest friend. Jesus dare not take the time to debate the issue. In a dramatic gesture, He turns His back on a friend, faces the other disciples and rebukes Peter for being a stooge of Satan and a backslider from the mind of God.

Twenty centuries later, we still do not know how to handle the paradox of confessing Christ and accepting His Cross. As Jesus tells Peter, it is a matter of the way we think and the things to which we give our attention. A secular mind, for instance, can juggle the ideas of God and man until a Christian confession rests compatibly with materialistic greed. Sermon after sermon extols secular success as the norm of the Christian life and guarantees either freedom or relief from suffering. Advanced one more step, Christianized secularism can limit the Gospel to one side of the Christ/Cross equation. By assuming the serving role of Christ through personal and social ministries, there is the danger of assuming that the saving work of Christ is automatic. Not so, according to the revelation in Mark's Gospel. Through the power of Christ's servanthood, we know the Incarnation; but only through the Passion of His suffering do we experience His redemption. Much attention in the contemporary Western church is given to the healing of human hurts, an expression of Christ's loving care for the traumas, tensions, and rifts that a secular society puts upon human bodies and human relationships. Equal attention needs to be given to the righting of human wrongs. Sin is never a popular subject because the blame cannot be transferred to other people or circumstances. Slow to recognize the Person of Christ in the healing of human hurts, Peter reacts with lightning speed against the Purpose of Christ in the righting of human wrongs. Do we share his guilt in confessing the Christ who serves us while rejecting the Savior who suffers for us? If so, the rebuke of Jesus still stands, *"Get behind Me, Satan! For you are not mindful of the things of God, but the things of men"* (v. 33).

AS THE EXEMPLARY PERSON

34 And when He had called the people to Him, with
His disciples also, He said to them, "Whoever desires

to come after Me, let him deny himself, take up his cross, and follow Me.

35 "For whoever desires to save his life will lose it, but whoever loses his life for My sake and the gospel's will save it.

36 "For what will it profit a man if he gains the whole world, and loses his own soul?

37 "Or what will a man give in exchange for his soul?

38 "For whoever is ashamed of Me and My words in this adulterous and sinful generation, of him the Son of Man will also be ashamed when He comes in the glory of His Father with the holy angels."

1 And He said to them, "Assuredly, I say to you that there are some standing here who shall not taste death till they see the kingdom of God come with power."

Mark 8:34—9:1

Jesus has come to another point of no return. Once and for all, He has to confront the secular and humanistic mind with the radical claims of the Gospel. Having told the disciples what it means for Him to be the Christ, He calls the crowd around Him to announce to the world and to all generations what it means to confess the Christ and take His name.

The Laws of Life. Four Laws of Life are given by Jesus which touch upon the psychological, physical, economic and spiritual nature of man. In *time* perspective, the four Laws extend from the present moment, through the end of physical life, into eternity, and on to the Day of the Lord. In *content,* they encompass all of the strivings that make up the human mind—motives, aims, values, and goals. By time and content, then, Jesus invokes the four Laws of Life to sever the mind of man from the mind of Christ. A secular and humanistic mind is motivated by selfishness; it needs security, values sucess, and sets a goal on status. The mind of Christ, however, takes up the Cross, loses its life, gains its soul, and glorifies God. Never again can a Christian be confused with a worldling. They live by conflicting laws and on a different time schedule. The distinction is seen in the following chart:

182

The Laws of Life
Mark 8:34–38

Nature of the Law	Time Perspective	Component of Mind	Mind of Man	Mind of Christ
Psychological	Present	Motives	Self	Take up your cross
Physical	Future	Aims	Security	Lose your life
Economic	Eternal	Values	Success	Gain your soul
Spiritual	Ultimate	Goal	Status	Glorify your God

The test of life. As Jesus throws down the gauntlet on the mind of man in the Laws of Life, He puts His hearers to a fourfold test. *First, what are your present motives?* Do you deny the desires for immediate and selfish gratification in order to take up your cross and follow Christ? *Second, what are your future aims?* Are you working to avoid death or willing to lose your life for the sake of Christ and the Gospel? *Third, where are your eternal values?* Is economic success the priority of your life or are you putting the premium upon the worth of the soul? *Fourth, what is your ultimate goal?* Is it limited to earthly status or projected toward the chief end of glorifying God?

Followers of Christ are susceptible to the influences of the secular and humanistic mind. Harry Blamires, in his book *The Christian Mind*,[1] exposes our failure to think Christianly. The marks of a Christian mind, according to Blamires, are an eternal time perspective, an awareness of evil, a concept of revealed Truth, an acceptance of God's authority, an incarnational concern for people, and a sacramental cast. Ideally, each of us subscribes to these marks of a Christian mind. In practice, however, we fall far short. Unconscious victims of the "Me" generation, we squeeze time into the immediate, downplay the power of evil, give lip-service to the great doctrines, negotiate God's authority, excuse our lack of compassion, and seek our joy only in the pleasures of life.

If we are consciously or unconsciously the victims of the secular and humanistic mind which dominates our day, Jesus has something to say to us. Every time that we repeat our confession that He is the Christ, the echo of His voice comes back across the chasm between His mind and ours, "Take up your cross, lose your life, gain your soul, and glorify your God." He takes away all of our excuses.

The goal of life. In the last of the four Laws of Life, Jesus lifts the veil on the doctrine of the Second Coming, when He adds, *"the Son of Man will also be ashamed when He comes in the glory of His Father with the holy angels"* (v. 38). He is not only giving the Law that makes the glory of God the ultimate goal of the mind of Christ, but He is also pointing forward to the end of time when He shall return in judgment. But as quickly as He stretches time to its ultimate, Jesus pulls it back into the present by saying, *"Assuredly, I say to you that there are some standing here who shall not taste death till they see the kingdom of God come with power"* (9:1). The meanings are multiple. Jesus puts an urgency upon the admonition to ". . . watch and pray; for you do not know when the time is" (13:33). He also foresees the disciples as witnesses of His Resurrection. Perhaps He refers to the power of the Holy Ghost which will carry the Gospel from Jerusalem, to Judea, and unto the uttermost parts of the earth. Even more immediately, Jesus anticipates the disciples joining Him in the Transfiguration that will take place in just six days.

As the Glorified Son

2 And after six days Jesus took Peter, James, and John, and led them up on a high mountain apart by themselves; and He was transfigured before them.

3 And His clothes became shining, exceedingly white, like snow, such as no launderer on earth can whiten them.

4 And Elijah appeared to them with Moses, and they were talking with Jesus.

5 And Peter answered and said to Jesus, "Rabbi, it is good for us to be here; and let us make three tabernacles: one for You, one for Moses, and one for Elijah"—

6 because he did not know what to say, for they were greatly afraid.

7 And a cloud came and overshadowed them; and a voice came out of the cloud, saying, "This is My beloved Son. Hear Him!"

8 And suddenly, when they had looked around, they saw no one anymore, but only Jesus with themselves.

9 And as they came down from the mountain, He

commanded them that they should tell no one the things they had seen, till the Son of Man had risen from the dead.

10 And they kept this word to themselves, disputing with one another what the rising from the dead meant.

11 And they asked Him, saying, "Why do the scribes say that Elijah must come first?"

12 And He answered and told them, "Elijah does come first, and restores all things. And how is it written concerning the Son of Man, that He must suffer many things and be treated with contempt?

13 "But I say to you that Elijah also has come, and they have done to him whatever they wished, as it is written of him."

Mark 9:2–13

Six days after Jesus promises the coming of the Son of Man in the glory of His Father, God affirms His Son in the resplendence of the Transfiguration with Peter, James and John as witnesses. All of the symbols of God's glory are present—a high mountain, shining garments, Biblical patriarchs, a shadowing cloud, and a voice from heaven. As God had affirmed Jesus for His servant ministry at the time of His baptism, He now prepares Him for His suffering. We understand the meaning of the Transfiguration for Jesus when we read, ". . . who for the joy that was set before Him endured the cross, despising the shame, and has sat down at the right hand of the throne of God" (Heb. 12:2). Our primary identification, however, is with the three disciples. They, too, need preparation for the Passion of Jesus. Prophecies of suffering, rejection and death have overwhelmed their minds and souls. How desperately they need to see what Christ means about His power and glory if they can ever break the hold of the temporal upon their lives. Unless they share a vision of the joy that Christ sees, they can never endure the cross or despise the shame that awaits them as well. Kierkegaard cites a parable in his book, *The Gospel of Suffering*,[2] in which he compares the rich man in his carriage at night, feeling safe because his lanterns light the dark that is close around him, but make a fright of the blackness just beyond the rays of his lanterns. The peasant in his wagon has no lanterns, but fixes his eyes upon the stars, and thus sees "gloriously in the dark but starry night."

God gives the three disciples a view of the stars that they will never forget in the dark days ahead. They are privileged to see the glory of the transfigured Christ. Pure light dances across Peter's vision as he lives and relives the event:

> For we have not followed cunningly devised fables when we made known to you the power and coming of our Lord Jesus Christ, but were eyewitnesses of His majesty.
>
> For He received from God the Father honor and glory when such a voice came to Him from the Excellent Glory: "This is My beloved Son, in whom I am well-pleased." And we heard this voice which came from heaven when we were with Him on the holy mountain.
>
> (2 Pet. 1:16–18)

What is the glory that they see?

They see the glory of His sinlessness. "And His clothes became shining, exceedingly white, like snow, such as no launderer on earth can whiten them" (v. 3). Even in exuberance, Mark chooses his words carefully. The *"shining"* to which he refers means outer splendor created by inner purity. In the glory with which God clothes Christ, the disciples see His sinlessness. Isaiah voices the comparison for every other member of the human race in his woeful words, ". . . all our righteousnesses are as filthy rags . . ." (Isa. 64:6, KJV). Christ and Christ alone has the purity to take upon Himself the sins of the world.

They see the glory of His Sonship. "And Elijah appeared to them with Moses, and they were talking with Jesus" (v. 4). William Blake said, "Great things are done when man and mountains meet." On Mount Sinai, Moses saw God face-to-face and lived to bring down the tablets of the Law. On Mount Carmel, Elijah called down the fire of the Lord to consume his sacrifice and bring Israel to its knees before God (1 Kings 18:38–39). Now, on another sacred mountain, Jesus converses with the most renowned names in Jewish history—Moses, the giver of the Law and Elijah, the greatest of the prophets. Except for Peter's tongue, the disciples are paralyzed. He rushes in where angels fear to tread by blurting out, *"Rabbi, it is good for us to be here; and let us make three tabernacles: one for You, one for Moses, and one for Elijah—"* (v. 5). For the second time in a few days, Peter is talking when he should be listening. In the first instance, Satan uses his officious air to tempt Jesus. This time, Peter errs on the side of the Spirit. Humbly, he acknowledges Jesus as Master and captures the sense of the moment by saying, *"it is good for us to be here"* (v. 5).

It is God's turn to interrupt. Enclosing the small company in the cloud of His presence, God sets Jesus apart by repeating the affirmation, *"This is My beloved Son"* (v. 7). An unbroken line of love between God the Father and God the Son joins the Baptism and the Transfiguration as part of an eternal relationship. Never again will the disciples mistake Jesus for a man. Firsthand, they are witnesses to the glory of the transcendent Son.

They see the glory of His suffering. "Hear Him!" God said (v. 7). As long as Jesus preaches the Good News of the Gospel, the disciples accept His Word as the Word of God. But when He predicts His suffering, rejection and death, they balk and become selective hearers of the Truth. Never again. By the command, *"Hear Him!"* God erases any distinction between His Revelation and the Revelation of Christ. On that same authority, Jesus will proclaim, "Heaven and earth will pass away, but My words will by no means pass away" (13:31). From now on, the disciples will know that every Word of Jesus, whether they like it or not, will carry the glory of transcendent Truth.

Suddenly, the glory is gone. Jesus stands alone. He, and He alone, will walk the path of suffering for our redemption. Such profound Truth must be reserved for the hearts and minds of Peter, James, and John. Jesus commands them to *"tell no one the things they had seen, till the Son of Man had risen from the dead"* (v. 9). Jesus never ceases to amaze us. Like a fisherman casting his bait just beyond the reach of the hungry fish, Jesus predicts again His Resurrection—an alien idea for the Jewish mind. His purpose is well served. The disciples begin to argue the idea among themselves. Educational studies of student achievement show that the most effective learning may not be in the formal classroom with a teacher, but in the informal debates with other students who are peers. Jesus has to be pleased with the new level of conversation among His disciples. Someone has said that great minds talk about ideas, average minds talk about things, and small minds talk about people. The quality of the disciples' debate is attested by the question that they bring to Jesus, *"Why do the scribes say that Elijah must come first?"* (v. 11). Their question represents an honest attempt to link the Revelation of Jesus the Messiah with the prophecies of Holy Scripture. Only advanced students draw such relationships between facts. Commending them for an intelligent question, Jesus answers the disciples in depth. He asks that they relate John the Baptist with Elijah and recognize the common mission of the two fiery prophets in preaching repentance, calling for social justice and suffering for the cause of righteousness. Elijah has come in the person of John the Baptist, Jesus says, and the Holy Scriptures have been fulfilled in his death. Without skipping a beat in the line of logic, Jesus takes the opportunity to remind the disciples that the same Holy Scriptures prophesy the Son of Man *"must suffer many things and be treated with contempt"* (v. 12). The return trip down the Mount of Transfiguration is the most meaningful teaching-learning encounter to date between Jesus and His disciples.

NOTES

1. Harry Blamires, *The Christian Mind* (Ann Arbor, MI: Servant Publications, 1978).

2. Søren Kierkegaard, *The Gospel of Suffering and the Lilies of the Field,* trans. David S. Swenson and Lillian Marvin Swenson (Minneapolis: Augsburg Publishing House, 1947), p. 123.

CHAPTER TWELVE

Teaching His Disciples

Mark 9:14–50

ABOUT PRAYER

14 And when He came to the disciples, He saw a great multitude around them, and the scribes disputing with them.

15 And immediately, when they saw Him, all the people were greatly amazed, and running to Him, greeted Him.

16 And He asked the scribes, "What are you discussing with them?"

17 And one from the multitude answered and said, "Teacher, I brought You my son, who has a mute spirit.

18 "And wherever he seizes him, he throws him down; he foams at the mouth, gnashes his teeth, and becomes rigid. And I spoke to Your disciples, that they should cast him out, and they could not."

19 He answered him and said, "O faithless generation, how long shall I be with you? How long shall I bear with you? Bring him to Me."

20 And they brought him to Him. And when he saw Him, immediately the spirit convulsed him, and he fell on the ground and wallowed, foaming at the mouth.

21 And He asked his father, "How long has this been happening to him?" And he said, "From childhood.

22 "And often he has thrown him both into the fire and into the water to destroy him. But if You can do anything, have compassion on us and help us."

23 Jesus said to him, "If you can believe, all things are possible to him who believes."

24 And immediately the father of the child cried out and said with tears, "Lord, I believe; help my unbelief!"

25 When Jesus saw that the people came running together, He rebuked the unclean spirit, saying to him, "You deaf and dumb spirit, I command you, come out of him, and enter him no more!"

26 And the spirit cried out, convulsed him greatly, and came out of him. And he became as one dead, so that many said, "He is dead."

27 But Jesus took him by the hand and lifted him up, and he arose.

28 And when He had come into the house, His disciples asked Him privately, "Why could we not cast him out?"

29 And He said to them, "This kind can come out by nothing except by prayer and fasting."

Mark 9:14–29

With the voices of glory still ringing in His ears, Jesus comes down from the mountain. His hearing is blasted by the grating noise of religious debate, human anguish and demonic possession.

Jesus hears the voice of the scribes in derision. A heated contest is raging between the nine disciples whom Jesus left on the plain and the scribes, probably another "truth squad" sent from Jerusalem. The scribes are not only winning the debate, but twisting the blade of ridicule with which they have stabbed the disciples. Jesus tries to come to the rescue of His disciples by asking the scribes, *"What are you discussing with them?"* (v. 16). Their silence is a smirk. No one answers until a man steps out of the crowd and tells Jesus about bringing his demon-possessed son to the disciples for healing, but finding that they lack the power to cast the evil spirit out.

Jesus hears His own voice in despair. Imagine basking in the glory of God one minute and dealing with the incompetence of the disciples the next minute. Following the principles of good leadership, Jesus has delegated His authority to the disciples, taken His hands off, and trusted them to act as He would act. The trust is awesome. If the disciples succeed, He succeeds; but if the disciples fail, Jesus fails. He has a right to lose His patience and voice His despair when He cries, *"O faithless generation, how long shall I be with you? How long shall I bear with you?"* (v. 19). Glum disciples, gloating scribes, and giddy crowd—all feel the depths of His despair.

Jesus hears the voice of the father in desperation. How ironic! In the midst of physical crisis, the disciples are arguing with the scribes. An outstanding professor with a sense of humor once told me, "You must understand the scholar's mind. We prefer debate over decision." But when a human being is screaming for help, debate must stop. Jesus takes action by instructing the desperate father, *"Bring him to Me"* (v. 19). Immediately, the evil spirit reacts in a *grand mal* convulsion. Jesus refuses to dignify the Devil. Instead, He calmly asks the father to talk about the history of his son's disgrace. Beginning with his childhood, the father traces the violence with which the family has lived until his desperation breaks through again, *"But if You can do anything, have compassion on us and help us"* (v. 22). Sadness sounds in his words. Whatever faith he had in Jesus when he brought his son to the disciples, their failure has undermined that faith. Restoration can only come as Jesus reasserts His power to heal and recalls the trust of the man. Mark's choice of words brings the scene alive, *"And immediately the father of the child cried out, and said with tears, 'Lord, I believe; help my unbelief!' "* (v. 24). No one has ever echoed that tearful cry without being healed by Jesus.

Jesus hears the voice of a demon in defeat. Shouts of victory are common to the triumph of God. At the coming of His Kingdom, the Psalmist exults, "God is gone up with a shout, the Lord with the sound of a trumpet" (Ps. 47:5, KJV). As the signal for His Second Coming, Paul foresees, ". . . the Lord Himself will descend from heaven with a shout, with the voice of an archangel, and with the trumpet of God . . ." (1 Thess. 4:16).

When God comes, there is another shout that is heard. Satan screams in defeat. At Jesus' command, the deaf and dumb spirit cries out and comes out of the writhing boy (v. 26). All of the signs of death sweep over the boy, *"But Jesus took him by the hand and lifted him up, and he arose"* (v. 27). By this act, Jesus keeps the theme of His death and Resurrection in the minds of the disciples. The demon's shriek, the boy's lifeless body, and the Lord's lifting hand will be remembered the next time that Jesus speaks of His Passion.

Jesus hears the voice of the disciples in dilemma. A private evaluation session follows the public crisis created by the disciples' failure. As a father who is frequently impatient with the public performance of my children and as an executive who is exposed to public criticism, I have learned the wisdom of Jesus' decision. If He had gone beyond His cry of general despair to single out the disciples for criticism, He would have magnified the damage to His own cause. Instead, He restores the credibility of His cause by casting out the demon and waiting until He is alone in a house with his disciples to deal with their failure.

Even the disciples who missed the Transfiguration are growing. Rather than hiding their failure, they admit it and ask for help, *"Why could we not cast him out?"* (v. 28). Jesus has to be encouraged by their question. They know that He has not given up on them and He knows that they want to change. So, rather than castigating them for their failure, Jesus points them to the source of their power. *"And He said to them, 'This kind can come out by nothing except by prayer and fasting' "* (v. 29). Scholars generally agree that *"fasting"* is a later addition to the New Testament text.

The lesson is profound because it is so simple. We can be called and gifted, prepared and ordained, to be the disciples of Jesus Christ, but if we do not remain in constant contact with the source of our power, we will fail in crisis. My son is a consulting psychologist for organizations that need performance evaluations to determine the effectiveness of their people. To approach this controversial problem, he develops a performance scale based upon "critical incidents" which test all of the resources of skills, experience, creativity, and intuition that a person brings to a job. Effectiveness is measured by the way in which the person responds to crisis. Contrary to the fears of some, performance evaluation is not intended to prove "failure," but to provide a means for growth and change.

When the father brings his demon-possessed son to the disciples for healing, they fail in the face of a "critical incident" because they lack the resources of spiritual power that are sustained only through constant prayer. The practice of the presence of God, as recommended by Brother Lawrence, is the discipline that makes effective disciples in the time of crisis.

ABOUT PASSION

30 And they departed from there and passed through Galilee, and He did not want anyone to know it.

31 For He taught His disciples and said to them,

"The Son of Man is being delivered into the hands
of men, and they will kill Him. And after He is killed,
He will rise the third day."
32 But they did not understand this saying, and
were afraid to ask Him.

Mark 9:30–32

Mark has led us through several turning points in his Gospel—
Peter's confession of Christ, Jesus' first prediction of His Passion,
and God's Transfiguration of His Son. Each is pointing toward Jerusalem and the cross. Not surprisingly, then, Jesus follows with His
feet. Turning south from Caesarea, He heads back toward Capernaum
along the western shore of the Sea of Galilee. Secrecy covers His
movements because Jesus values the teaching time with His disciples.

Truth taught. Many subjects must have been covered in the walking
seminar that Jesus held with His disciples. Mark records only the
essence of the teaching in which Jesus repeats the prophecy of His
Passion. Again, Jesus refers to Himself as the Son of Man, forecasts
a violent death, and promises to rise on the third day. The first time
that He makes this prediction, the disciples stop their ears and Peter
rebukes Him. Yet, the influence of His words remains just below
the level of consciousness, ready for recall. After the Transfiguration,
Jesus brings the subject up again, piquing the curiosity of Peter, James,
and John. When He takes the epileptic boy by the hand and lifts
him up from apparent death, the disciples see a symbol of the Resurrection, so when Jesus repeats His prophecy, He tugs at the thread
of continuity between His teaching and the events which the disciples
witnessed. It cannot be said too frequently: the teaching of Truth
must be a repetitive and consistent experience engaging mind, emotion
and will in all the aspects of life.

Truth advanced. Jesus also gives the disciples something new for their
reflective thoughts. He predicts, *"The Son of Man is being delivered into
the hands of men"* (v. 31). Treachery is in the air. For the first time
with His friends, Jesus speaks of betrayal as a point of fact and perhaps
as a warning. Mark's choice of words, *"being delivered into the hands of
men,"* has a double-edged meaning. By a conscious act of will, man
may perpetrate betrayal, but only as the will of God permits it in
order to fulfill the divine purpose. In the days just ahead, the disciples
must be assured that evil's victory is never permanent. God is still
in control.

193

Truth feared. At first, it appears as if the disciples will wallow in the doldrums of dullness because *"they did not understand this saying and were afraid to ask Him"* (v. 32). Anyone who has been in a similar situation, knows that the fear of asking Jesus what He means is in itself a sign of hope. Why not ask? Most likely, the disciples are afraid to know. After Jesus' first prediction of His suffering, they counter with rebuke. After the Transfiguration, the disciples tie the suffering of the Messiah to the coming of Elijah. Following the healing of the epileptic boy, the faltering followers ask, *"Why could we not cast him out?"* (9:28). In other words, they do not understand fully what Jesus means, but they know enough to fear what it means to ask for more Truth. As with us, their understanding is selective. If they ask what Jesus means about betrayal, they will find Judas in their hearts. If they ask about His killing, their dreams of the Messiah's Kingdom on earth will be destroyed. If they ask about the Resurrection, they will leap beyond the bounds of their comprehension. Most of all, if they ask about the cross, they will have to make a commitment as radical as the denial of self and follow Jesus to their deaths.

We must go easy on the disciples. They are in the middle of reworking every concept of the Messiah by which they have been taught. We who live on the other side of the Resurrection do not have the same excuse. When Jesus calls us to suffer betrayal and death with Him in order to rise in the newness of His life, do we still claim ignorance and fear to ask the critical question?

ABOUT PRIDE

33 And He came to Capernaum. And when He was in the house He asked them, "What was it you disputed among yourselves on the road?"
34 But they kept silent, for on the road they had disputed among themselves who would be the greatest.
35 And He sat down, called the twelve, and said to them, "If anyone desires to be first, he shall be last of all and servant of all."
36 And He took a little child and set him in the midst of them. And when He had taken him in His arms, He said to them,
37 "Whoever receives one of these little children

in My name receives Me; and whoever receives Me,
receives not Me but Him who sent Me."

Mark 9:33-37

One by one, the spiritual flaws of the disciples are being exposed.
First, it is their prayerlessness; next, it is their fear; now, it is their
pride. We know why the disciples are afraid to ask a question after
Jesus speaks of His betrayal, death and Resurrection. Everything that
He says is screened through the filter of their selfish ambition.

Ambition has an appetite that can never be satisfied. Pretenders
to the throne of worldly power will stop at nothing to achieve their
goal. A brief encounter with politics in Washington, DC, is a quick
lesson in the power of ambition. After a presidential election, all
the chairs of high office are up for grabs. As one senator described
the scene, "Everyone is scratching, drooling and lusting for a presidential appointment." Insiders call it "Potomac fever," a catch-phrase
for unbridled ambition that only asks, "Who do you know?" and
"What can you do for me?" Under the intoxicating spell of ambition,
the disciples fell prey to the same insatiable appetite.

By inference, the disciples who are competing for first place in
the coming Kingdom are Peter, James, and John, the inner circle of
trusted friends whom Jesus had chosen to climb the Mount of Transfiguration with Him. Their rivalry illustrates the truth that God cannot
trust most of us with greatness. Imagine the disciples in debate. Who
stood closest to Jesus when He shone with glory, someone asks?
Did He hint at His successor by the way He looked or what He
did? Is Peter His favorite? If they entertain such thoughts, a cloud
of ambition soon overshadows the glory of the Transfiguration.

Taking Peter, James, and John aside, He asks a question for which
He already has the answer, *"What was it you disputed among yourselves
on the road?"* (v. 33). Shame keeps them silent. They have been with
Jesus long enough to know that their thoughts are not His thoughts.
Why, then, do they persist in doing what they know to be wrong?
One reason might be the false assumption that Jesus is out of the
range of hearing or seeing. On the road, either Jesus has walked
ahead or they have lagged behind during their dispute. If they had
known that He heard or saw them, their conversation would have
become pious and pure.

As part of my training for the hospital chaplaincy, I had to serve,
first, for two weeks as an orderly, with only the head nurse knowing

that I was a minister. One of my patients had a vulgar tongue and he spared no one, not even me, when I tried to serve him. Two weeks later, I switched uniforms from the orderly's gray to the chaplain's white and added the blue symbol of a cross on the pocket. When I returned to the ward, the same patient failed to recognize me at first because his eyes were fixed on the jacket and the cross. To my utter astonishment, I heard him say, "God bless you, chaplain, I love my Jesus." Then, looking up at the same face that had been subjected to his curses, he lapsed into an awkward silence. He illustrated the guilt that we all know. If we suddenly realized that Jesus heard all of our words and saw all of our actions, wouldn't our guilt cause us also to lapse into embarrassed silence?

When his followers falter, a leader has the opportunity to exploit the situation to his own advantage or turn it into a positive learning experience. Jesus sets the example for all leaders who love their people by sitting down, calling the Twelve about Him and giving them the principle of true greatness, *"If anyone desires to be first, he shall be last of all and servant of all"* (v. 35). Raw ambition works on the opposite principle: if anyone desires to be first, he shall be first and served by all.

To illustrate the principle, Jesus shows the disciples the person of greatness. As only Mark records, He takes up a little child into His arms in a show of love and says, *"Whoever receives one of these little children in My name receives Me; and whoever receives Me, receives not Me but Him who sent Me"* (v. 37). Much has been written about the humility, openness, and obedience of a childlike spirit. Jesus' choice of words in this instance, however, has a special meaning. In the Aramaic, the same word is used for "child" that is used for "servant." Thus, the meaning of the word extends beyond the common virtues of a child to the qualities that a child and a servant share. Each receives his or her identity from the father or the master. The lesson cannot be avoided. To take the least and last of God's people into our arms is to be incarnationally identified with Jesus and through Him with God the Father. In other words, as a servant loses his identity by serving others, he takes on the identity of his master. Likewise, as a child acts in obedience to the father, it is the identity of the father which is read into the action. We are the children of our father and bear his identity by the way we live. If power and position drive us, we do not belong to Christ; but if we are the *"last of all and servant of all"* (v. 35), we are identified with Christ as the sons of God. Greatness is incidental.

ABOUT PREJUDICE

38 And John answered Him, saying, "Teacher, we saw someone who does not follow us casting out demons in Your name, and we forbade him because he does not follow us."

39 But Jesus said, "Do not forbid him, for no one who works a miracle in My name can soon afterward speak evil of Me.

40 "For he who is not against us is on our side.

41 "For whoever gives you a cup of water to drink in My name, because you belong to Christ, assuredly, I say to you, he will by no means lose his reward.

42 "And whoever causes one of these little ones who believe in Me to stumble, it would be better for him if a millstone were hung around his neck, and he were thrown into the sea.

43 "And if your hand makes you sin, cut it off. It is better for you to enter into life maimed, than having two hands, to go to hell, into the fire that never shall be quenched—

44 "where *'their worm does not die and the fire is not quenched.'*

45 "And if your foot makes you sin, cut it off. It is better for you to enter life lame, than having two feet, to be cast into hell, into the fire that never shall be quenched—

46 "where *'their worm does not die and the fire is not quenched.'*

47 "And if your eye makes you sin, pluck it out. It is better for you to enter the kingdom of God with one eye, than having two eyes, to be cast into hell fire—

48 "where *'their worm does not die and the fire is not quenched.'*

49 "For everyone will be seasoned with fire, and every sacrifice will be seasoned with salt.

50 "Salt is good, but if the salt loses its saltiness,

197

how will you season it? Have salt in yourselves, and
have peace with one another."

In response to Jesus' statement *"Whoever receives one of these little children
in My name receives Me; and whoever receives Me, receives not Me but Him
who sent Me"* (9:37), John asks the only direct question that is attributed
to him in the Gospels. It is a good question because it extends the
principle of receiving others to a specific case on which the disciples
had already acted. John's intelligence is to be credited with his ability
to see the wider implications of Jesus' teaching. At the same time,
his question may be partially prompted by guilt. As one of the three
disciples contending for greatness in the Kingdom of God, John may
have asked the question as a diversionary tactic to take Jesus' attention
away from his own show of competitive self-interest. Guilt has a
way of seeking straw men who will take the blame for us.

Whatever motive prompts John to ask his question, Jesus tempers
His rebuke in order to use the incident to enunciate four principles
for internal relationships among His disciples in the Kingdom of God.
The general subject is prejudice; the specific cases relate to those
members of the Body of Christ who are *different, needy, weak,* or *contentious.*

Relating to disciples who are different ("we" vs. "them"). John tips the
answer to his own question when he reports, *"Teacher, we saw someone
who does not follow us casting out demons in Your name, and we forbade him
because he does not follow us"* (v. 38). For John, the crux of the issue is
the fact that the unnamed exorcist does not belong to the company
of the Twelve. For Jesus, the issue centers in the fact that His name
is invoked and devils are cast out. Whoever the exorcist, he accurately
perceives the power of Jesus' name and in that name performs miracles. Jesus' own disciples had failed precisely in these points just
days before when they stood powerless before the demons who possessed the epileptic boy. So, applying the twofold test of invoking
His name and casting out demons, Jesus opens the circle of discipleship
to admit a stranger by saying, *"For he who is not against us is on our
side"* (v. 40).

"We" vs. "them" is a common fault, even among Christians. Labels
are attached to denominations, theological differences, and ministerial
styles that put people just outside the circle of true faith. On more
than one occasion, I have felt the sting of discrimination within the

circle of faith when brothers of a different theological tradition accept me up to a point and then draw a line. With tongue in cheek, I have likened myself in these moments to a black man who moves into a white neighborhood, "He's a nice guy and a brother in Christ, but I wouldn't want him to marry my daughter." Presumably, theological values in the neighborhood will go down if I move in.

Labels of "we" and "them" are reserved for distinctions between Christians and the world. They have no place in the Kingdom of God, particularly when disciples share His name and show His miracles.

Relating to disciples who are needy ("ours" vs. "theirs"). Needs vary as much as ideas among the disciples of Christ. Some are rich and some are poor. Some have all their wants supplied and others have few of their needs met. So, within the Body of Christ, we have a responsibility for each other. Is it too radical to assume that no Christian should be naked, thirsty, or hungry as long as other Christians have clothes, water, and food?

Putting the question in unmistakable terms, Jesus places eternal value upon a cup of water given in His name. Great and humble tasks merge in the Kingdom of God. Almost daily, I drive past our church on the way to the president's office of a Christian university. Vice presidents are waiting to see me and secretaries are waiting to serve me. At my fingertips are computers, word processors, three telephone lines, a dictating machine, and an instant intercom. Yet, as I drive past the church, I see the wisp of a gray-haired woman bending over the shrubs with pruning shears in her hand and a lawn basket at her back. Her ministry is to keep the lawn of God's house worthy of His name. Her task is as simple and as humble as giving a cup of water in Jesus' name. I pray each day that God will give me the honor of following her through the gates into His kingdom.

Relating to disciples who are weak ("me" vs. "you"). Jesus' disciples range along a wide spectrum of spiritual maturity. Those who are blessed with seniority, experience, insight, and leadership in the Kingdom have a special responsibility to those who are "babes in Christ." In fact, Jesus goes so far as to make the disciples' accountability for weaker members of the Body a matter of eternal life and death. Whatever the sacrifice, a disciple dare not put a stumbling block or an ensnaring trap along the growth line of a new, weak, or struggling believer. The attitude of "me" vs. "you" has no part in the Kingdom of God. Therefore, the stronger disciple will discipline the work of his hands, the way of his feet, and the watch of his eyes with the least of God's children in mind. And if necessary, the stronger disciple will perform radical surgery on the things he does, the direction he pursues, and the views he takes in order to avoid offending a weaker brother. Paul follows this principle when he refuses to eat meat offered to idols, not because of his convictions about the meat, but because of his concern for new believers who still struggle to shake off the remnants of idolatry.

Three times, Jesus warns against offending the least of those in the Kingdom of God. Each time, He calls for the discipline of radical surgery on the hand, the foot, or the eye as the preferable alternative to hell, *"where their worm does not die and the fire is not quenched"* (9:44, 46, 48).

Relating to disciples who are contentious ("I" vs. "I"). Jesus has not forgotten the dispute over greatness that gave Him the opportunity to teach His disciples about their relationships, one with another, as well as with other disciples in the Kingdom of God. Nor has He forgotten the fact that the disciples need a direct answer to their competitive "I" vs. "I" spirit which provoked their dispute. Salt is the symbol that He chooses to press home His point. Although scholars concede that Mark 9:49–50 is one of the most difficult passages in the Gospels to interpret, three perspectives on the meaning of salt give us some insight into the principle that Jesus proposes.

First, meat sacrifices in the Old Testament were seasoned with salt as an essential part of the purification process. Projected forward into Jesus' time, the seasoning of the sacrifice became another prediction of His suffering which the disciples would share. Suffering has a way of bringing people together. Missionaries on the foreign field who are working against overwhelming odds have no time for denominational differences. Together, in the name of Christ, they are as one Body. Sooner or later, Jesus is saying, suffering, as represented by the salted sacrifice, will be the means which brings the disciples together.

Second, salt is the flavoring and preserving ingredient in the meat. From the prospect of their common suffering, Jesus leads the minds of the disciples to think about their common task. They are in the midst of a dying and corrupt culture in which their joyous and saving witness is the only hope. Therefore, to counterbalance the commonality of suffering that will bring them together, Jesus reminds the disciples that their common task to be the salt of the earth is far greater than their personal ambitions.

Third, salt represents a covenant relationship among men that binds them as brothers. In the ancient East, courtesy dictated that a stranger be invited for a meal that included a ritual of eating bread and salt as a symbol of brotherhood, even though the stranger and his host had never met before and might never meet again. Arabs who are brothers by covenant rather than blood still say, "There is salt between us."

Only one conclusion can be drawn from Jesus' teaching about salt as the symbol of the brotherly covenant. If nonbelievers who are strangers and even enemies have salt between them, surely the disciples can *"have peace with one another"* (v. 50).

The depth of Jesus' teaching in these verses is unfathomable. At best, we conclude with a personal application. Our relationships with other disciples are often like the dispute of Peter, James, and John over greatness in the Kingdom of God. Jesus enters the scene to give us a totally different set of principles by which to live with one another. The child-servant is our model and the name of Jesus is our test. He asks us to be tough on ourselves and tender with others. Then, in our relationships, we find that when we receive the least and the littlest of God's children, we receive Christ and the Father who sent Him. As radical as it may be, our identification as disciples of Christ begins not with the grandeur of confessing God the Father, but in the humility of serving the least of all His children. Are we any different than the disciples? The truth is almost more than we can bear.

CHAPTER THIRTEEN

Addressing His Society

Mark 10:1–31

DIVORCE: THE STING OF SOPHISTRY

1 And He arose from there and came to the region of Judea by the other side of the Jordan. And the people gathered to Him again, and as He was accustomed, He taught them again.

2 And the Pharisees came and asked Him, "Is it lawful for a man to divorce his wife?" testing Him.

3 And He answered and said to them, "What did Moses command you?"

4 And they said, "Moses permitted writing a certificate of divorce, and to put her away."

5 And Jesus answered and said to them, "Because of the hardness of your heart he wrote you this precept.

6 "But from the beginning of the creation, God *'made them male and female.'*

7 *'For this reason a man shall leave his father and mother and be joined to his wife,*

8 *and the two shall become one flesh';* so then they are no longer two, but one flesh.

9 "Therefore what God has joined together, let not man divide."

10 And in the house His disciples asked Him again about the same matter.

11 And He said to them, "Whoever divorces his wife and marries another commits adultery against her.

12 "And if a woman divorces her husband and marries another, she commits adultery."

Mark 10:1–12

Speed and intensity take over as Jesus moves toward Jerusalem. Leaving Galilee for the last time, He journeys south through Samaria and east over the Jordan into the Peraean region of Judea. Here Jesus reopens His public ministry and the Pharisees reopen their public attack.

While Jesus is teaching the people, the Pharisees arrive with another of their loaded questions, *"Is it lawful for a man to divorce his wife?"* (v. 2). Satan has many agents and comes in many forms. Mark informs us that the Pharisees are again *"testing Him"* (v. 2), not with an honest question, but with the intent to do evil. The motive of the Pharisees does not differ from Satan's attack in the wilderness. Probe after probe is being aimed at Jesus to find the spot where He will either sin against God or give His enemies a reason for putting Him to death.

This time, the Pharisees test Jesus with a probe of many prongs. By posing the question about divorce, they try to force Jesus into a corner where He has to alienate someone with His answer. If He opposes divorce on legal grounds, He contradicts the law of Moses. If He makes divorce a moral issue, He exposes Himself to the same fate as John the Baptist at the hands of the adulterer, Herod Antipas. At the same time, if He accepts divorce on legal grounds, He subjects Himself to the law of Moses and the interpretation of the Pharisees. But if He refuses to accept divorce on moral grounds, He chooses to side with the Shammai faction of the rabbinical school in their heated debate with the students of Hillel. Scholars of the high priest, Shammai, contended that divorce could be granted only for immorality on the part of the husband, while the more liberal Hillelites interpreted the law of Moses to permit a man to divorce his wife for any reason of dissatisfaction, including burnt bread or a fairer female.

Wisdom and experience have taught Jesus to lead the Pharisees into their own trap by asking a counterquestion rather than giving them a direct answer. Choosing His words carefully, He turns the question back to them, *"What did Moses command you?"* (v. 3). Feeling false security in their knowledge of Mosaic law, the Pharisees recite the provision for divorce that Moses *"permitted."* They do not say "commanded." Jesus takes advantage of their choice of words to address the question of divorce from God's perspective.

Moses' permission for divorce is an indictment on the human condition. Jesus acknowledges Moses' provision for a certificate of divorce that spells out the conditions of separation. Divorce had become the mode among his people and, as their leader, he had the responsibility to limit and regulate a behavior that threatened to destroy a nation built upon the family. At best, Moses hoped that his temporary legislation would be superseded by a revival among the Jews that would once again put the Spirit of love above the letter of the Law.

God's purpose for marriage has not changed. Jesus calls a spade a spade. Moses' temporary provision for divorce is not God's norm; it is proof of man's sin. Jesus might have launched into a fiery sermon on divorce, as evidence of the blackness and hardness of man's heart. But instead of dignifying divorce, with all its grubby details, He chooses to elevate the sacredness of marriage. God's intention for marriage, Jesus says, is revealed in the very beginning. Two distinct sexes were created by God for the purpose of marriage. Thus, a man is to break away from his parents and be joined to his wife so that "1 + 1 = 1" in their relationship. Yoked together by marriage vows taken in the presence of God, the relationship of husband and wife is permanent. Jesus has not dodged the Pharisees' question. By their own scriptures, they must admit that God's original intention for marriage has not changed.

Later on, when Jesus and His disciples are alone in the house, the conversation continues in detail. Confusion still exists in the disciples' minds about divorce. If Jesus' public statement is taken literally, divorce is not permissible under any circumstances. Jesus' response to their continuing question is difficult to interpret. Some take it as new legalism in which divorce and remarriage on the part of either husband or wife is adultery. Others refer to Matthew's account of the same conversation in which He makes "sexual immorality" a legitimate exception for divorce and remarriage. Still others find Jesus correcting the anti-feminism of Jewish law which let a man divorce his wife for any reason, but left no recourse for her, even if the husband were guilty of adultery.

The spirit of the law has contemporary meaning. We need to rethink this difficult passage in terms of the Spirit, rather than the letter of the Law. Never once does Jesus introduce a new legalism that would be the stuff out of which Pharisees of the future could be made. At the same time, He does not back away from the truth that divorce is a symptom of man's sin and permanent marriage is God's intention. Thus, the Spirit of the Law still prevails. Divorce may have to be recognized in a secular society. Whether we like it or not, legislation may be necessary to limit and regulate its spread. For instance, a law calling for a six-month waiting period and counseling on "irreconcilable differences" may not be Christian, but it may be best under the circumstances of human nature to declare formally the primacy of the family and informally the seriousness of the marriage vows. Jesus would be the first to recognize divorce as a fact of life which may have to be permitted under certain circumstances, but the last to condone it as God's original purpose. Divorce is still a primary symptom of our sclerotic hearts. We continue to ask, "Is it legally permissible?" when we should be asking, "Is it God's intention?"

hardened

CHILDREN: THE STIGMA OF SMALLNESS

13 And they brought young children to Him, that He might touch them; but the disciples rebuked those who brought them.

14 But when Jesus saw it, He was greatly displeased and said to them, "Let the little children come to Me, and do not forbid them; for of such is the kingdom of God.

15 "Assuredly, I say to you, whoever does not receive the kingdom of God as a little child will by no means enter it."

16 And He took them up in His arms, put His hands on them, and blessed them.

Mark 10:13–16

"Murphy's Law" seems to rule everything the disciples say and do. If anything can be said that is wrong, they will say it; if anything can be done that is wrong, they will do it. Both blunders are illustrated when mothers bring their young children to Jesus that He might touch them. Emotions run high as parents push and tempers flare, and innocent children, as always, are caught in the middle. The feelings of the participants reveal the Truth that Jesus teaches by His words and action.

Persistent parents bring their small children to Jesus. According to the custom of the time, mothers made sure that their children were touched and blessed by a distinguished rabbi after their first birthday. Although Mark's word for "children" includes a range from one to twelve years of age, his later reference to Jesus' taking them up and folding them into His arms suggests that infants are involved. The persistence of those who brought the children is inferred by Mark's choice of a verb tense that means they "kept on bringing their small children" to Jesus. Putting these two thoughts together, the scene that provokes the disciples to strong action can be visualized. Anxious mothers with squirming and squealing babies push for a place in line to feel Jesus' touch and receive His blessing. The noise disturbs His teaching and the demand upsets His schedule. Only parents with the highest hopes for their children can fully understand the persistence and the anxiety that makes the touch of Jesus so important.

Several faculty families had their first children at the same time that we did. Whenever the women got together, unspoken competition dominated their conversation. The first tooth, the first step, the first word—all became extensions of the mother's ego. Later on, fathers took over to brag about grade points, batting averages, and spelling bees. Pride is a privilege of parenthood that persists from generation to generation.

Disgusted disciples rebuke the parents. To protect Jesus and His priorities, the disciples take strong and decisive action against the people who bring their young children for a blessing. Teaching and miracles should preoccupy His time and attention, not the touching of children to satisfy a mother's whims. The disciples' motive may have been right, but their feelings are wrong. Disdain fills their voices as they rebuke the parents. They also betray the low value that they place upon the personality of a small child. Despite the fact that they have lived with Jesus more than two years, hearing Him teach and seeing Him perform miracles, they still have not caught His spirit. Even His most recent words about receiving a little child as the way of receiving Him and His Father have gone for naught. Behind the caustic rebuke of the disciples lingers their arrogant humanity and the un-Christly attitudes of their age.

An angry Jesus rebukes the disciples. When the disciples' attitude unmasks their true values, Jesus flashes instant anger. Not only does He come to the defense of the children, but He advances them to the top of the scale of values by which a person enters the Kingdom of God. Contrary to the usual interpretation of this passage, the qualities of humility, peace and joy do not earn the child a first place in the Kingdom. Children, in their own way, can be the most arrogant, hostile and sullen of all creatures. Their identification with the Kingdom of God is their lack of power and their need for help. A child in arms has neither social influence nor personal strength upon which to rely. Utter trust relaxes the child in the arms of the parent. So it is with all who enter the Kingdom of God.

A loving Jesus embraces the children. As always, Jesus backs up His words with an act of love. Peter's memory of the event gives us unique insight into the depth of Jesus' feelings when Mark alone records, *"And He took them up in His arms, put His hands on them, and blessed them"* (v. 16). The words, *"took them up,"* can be amplified to mean, "He folded them into His arms."

Children who know they are loved will return the love. Early one morning, in a Cambodian refugee camp, my wife and I picked our way through the mud and among hunkering people who had waited through the night for the bus that would take them back to their homeland, even though returning meant starvation and violent death. We came to a clearing where our guide suggested that we take a picture with our students who were serving food to the people. Lining up for a typical camera shot, we noticed that two Cambodian children had followed us into the center of the circle. I stopped the picture and beckoned to the little brown boy, asking that he come and pose with me. At first he hesitated; then, looking at his sister for approval, he took half-steps toward me. I went over and scooped him up with my hand under his buttocks. Bare bones protruded through the flesh into my hands as I felt starvation for the first time. Emotions that I had known only at the dedication of my own children engulfed me as I folded that boy into my arms. Then, just before the shutter clicked, he snuggled his head into the crook of my neck in a show of love that I will feel through eternity. At that moment, our love was perfect and our trust was complete. I would have walked a continent with him in my arms in order to claim him as my son or I would have taken his place in a Cambodian hut if I could have been assured of his future. Neither of these choices was mine, but the meaning of the moment can never be taken away from me. Heaven will be complete when I take him in my arms again. For the present, I am content to know that I have had the privilege of entering into the Spirit of Jesus Christ when He folded the children into His arms and they snuggled their heads into the crook of His neck.

WEALTH: THE SADNESS OF SUCCESS

17 And as He was going out on the road, one came running, knelt before Him, and asked Him, "Good Teacher, what shall I do that I may inherit eternal life?"

18 And Jesus said to him, "Why do you call Me good? No one is good but One, that is, God.

19 "You know the commandments: *'Do not commit adultery,' 'Do not murder,' 'Do not steal,' 'Do not bear false witness,' 'Do not defraud,' 'Honor your father and your mother.'* "

20 And he answered and said to Him, "Teacher, all these I have observed from my youth."

21 Then Jesus, looking at him, loved him, and said to him, "One thing you lack: Go your way, sell whatever you have and give to the poor, and you will have treasure in heaven; and come, take up the cross, and follow Me."

22 And he was sad at this word, and went away grieved, for he had great possessions.

23 And Jesus looked around and said to His disciples, "How hard it is for those who have riches to enter the kingdom of God!"

24 And the disciples were astonished at His words. But Jesus answered again and said to them, "Children, how hard it is for those who trust in riches to enter the kingdom of God!

25 "It is easier for a camel to go through the eye of a needle than for a rich man to enter the kingdom of God."

26 And they were astonished beyond measure, saying among themselves, "Who then can be saved?"

27 And Jesus looking at them said, "With men it is impossible, but not with God; for with God all things are possible."

28 And Peter began to say to Him, "See, we have left all and followed You."

29 And Jesus answered and said, "Assuredly, I say to you, there is no one who has left house or brothers or sisters or father or mother or wife or children or lands, for My sake and the gospel's,

30 "who shall not receive a hundredfold now in this time—houses and brothers and sisters and mothers and children and lands, with persecutions—and in the age to come, eternal life.

31 "But many who are first will be last, and the last first."

Mark 10:17–31

Contrast is a keen tool for teaching the truth. Mark shows us his mastery of this instrument when he records the encounter of Jesus with the rich, young ruler immediately after blessing the small children. Helpless babies without power or status are seen in sharp relief against the stunning achievements and swaggering confidence of the young man who runs to Jesus and kneels before Him. The story unfolds in: (1) the false economy of human achievement; (2) the sad truth of human pursuits; and (3) the great reversal of human values.

The false economy of human achievement. Matthew and Luke tell us that the man who runs to Jesus and bows before Him is young, rich, and powerful. In current terms, he would be classified as a "high achiever." By his own efforts, he has gained money and power. Luke identifies him as "a certain ruler" (Luke 18:18), implying that he was the chief of the synagogue or a respected member of the Sanhedrin.

Despite his wealth and position, the young man still exhibits the exuberance of youth. A vision of the future sparkles in his eyes. The fact that he comes running to Jesus tells us something about his attitude toward life. Early on, he has learned that you get what you want by running toward your goal at the head of the pack. More than that, he has learned that you run with a "proactive" attitude in all of your relationships. Everyone would enjoy being in the company of this person—not just because he is rich and powerful, but because he has a fast-moving and forward-looking view of the world.

Rich, young, and powerful. Most of us would succumb to the temptations of having too much, too soon. Not this young man. Wealth did not undermine his virtue, and power did not smother his respect for authority. He can still kneel before a master Teacher and claim obedience to the Law from the time of his youth.

Wisdom beyond his years also sets the young man apart. When he stops running and winning, he reflects upon his future. What more can he achieve? What virtue still eludes him? What satisfaction does he not yet know? The answer echoes through the chambers of the only empty spot in his life. He longs for spiritual satisfaction and the assurance of eternal life.

The sad truth of human pursuits. Hearing about the rabbi whose teaching emphasizes eternal life, the young man determines to achieve this elusive goal by the same effort, style, and assumptions by which he has brought the rest of the world to his doorstep. Running, bowing, flattering and deferring, he asks Jesus the timeless question, *"Good Teacher, what shall I do that I may inherit eternal life?"* (v. 17). His question is right, but his assumptions are wrong. First, he assumes that *goodness can be achieved.* When he salutes Jesus as "Good Teacher," he is commending His achievements rather than His character. Such a thought is quickly refuted by Jesus. *"Why do you call Me good? No one is good but One, that is, God"* (v. 18). Critics who try to use this response to prove that Jesus does not think of Himself as God miss the point. He is only responding to the misconception that good is achievable by human effort, rather than possessed and given by God's grace.

Another false assumption is that *eternal life can be earned.* If Jesus' reaction to the attempt at flattery shakes up the young man, his confidence comes back when Jesus cites the foundation for goodness in the commandments that deal with a person's responsibility to a neighbor. Puffing with justifiable pride, the young man must feel as if he is on the threshold of eternal life when he gives the ready answer, *"Teacher, all these I have carefully observed from my youth"* (v. 20).

What more can Jesus ask? Mark's uncanny perception of the "feeling tones" between Jesus and the young man speaks volumes. He reports that Jesus locks eyes with the man, looks deeply into his soul, and loves what He sees. Not only does Jesus admire the rare virtue of his exemplary character, but He foresees the potential of his drive and vision for the advancement of the Kingdom of God. One can speculate that this young man might have been God's first choice for the role that Saul of Tarsus would eventually take. In both cases, love prompts Jesus to speak the Truth to them. To Saul, He says, "I am Jesus whom you are persecuting" (Acts 9:5). Speaking to the rich young ruler, He diagnoses his need: *"One thing you lack"*; prescribes the remedy, *"Go your way, sell whatever you have and give to the poor"*; promises the reward, *"and you will have treasure in heaven"*; and puts out the challenge, *"come, take up the cross, and follow Me"* (v. 21).

With the Word of Truth spoken in love, Jesus shatters the high hopes which the young man holds for human achievement. He thinks, as the third false assumption, that *everything can be bought for a price, including eternal life.* Jesus teaches him a basic lesson in economics. Price and cost are not the same. Price is written in dollars, but cost is spelled out in values. No price tag can be put upon eternal life, but it does have what economists call an "opportunity cost." Every time we buy anything, we are asking, "What opportunity am I willing to sacrifice in order to make this purchase?" For the poor man, a pair of shoes may be the "opportunity cost" for buying a loaf of bread. For the rich man, investment in a new enterprise may be the "opportunity cost" for the expansion of an old business. When Jesus applies the principle of "opportunity cost" to the value of eternal life, He pierces the heart of the young man. Everything is to be sacrificed, including the fruits of human achievement. In other words, eternal life is a value that cannot be bought, but costs our all.

A deep cloud of gloom crosses over the countenance of the rich young ruler. His wealth and his power represent a cost that he will not pay. Hope disappears in pain as he turns away. He has made his choice.

The great reversal of human values. Acting out His look of love, Jesus gives the young man His full attention during the time that they are engaged in conversation. But when the young man makes his decision and goes away grieved, Jesus responds with the same air of finality. Looking around, He turns His attention back to the disciples, realizing once again that the future of the Gospel depends upon His teaching and their learning. So, sparing no sting of Truth, He reverses the expectations, rewards and values of wealth which have become confused with spirituality among the Jews. The shock waves of this great reversal still reverberate through the twentieth century.

Jesus reduces the *expectations* attached to wealth. Jewish law and its interpretations made wealth a sign of God's special favor and a qualification for spirituality. True piety, according to the Jews, consisted of the practices of prayer, fasting and almsgiving. Poverty-stricken people could pray, but only the rich had the food to fast and the money to give. In the economics of the Jews, wealth had become the stuff out of which spirituality was made.

Putting spirituality and wealth together eases a rich man's entry into the Kingdom of God. Jesus turns this false expectation upside down. *"How hard it is for those who trust in riches to enter the kingdom of God!"* (v. 23), He declares. Then, when the mouths of the disciples drop open, He adds shock to shock by picking up on a current quip that the people use to express the ludicrous, *"It is easier for a camel to go through the eye of a needle than for a rich man to enter the kingdom of God"* (v. 25). His point is well taken. Wealth is a human value with a voracious appetite which binds a person to earth and, as Dr. Samuel Johnson said, ". . . makes it difficult to die."

The disciples cannot absorb the Truth. Astonished beyond measure, they blurt out, *"Who then can be saved?"* (v. 26). Jesus looks at them again with laser eyes that burn the Truth into their minds, *"With men it is impossible, but not with God; for with God all things are possible"* (v. 27). Rich man, poor man, beggar man, thief—none can enter by their own merit or need, but all can be saved by the gift of God.

Jesus reverses the *rewards* attached to wealth. When Peter sees the reversal of expectations associated with wealth, he quickly aligns himself and his fellow disciples on the side of poverty, *"See, we have left all and followed You"* (v. 28). His plea contains a plaintive note. Just as quickly, Jesus makes it plain that His disciples have no room for self-pity. Their rewards are in the multiples of spiritual values that are priceless. Think of it! Homes, family, children and lands by the hundreds. Anyone who has experienced the worldwide relationships in the family of God knows what Jesus means.

Contrary to our standard system of rewards, Jesus also includes persecution among the spiritual values His disciples will receive. Strange, isn't it? Jesus promises a hundredfold what we try to avoid at all costs. Yet, He is consistent with His own beatitude: "Blessed are those who are persecuted for righteousness' sake, For theirs is the kingdom of heaven" (Matt. 5:10). Of course, the reward of persecution can only be seen in the perspective of the value of values, *"and in the age to come, eternal life"* (v. 30).

Finally, Jesus reverses the *position* attached to wealth when He repeats the premise, *"But many who are first will be last, and the last first"* (v. 31). Someone has said that Jesus threw the whole human parade into reverse. Generals will ride white horses behind marching foot soldiers, bishops will bring up the end of the processional behind the lowliest of the parishioners, and the wealthy in their purple robes will follow ragged peasants into the Kingdom of God. Death is the great equalizer.

What started out as the grand hope of the rich young ruler has become the sad truth which he cannot face and the great reversal of human values in the coinage of the Kingdom and the economy of eternal life.

CHAPTER FOURTEEN

Personalizing His Purpose

Mark 10:32–52

To Die

32 And they were on the road, going up to
Jerusalem, and Jesus was going before them; and they
were amazed. And as they followed they were afraid.
And He took the twelve aside again and began to tell
them the things that would happen to Him:
33 "Behold, we are going up to Jerusalem; and the
Son of Man will be delivered to the chief priests and
to the scribes, and they will condemn Him to death
and deliver Him to the Gentiles;
34 "and they will mock Him and scourge Him and
spit on Him and kill Him. And the third day He will
rise again."

Mark 10:32–34

Mark continues to amaze us with his ability to fill up a scene
with images and emotions by using just a few, simple words. Almost
as a matter of fact, he informs us that Jesus, His disciples and a
crowd of followers are *"on the road, going up to Jerusalem, and Jesus was
going before them"* (v. 32). Nothing seems unusual about this scene.
Jesus often walks ahead of the crowd and He has already committed
Himself to go to Jerusalem. What, then, causes Mark to report so
vividly, *"and they were amazed. And as they followed they were afraid"*
(v. 32)? Something in the demeanor of Jesus must have charged all
the ions of the air with the weight of impending doom. Do Jesus'
steps suddenly become heavy? Does He throw His shoulders back

and thrust His chin forward in an act of high resolve? The scene is reminiscent of the musical drama *The Man of La Mancha*. As Cervantes mounts the ladder leading from the dungeon to his death, he stretches to his full stature in the image of Don Quixote and lifts his eyes upward to a goal beyond the guillotine. Lagging behind him is his dim-witted and hunchbacked squire, Sancho Panza. Cowardice comes across his face as he measures the consequences of following his master. But then, seeing the courage, the resolute spine, the vision, and the uplifted eyes of a man with the "impossible dream," Sancho begins to imitate Don Quixote. Suddenly, his back is straight, his eyes are clear, and his joy is full as he steps on the first rung of the ladder on the way to death and glory.

Mark's picture of the resolute Jesus leading the way to Jerusalem in order to fulfill the will of God packs the same emotion. By His position ahead of the crowd and the posture of His walk, Jesus communicates the meaning of leadership as a position, a tone, and a responsibility. As always, when these qualities are displayed, close followers are amazed and the masses are paralyzed with fear.

Leadership is being alone and ahead of the crowd. James McGregor Burns divides leaders into two types: "transformational" leaders and "transactional" leaders. A transformational leader has an all-consuming vision to which he calls his followers and a charismatic personality by which he leads them. A transactional leader, on the other hand, searches for the goals of the group and negotiates a program to achieve them. Neither leadership style is right for all situations. In crisis, people look for a transformational leader; in calm, they want the transactional type.

On the road to Jerusalem and toward the crisis of the cross, Jesus walks ahead and alone in the position of a transformational leader. Nothing can turn His head from His purpose. Isaiah prophesies this moment when he puts words into the mouth of the Messiah, ". . . I set my face like a flint . . ." (Isa. 50:7, KJV). And the author of Hebrews looks back upon this scene when he describes Jesus as the "author," or, according to some translations, the "pioneer," of our faith (Heb. 12:2). Using the analogy of the wagon train moving across hostile territory, someone has to "ride point" if the pioneers are to reach their destination safely.

Leadership is the tone of courage in the midst of fear. Whatever Jesus communicates from the head of the procession, two emotions sweep over the company. The disciples are amazed and the crowds are filled

with fear. Amazement is a mixed emotion, arising out of two contradictory feelings: admiration and fear. The disciples must have seen
dread mingled with joy in the face of Jesus. Their meager understanding of His Passion prophecies gives them just enough information
to leave them baffled. The rest of the crowd, however, reacts to the
same look and gazes with pure fear, bordering on panic. They have
nothing to go on, except their feelings.

Jesus shows us the positive side of resolute courage. Out in front
of the fearful crowd, He finds strength and determination to do the
will of God. Fear, the natural reaction of mixed motives, keeps us
from closing the gap between Him and us. Yet, if we want the courage
to walk with Jesus on the way to the cross, we too must become
obsessed with the single-mindedness of doing the will of God.

Leadership is the responsibility for living with the consequences of our decisions.
A leader is a person who has a realistic understanding of the issues,
knows the implications of decision-making and is still willing to take
the risk of being out in front. President Lyndon Johnson spoke from
experience when he told Billy Graham, "Billy, there comes a time
when you have to stand like a jackass in a hailstorm and *take it!*"
Known for his plain speech and practical wisdom, Johnson knew
what it meant to stand in hailstorms. A president must make decisions
and live with the consequences.

Jesus sees the hailstorm of consequences that are ahead of Him.
Sensing the pitched emotions that He has created on His approach
to Jerusalem, He takes the disciples aside and reveals to them the
reason for His awesome resolve. For the third time, He predicts His
Passion. Now the details are complete. At Jerusalem, He will be betrayed; condemned by the Sanhedrin; transferred to a Roman court;
subjected to mocking, spitting, and scourging; crucified and resurrected on the third day.

Two new facts are introduced in this third prophecy of Jesus' Passion that are not included in the first two. One is the transfer to
the Roman court; the other is the ridicule, contempt, and beating
that will follow. For a Jew, the ultimate disgrace is to be rejected
by his own people and humiliated by the Gentiles. Put yourself in
Jesus' place. Knowing that He will be mocked as a king, spit upon
as a dog, and scourged as a criminal, He has to anticipate as well
as experience His suffering.

Leaders who have to live with the implications of their decisions
often find themselves alone and ahead of the fearful crowd. Moments

ago, I made a personnel decision I believe to be right, even though it was not easy. Because it dealt with a person, a career, and a brother in Christ, I consulted with superiors and confidants before finalizing the decision. After it was made, the same people with whom I consulted had second thoughts and left me all alone with the consequences.

Do we put Jesus in the same spot? Intellectually, we consent to follow Him and take up His cross. Emotionally, a lot of fear, mixed with a little wonder, still separates us from Him when we consider the consequences. While we would never be the rich young ruler and turn deliberately away, we do our best to reduce the demands and relieve the suffering. If so, Jesus' command comes back to us, "For whoever desires to save his life will lose it, but whoever loses his life for My sake and the gospel's will save it" (8:35). To follow Christ is to lead with Him—alone, courageous and realistic.

To Serve

35 And James and John, the sons of Zebedee, came to Him, saying, "Teacher, we want You to do for us whatever we ask."

36 And He said to them, "What do you want Me to do for you?"

37 They said to Him, "Grant us that we may sit, one on Your right hand and the other on Your left, in Your glory."

38 But Jesus said to them, "You do not know what you ask. Can you drink the cup that I drink, and be baptized with the baptism that I am baptized with?"

39 And they said to Him, "We can." And Jesus said to them, "You shall indeed drink the cup that I drink, and with the baptism I am baptized with you will be baptized;

40 "but to sit on My right hand and on My left is not Mine to give, but it is for those for whom it is prepared."

41 And when the ten heard it, they began to be greatly displeased with James and John.

42 But Jesus called them to Himself and said to them, "You know that those who are considered rulers

over the Gentiles lord it over them, and their great
ones exercise authority over them.

43 "Yet it shall not be so among you; but whoever
desires to become great among you shall be your
servant.

44 "And whoever of you desires to be first shall
be slave of all.

45 "For even the Son of Man did not come to be
served, but to serve, and to give His life a ransom
for many."

Mark 10:35–45

Each of the three Passion prophecies is followed by an inappropriate
rebuke or request from one of the three disciples of Jesus' inner circle.
Peter took it upon himself to rebuke Jesus after the first announcement
of the Son of Man's forthcoming suffering. John assumed the role
of spokesman, following the second prediction, when he indirectly
contested with Jesus about an exorcist who cast out demons in Jesus'
name, but did not belong to the Twelve. James and John come together
to make a personal request, following the third and final Passion
prophecy. Matthew, in his Gospel, tells us that Salome, the mother,
also comes with her sons and actually speaks for them. Although
the request may have been mutual, Mark lets the sons speak for
themselves, *"Teacher, we want You to do for us whatever we ask"* (v. 35).
Such an open-ended request is presumptuous under any circumstances, but Jesus is willing to listen. James and John want nothing
less than the right and left hand next to Christ's throne when He
reigns in glory.

A lust for greatness lurks behind the request of James and John.
The same lust shows through Peter's rebuke and John's rebuttal. Each
wants to protect his legacy of power and position in an earthly kingdom. In doing so, each exposes his lust for greatness as a two-sided
coin. One side is ambition; the other side is jealousy. Jesus has a
right to be impatient and angry with them, but instead, He recognizes
their progress in open questions and inch-by-inch understanding.
So He chooses to teach them the meaning of true greatness by comparing the human standards of rank and power with His standard of
servanthood.

The standard of rank. James and John are thinking about the Jewish
standard of rank when they ask for seats on the right and the left
hand of the reigning Jesus. Although their brotherly request assumes

that either James or John would be satisfied with either seat, the fact is that a bloody fratricidal battle would follow because the right-hand seat is the place of highest honor.

Greatness defined by the standard of rank degenerates into nitpicking protocol. In a monarchy, no one walks ahead of the queen; in a democracy, no one leaves the building until the president is escorted out; in a board of directors meeting, the brass plate on the back of a chair and its position at the table identifies the locus of power.

Jesus does not deny the standard of rank as a measure of greatness in the Kingdom of God. He bases the positioning, however, on the participation of the disciples in sharing the cup of His suffering and being submerged in the baptism of His death. Later on, this Truth will become the faithful saying:

> For if we died with Him,
>   We shall also live with Him.
> If we endure,
>   We shall also reign with Him . . .
>   (2 Tim. 2:11, 12)

Jesus also leaves the prerogative for positioning to God, the Father. Without diluting His deity in the slightest, Jesus takes Himself out of the decision to judge greatness among His disciples. Wisdom guides the decision because He is too close to the situation. As a father of four, I have no favorite children. Each is fully loved and each is uniquely great. Someone with a more objective viewpoint would have to judge their qualities and rank them in order. It is equally unfair to expect that Jesus will rank order the disciples whom He loves and in whom He sees differing qualities of greatness.

The standard of power. Word leaks out that James and John are conspiring for the top positions in the coming Kingdom. Their ambition has isolated Peter and caused jealousy among the other disciples. A power struggle threatens to destroy all the work that Jesus has done to weld the Twelve into a unified, working body. He has to nip the rebellion in the bud. Calling the Twelve together, Jesus talks to them about the standard of power which the Gentiles use to determine greatness. Touching on the tender spot of men who have been ground under the heel of Roman oppression, Jesus reminds them of the Gentile rulers who use their power to "lord it over" them. His point is well taken. The disciples know that they have fallen victim to the same corrupting power that they suffer from the Romans, and they want none of it.

Power as the standard of greatness is still corrupting. We fail to realize that power is a limited commodity. There is only so much to go around. Those who are in power want to protect their position; those who are out of power always want more. The prediction is sure. If power is a standard of greatness in any church or Christian organization, ambition will rule and jealousy will reign.

The standard of servanthood. Jesus is in the business of upsetting all the accepted standards of the world. Categorically rejecting rank and power, He establishes servanthood as His standard of greatness. By rank, a servant is last of all. In power, a servant has none.

"Service" is too impersonal and too limited a term to describe the standard of greatness set by Jesus for His disciples. In a single sentence that rises like a mountain peak above all previous statements about His purpose, Jesus personalizes "servanthood" as the standard of greatness when He says, *"For even the Son of Man did not come to be served, but to serve, and to give His life a ransom for many"* (v. 45). Greatness is not to be sought; if it comes, it comes through giving. *Life* magazine carried an editorial comparing the lives of great people, such as Winston Churchill, Pope John XXIII, and Albert Schweitzer. None of them aspired to greatness as his primary goal. Each of them sacrificed himself in order to be a servant of the people. According to the conclusion of the editorial, they were great because they chose first to be good.

Ultimate good rules the servanthood of Jesus. Without rank and without power, He gives up His life as *"a ransom for many."* College students often seek counsel concerning their future careers. Almost without exception, they want to know how they can "serve." Sometimes, "service" is mixed with salary, status and security. Seldom is the risk of service fully considered, and even less often do the students think forward to the lasting benefits and the ever-expanding circle of those whom they will serve. The perspective is too big and too distant for youthful minds to grasp. They need an example, not advice. Greatness is theirs if they follow the Son of Man who *"did not come to be served, but to serve, and to give His life a ransom for many."*

To Heal

46 And they came to Jericho. And as He went out of Jericho with His disciples and a great multitude, blind Bartimaeus, the son of Timaeus, sat by the road begging.

47 And when he heard that it was Jesus of Nazareth, he began to cry out and say, "Jesus, Son of David, have mercy on me!"

48 And many warned him that he should be quiet; but he cried out all the more, "Son of David, have mercy on me!"

49 And Jesus stood still and commanded him to be called. And they called the blind man, saying to him, "Be of good cheer. Rise, He is calling you."

50 And throwing aside his garment, he rose and came to Jesus.

51 And Jesus answered and said to him, "What do you want Me to do for you?" The blind man said to Him, "*Rabboni,* that I may receive my sight."

52 And Jesus said to him, "Go your way; your faith has made you well." And immediately he received his sight and followed Jesus on the road.

Mark 10:46–52

The healing of the blind beggar Bartimaeus is significant because it is the final healing that Mark reports and it enters as an interruption into the events of Jesus' Passion. Mark sets the scene when Jesus is leaving Jericho on the last leg of His journey to Jerusalem, just fifteen miles away. Passover is approaching and the road is jammed with pilgrims chanting on the way to the Holy City. Alongside the road is another crowd—parade watchers, curiosity seekers, and those who are too poor, sinful, diseased, or handicapped to make the journey to Jerusalem. By now, the size of the crowd following after Jesus has swelled to *"a great multitude"* (v. 46). Putting all the dynamics of milling, moving people together in a festival atmosphere must have filled the air with a tingle of triumph. After all, the news that the young rabbi who has challenged the religious establishment of the Jews is on His way to Jerusalem would create its own excitement. The promise of a confrontation always draws a crowd.

Amid the cacophony of sound, a disrupting voice grates against the ears, *"Jesus, Son of David, have mercy on me!"* (v. 47). Someone has told Bartimaeus—blind man, beggar, and public nuisance—that the passing of Jesus caused the commotion. To avoid a smear on the reputation of Jericho or a blight on the festivities, many citizens try to silence the voice of Bartimaeus. But the blind man sees something that no one else has seen and cries all the more, *"Son of David, have mercy on me!"* For the first time, Jesus is publicly called the Son of David. Whether Bartimaeus knows it or not, he introduces Jesus to Jerusalem and strikes the keynote for the triumphal entry. Jews in Jerusalem claim David as their father and his son as their Messiah.

Both the plaintive sound and the prophetic salute of Bartimaeus stop Jesus in His tracks. Presumably, His healing ministry has been left behind Him and all of His energy now has to be marshaled for His own suffering. Nothing can deter or interrupt Him—except a needy man crying for mercy. In His hearing Bartimaeus's pleas above the noise of the crowd, stopping the processional for a blind beggar, and calling the pitiful creature to come to Him while on the way to Jerusalem there is proof enough that Jesus, the Servant, and Jesus, the Savior, are inseparable.

A call to faith. On Jesus' instruction, someone tells the blind man that he is being summoned. Whoever carries the call sounds like Jesus Himself, *"Be of good cheer. Rise, He is calling you"* (v. 49). *"Be of good cheer"* is an appeal to emotions that Bartimaeus thought were gone forever. He has heard "Cheer up" before from callous people who tossed it into his face rather than throwing a coin into his begging blanket. Never before has he heard words of encouragement combined with the command, "Rise." A serious call to faith requires an act of will as well as a word of hope. The information, then, that *"He is calling you"* (v. 49) tests the level of Bartimaeus's cognitive skills. In his past experience, no one has ever responded to his call, except to demand silence. Perhaps even now, he thinks, a cruel hoax is in the making. Raw intelligence and refined intuition, however, tell Bartimaeus the truth. As a blind beggar, he has no place to go but up. The risk is minimal. As simple as it seems, the call to "Look up, get up, and go up" defines faith as an act of hope based upon limited information.

A show of faith. If ever a person enthusiastically demonstrates a holistic show of faith, Bartimaeus does. Feeling for feeling, will for will, mind for mind, he answers the call from Jesus. In response to the word of encouragement, *"Be of good cheer"* (v. 49), he goes a step further to the daring act of throwing aside the ragged garment that serves functionally to catch coins and symbolically as a sign of his beggarliness. Equally bold, on the command, "Rise," he abandons his sitting position as a beggar by springing up and standing like a man. Posture always gives clues to self-esteem. Never again will Bartimaeus be looked down upon as the scum of the earth. As Job responded to God's challenge, Bartimaeus stands ready to answer as a man.

To complete his show of faith, Bartimaeus comes to Jesus. All of his life, the blind beggar has counted on others to lead and feed him. If he still needed help, Peter would have remembered it and Mark would have reported it. No. Although still blind, Bartimaeus walks out his own Emancipation Proclamation. What a sight it must have been to see the crowd open a path for Bartimaeus as he comes to Jesus! In one sense, faith has already made him a whole man. His feelings, his will, and his mind are healed.

The result of faith. Jesus meets the ready faith of Bartimaeus with the open-ended question, *"What do you want Me to do for you?"* (v. 51). Not long before, James and John had asked Him to grant them whatsoever they asked. The difference between Bartimaeus's answer and the disciples' request is the difference between faith and ambition. Faith asks for needs; ambition begs for wants. Bartimaeus needed his sight; James and John wanted the places of honor in the coming Kingdom of God.

Jesus exempted Himself from responding to the disciples' wants, but He wastes no time in meeting Bartimaeus' need. *"Go your way; your faith has made you well"* (v. 52) not only gives instant sight to a blind man, but recognizes the total healing of a person with a ready faith. Spiritually free, physically sound, and humanly dignified, Bartimaeus is pronounced "well" and "whole."

Mark reinforces the total healing of Bartimaeus by bringing the story full cycle in the conclusion, *"And immediately he received his sight and followed Jesus on the road"* (v. 52). A beggar becomes a disciple and a squatter becomes a pilgrim—living, seeing, walking, and singing proof that Jesus is Servant and Savior.

CHAPTER FIFTEEN

Claiming His Lordship

Mark 11:1–26

LORD OF THE PEOPLE

1 And when they came near to Jerusalem, to
Bethphage and Bethany, at the Mount of Olives, He
sent out two of His disciples;

2 and He said to them, "Go your way into the
village opposite you; and as soon as you have entered
it, you will find a colt tied, on which no one has ever
sat. Loose it and bring it.

3 "And if anyone says to you, 'Why are you doing
this?' say, 'The Lord has need of it,' and immediately
he will send it here."

4 And they went their way and found the colt
tied by the door outside on the street, and they loosed
it.

5 And some of those who stood there said to them,
"What are you doing, loosing the colt?"

6 And they spoke to them just as Jesus had
commanded. And they let them go.

7 And they brought the colt to Jesus and threw
their garments on it, and He sat on it.

8 And many spread their garments on the road,
and others cut down leafy branches off the trees and
spread them on the road.

9 And those who went before and those who
followed cried out, saying:

"Hosanna!

'Blessed is He who comes in the name of the
LORD!'

10 Blessed is the kingdom of our father David
That comes in the name of the Lord!
Hosanna in the highest!"

11 And Jesus entered into Jerusalem and into the
temple. And when He had looked around at all things,
as the hour was already late, He went out to Bethany
with the twelve.

Mark 11:1–11

A prophetic ministry in Jerusalem leads Jesus to His Passion. Entering the city in triumph, cursing the fig tree, and cleansing the Temple are events continuous with prophetic revelation. In each of these events by which He introduces Himself to Jerusalem, He is the subject of the *prophetic Word,* the leader of *prophetic fulfillment* and the object of the *prophetic future.* Through these events, He claims His Lordship over people, nature and the church. His prophetic ministry begins when He enters Jerusalem in triumph.

The prophetic Word. Anticipation edges upward to a fever pitch when Jews on a pilgrimage to Jerusalem climb the east side of the Mount of Olives just out of sight from the city. They know that their path will lead them to a turn in the road at the crest of the mountain where suddenly a vista of the Holy City bursts into panoramic view before their eyes.

While eating breakfast on the veranda of a hotel on the Mount of Olives, we were startled to hear muffled and distant sounds of shouting. Fear led us to think that commandos were on the attack. "No," our waiter assured us, "You are hearing the shouts of pilgrims who have just caught their first glimpse of Jerusalem." Soon, on a nearby path, we saw the pilgrims coming, watched them as they wound their singing way down the mountain, across the valley and, with a final shout, through the eastern gate into the city.

Prophecy says that the Messiah will enter Jerusalem on the same note of triumph. Zechariah 9:9 (KJV) rings out: "Rejoice greatly, O daughter of Zion; shout, O daughter of Jerusalem: behold, thy King cometh unto thee: he is just, and having salvation; lowly, and riding upon an ass, and upon a colt the foal of an ass."

The prophetic fulfillment. Jesus cannot be accused of being a political animal. He refuses to compromise His purpose for the sake of tradi-

224

tion, popularity, controversy, misunderstanding, or the threat of death. But now, when He is the leader in prophetic fulfillment, He becomes a strategist of the first order. Mark, in fact, records in detail the preparations for the entry into Jerusalem that Jesus personally supervises. Usually, He leaves the details for His arrangements to the disciples. Not this time. The entry into Jerusalem has to be perfect in every detail—not for His sake, but for the sake of those who will critically analyze His entry to see if it conforms exactly to the specifics of Zechariah's prediction.

Jesus knows that the style of leadership He establishes on His entry into Jerusalem will affect everything He says and does in the days ahead. So, with the precision of a perfectionist, He walks His disciples through every detail for finding the colt of an ass, untying it, assuring the owner that it will be properly returned, and bringing it to Him as the unbroken animal that only a king would ride. Other details are secondary in Mark's mind. Disciples throw their garments on the beast as a makeshift saddle and the processional moves to the gate of entry. Instinct leads the people along the way to break forth with a natural response to the entry of a king—garments are strewn in His path, palm leaves are plucked and waved, and an impromptu choir begins its antiphonal chant:

Hosanna!

Blessed is He who
comes in the name of
the Lord!

Blessed is the
kingdom of our
father David

That comes in the
name of the Lord!

*Hosanna in the
Highest!*

Mark 11:9-10

Even though they stop short of lauding Jesus as the Messiah and even though their shouts of "Hosanna!" mean "Save Us" with an earthly Kingdom in mind, at least they acknowledge Jesus as King. Later on, we learn that the chief priests and scribes would have speeded their nefarious death plot against the Man from Galilee except for their fear of the people. The emotions of masses invariably create problems for leadership. Wisdom says, "The feelings of the people may be fickle or wrong, but they must be respected as fact." As long as the people feel that Jesus promises them a king, the hands of His enemies are tied. In the triumphal entry, Jesus claims His Lordship with the people and temporarily, at least, wins their acclaim.

The prophetic future. We can now understand why Jesus pays personal attention to the details of getting, preparing, and returning the animal upon which to ride through the gates into Jerusalem. In the symbol of the foal of an ass, He predicts His role as the King who comes in dignity and peace. Roman Christians to whom Mark writes can visualize the contrast between the triumphal entry of Jesus and the pageantry that greeted Roman Emperors on return from their wars. As a symbol of bloody conquest, Caesar chose a prancing horse at the head of a processional that included his warriors, a shackled contingent of the conquered people, and an extravagant display of the booty that the army had taken by force. Jesus makes His triumphal entry on a donkey—a symbol of peace, not war; of humility, not pride. Behind Him comes an entourage of twelve fishermen, called to be disciples, and a rabble of common people whom He has healed and set free. They serve as trophies of His conquest—not by bloody violence, but by unremitting love.

In our day, a donkey is the butt of our jokes and the symbol of stupidity. Someplace in the history of changing symbols, we went awry. By choosing the foal of an ass, Jesus gives us the symbol for His prophetic future. He comes in peace, not war, and He conquers by His Spirit, not by might nor power. For those of us who want to see Christianity represented by a leader on a prancing horse at the head of a conquering army showing off its trophies, Jesus' entry into Jerusalem is a defeat rather than a triumph.

LORD OF NATURE

12 And the next day, when they had come out from Bethany, He was hungry.

13 And seeing from afar a fig tree having leaves, He went to see if perhaps He might find something on it. And when He came to it, He found nothing but leaves, for it was not the season for figs.

14 And Jesus answered and said to it, "Let no one eat fruit from you anymore forever." And His disciples heard it.

Mark 11:12-14

Jesus does not claim His Lordship all at once. From the information that Mark gives us, the triumphal entry comes off as a local affair, attracting little attention outside the immediate participants. This is attested by the fact that Jesus goes without incident to the Temple at the end of the day. After surveying the scene, Jesus leaves the city and returns to Bethany, where He probably stays at the home of His close friends, Lazarus, Martha and Mary. The next morning, then, Jesus travels back to Jerusalem to place another claim upon His Lordship. On the way, hunger prompts Him to look for fruit on a fig tree whose mature leaves promise early fruit. Thus begins the story that some scholars doubt is true. Others read it only as a parable and all admit that it is difficult to interpret. Perhaps our outline of the *prophetic Word,* the *prophetic fulfillment* and the *prophetic future* will help.

The prophetic Word. Figs have a special meaning in Old Testament prophecy. They symbolized the fruit of spiritual fulfillment, based upon Israel's promise as God's chosen people. Yet, most frequently in prophecy, figs represent apostasy, all the more tragic because of unfulfilled promises. Micah 7:1 forecasts Jesus' hunger and disappointment: "Woe is me! for I am as when they have gathered the summer fruits, as the grapegleanings of the vintage: there is no cluster to eat: my soul desired the first ripe fruit" (KJV).

Finding nothing but leaves on the promising fig tree, Jesus' disappointment turns to judgment as the prophet Jeremiah predicted: "I will surely consume them, saith the Lord: there shall be no grapes on the vine, nor figs on the fig tree, and the leaf shall fade; and the things that I have given them shall pass away from them" (Jer. 8:13, KJV).

Like the fig tree, Israel had been chosen as God's people and blessed beyond measure. If only they had lived up to their potential!

The prophetic fulfillment. The enigma of the fig tree will never be resolved, short of eternity. According to Mark's own statement, the time for figs has not yet come. Why, then, does Jesus hold the tree responsible for something that is contrary to its nature? Even more, why does He expect fruit out of season to satisfy His own hunger?

From every human standpoint, it appears as if the cursing of the fig tree is arbitrary, unreasonable and unjustified.

Jesus' character is in question. After spending so much time dealing with the selfishness of His disciples, does He succumb to the same temptation? Certainly, it is not fair to curse a fig tree for failure to bear fruit out of season just to satisfy His hunger.

What really happens? A combination of Micah's prophecy and Mark's Gospel sheds some light on the dilemma. Prophetically, Micah hears the Messiah say, ". . . my soul desired the firstripe fruit" (Mic. 7:1, KJV) and, practically, Mark has Jesus seeing the leaves on the fig tree and going over to it to see *"if perhaps He might find something on it"* (v. 13). On the basis of what Jesus sees in the maturity of the leaves, He has reason to expect the firstripe fruits with which to satisfy His hunger. The fig tree is cursed for the pretense of its leaves, not for its lack of fruit. Hypocrisy is more than being what a person is not; it is also failing to produce what is promised. A wise counselor told a young man, "You have such a gift with words. Do not let your eloquence become a substitute for substance." Spiritual style can produce *"nothing but leaves"* (v. 13) if it raises expectations, but fails to produce fruit to feed the hungry.

A media age has a tendency to mistake spiritual style for spiritual substance. Marshall McLuhan, in his serious thoughts about television and its social impact, uttered an indictment as much as an observation when he entitled one of his books, *Understanding Media: The Extensions of Man.* In the six short words of his title, McLuhan proposes the revolutionary idea that the way in which a message is relayed becomes the message itself. How true! How false! Communicating with style may enhance the message, but it cannot take its place, at least where the Gospel is concerned. Otherwise, we fall into the Pharisees' trap of making religious means a spiritual end in itself. Leaves are a sad substitute for fruit—whether talking about fig trees, Pharisees, or any of us who have style without substance.

The prophetic future. In the last miracle recorded by Mark, Jesus curses the fig tree, *"Let no one eat fruit from you anymore forever"* (v. 14). All other miracles had been performed for human benefit. Why, then, did Jesus leave us with a destructive show of power as the final reminder of His miracles? The generally accepted reason is that Jesus chooses the fig tree as a parable of His coming to Jerusalem as the Lord of Judgment. Chosen by divine appointment, given God's Law, protected from annihilation, led to a new land, disciplined in exile, blessed beyond measure, Israel stands at the center of the world as the source of God's redemptive hope. Alas, instead of fulfilling the hope by accepting Jesus as the Messiah, God's own people counter His coming with a rigid display of empty rituals, human interpretations, and meaningless symbols.

The nature of God calls for severe judgment as the other side of His longsuffering love. Even then, Jesus chooses a fig tree, rather than a person, on which to pronounce His curse. As spiritually barren as Israel had proved to be, one more warning is given by a parable. God's judgment is still restrained, but as the poet wrote, "The mills of the gods grind slowly, but they grind exceedingly fine."[1] Seventy years later, the judgment on Jerusalem will be so devastatingly complete that Josephus will remember that the Romans will run out of space in which to erect one more cross. A fig tree with nothing but leaves remains as a grim reminder of Jesus as the Lord of Judgment as well as the King of Life.

LORD OF THE CHURCH

15 And they came to Jerusalem. And Jesus went into the temple and began to drive out those who bought and sold in the temple, and overturned the tables of the moneychangers and the seats of those who sold doves.
16 And He would not allow anyone to carry a vessel through the temple.
17 And He taught, saying to them, "Is it not written, *'My house shall be called a house of prayer for all nations'*? But you have made it a *'den of thieves.'*"
18 And the scribes and chief priests heard it and sought how they might destroy Him; for they feared Him, because all the people were astonished at His teaching.
19 And when evening had come, He went out of the city.

Mark 11:15–19

In the glorious moment of the triumphal entry, we sometimes forget the line of march that took Jesus directly to the Temple. Mark reports that ". . . He had looked around at all things, as the hour was already late . . ." (10:11). What Jesus sees displeases Him. Although the Holy of Holies remains inviolate, the outer Court of the Gentiles has been turned into a bazaar for selling sacrificial animals and taxing worshipers. By the time that Jesus arrives after first entering Jerusalem, all of the merchants and moneychangers have closed up shop for the night. Nothing can be done at that time, so Jesus leaves the city for an overnight stay in Bethany—but not without firm intentions for future actions. As Lord of the Temple, He sees that a therapeutic cleansing is needed.

The prophetic Word. Strong prophetic passages give authority to Jesus' actions in the Temple. As if looking through Jesus' eyes, Jeremiah writes: "Is this house, which is called by my name, become a den of robbers in your eyes? Behold, even I have seen it, saith the Lord" (Jer. 7:11, KJV).

His return to the Temple with the intention of cleaning house is also foreseen by Malachi's prophecy: ". . . and the Lord, whom ye seek, shall suddenly come to his temple, even the messenger of the covenant, whom ye delight in: behold, he shall come, saith the Lord of hosts" (Mal. 3:1, KJV).

Going on, Malachi graphically describes the anger with which Jesus purges His Temple: "But who may abide the day of his coming? and who shall stand when he appeareth? for he is like a refiner's fire, and like fullers' soap" (Mal. 3:2, KJV).

The object of His anger? Malachi lays the blame for the corruption of the Temple at the feet of the priests: ". . . And he shall purify the sons of Levi, and purge them as gold and silver, that they may offer unto the Lord an offering in righteousness" (Mal. 3:3, KJV).

Finally, the reason behind Jesus' rage is found in Isaiah's prophecy. Speaking of the Gentiles, God says: "Even them will I bring to my holy mountain, and make them joyful in my house of prayer: their burnt offerings and their sacrifices shall be accepted upon mine altar; for mine house shall be called a house of prayer for all people" (Isa. 56:7, KJV).

In unusual and accurate detail, the prophetic Word sets the stage for Jesus to cleanse His Temple.

The prophetic fulfillment. In the Court of the Gentiles, Jesus sees violations against the sanctity of the Temple. Merchants sell sacrificial animals at exorbitant prices, and priests serve as moneychangers to collect a Temple tax from the worshipers. The courtyard also serves as a shortcut for business traffic through the Temple. A Jewish mind might rationalize these violations by thinking that the Court of the Gentiles is least holy among the outer courts of the Temple. As long as the inner court which houses the Holy of Holies remains sacrosanct, no harm is done. Jesus has another view of the Temple. All of its precincts are holy, and for priests to choose the Court of the Gentiles for merchandising speaks again of their corruption.

Rationalized encroachment upon holy centers through peripheral areas is still a way of spiritual corruption. What are the peripheral areas of the church that are open to violation? More and more functions are being added to the traditional ministries of the church, such as day care centers, Christian schools, senior citizen centers, singles activities, counseling clinics, and food banks. Are their policies consistent with the standards of the holy place? Does the same sacred spirit pervade their space? Are ministers diverted from prayer, visitation, counseling, and the preaching of the Word by these activities? In higher education, the term "veto groups" is used to describe factions on campus whose purposes run counter to the mission of the college or the university. In the Court of the Gentiles, merchants and priests formed a "veto group" whose policies and practices countered the purpose and corrupted the spirit of the Temple. For them, and sometimes for us, a therapeutic cleansing is in order.

The corruption goes deeper than evidenced by merchants selling sacrificial doves and animals at outrageous prices to the poor who come to worship. Priests exploit their position by taking a share of the profits and collecting an artificially contrived Temple tax from the pilgrims and worshipers. The scene is reminiscent of a big-time gambling operation. Cheating and crime are companions to the gambling industry, but they cannot continue without the corruption of police and public officials. Likewise, the Temple could not have been corrupted without the collusion of the priests. Heavy responsibility rests upon those who are called to be keepers of the courts that surround the Holy place.

The prophetic future. A purging must have a purpose. Otherwise, seven devils return to replace each one that is cast out. Jesus has more in mind than just clearing out the merchants and repudiating the priests. By His action in the Court of the Gentiles, He restores the space given to God's purpose of making His Temple *"a house of prayer for all nations"* (v. 17). Corruption in the courtyard has blocked Gentiles from entering into faith. Never again. The Lord of the Temple comes— not just to restore His Temple as a house of prayer, but to reopen the promise that His salvation is for all nations.

A purging also brings out hate. Because Jesus undercuts the profits and publicly embarrasses the agents of the high priests, the hierarchy of the Temple joins in conspiracy with the scribes to kill Him. Strange, isn't it? Jesus has denied their tradition, repudiated their teaching, and condemned their spirit, but the chief priests do not think about violence until He touches their pocketbook. As the forces line up, the people are on Jesus' side. And opposite them are His enemies, now including the chief priests who will stop at nothing to eliminate the man who is taking away their profits and their power.

LORD OF FAITH

20 And in the morning, as they passed by, they saw the fig tree dried up from the roots.

21 And Peter, remembering, said to Him, "Rabbi, look! The fig tree which You cursed has withered away."

22 And Jesus answered and said to them, "Have faith in God.

23 "For assuredly, I say to you, whoever says to this mountain, 'Be removed and be cast into the sea,' and does not doubt in his heart, but believes that those things he says will come to pass, he will have whatever he says.

24 "Therefore I say to you, whatever things you ask when you pray, believe that you receive them, and you will have them.

25 "And whenever you stand praying, if you have anything against anyone, forgive him, that your Father who is in heaven may also forgive you your trespasses.

26 "But if you do not forgive, neither will your Father who is in heaven forgive your trespasses."

Mark 11:20–26

After spending another night in Bethany, Jesus and His disciples are wending their way over the Mount of Olives on the same path that had taken them to Jerusalem the day before. Probably at the crest of the mountain, Peter notices the fig tree that Jesus has cursed. Dry leaves and dead branches tell him that the roots have withered. When he calls the fact to Jesus' attention, he sparks a succession of thoughts that begin with the power of God, lead to prayer, advance to faith, and end with forgiveness.

To teach such a comprehensive lesson, Jesus turns from the withered fig tree, which symbolizes His judgment on Israel, to the glory of the larger scene around them. Looking back toward the East where the Dead Sea can be seen as a large, mirrored pool on the desert floor, He begins to talk about "removing a mountain" into the midst of the sea by the power of God and the prayer of faith. "Removing a mountain" served as a common figure of speech among the Jews who wanted to describe a situation that was well-nigh impossible. Pointing to the end of time, Zechariah saw the Lord standing on the Mount of Olives, cleaving it with a valley from east to west, and moving its bulk north and south until the place upon which the mountain stood became a plain (Zech. 14:3–10, KJV). With this image of the impossible fixed in their minds, the Lord of Nature teaches His disciples about the power of prayer that is based upon faith in God and backed up by the spirit of forgiveness.

The creative mind of Christ. At first, the way in which Jesus turns the sight of the withered fig tree into a lesson on the power of prayer seems to be too much for us. If we divide the episode into separate steps, however, we see the creative mind of Christ at work.

Timing is a quality of creativity. Rather than living in the past, Jesus finds relevance in the present and hope in the future. He might have fixed His attention on the withered fig tree, teaching its symbolic meaning and reinforcing His role as Lord of Judgment over nature and nations. Instead, He puts the past behind Him and uses the present to move on.

Attitude is also a qualification for creativity. Everything surrounding the incident of the fig tree smacks of negativism—cursing, withering, judgment, and death. A creative mind does not dwell on the negative. Jesus hardly acknowledges Peter's comment about the withered tree. Rather, He turns immediately to the positive thoughts about moving mountains and says, *"whatever things you ask when you pray, believe that you receive them, and you will have them"* (v. 24).

Viewpoint is another characteristic of creativity. How quickly Jesus diverts the disciples' eyes from the withered fig tree to the grand eastern view from the mountaintop. Is it one of those days in Palestine when the sky is so clear that you feel as if you can see forever? God's view is large and long. The disciples need to see the full potential of faith from the mountaintop in order to survive the days just ahead. Jesus' ability to use that view as a spiritual promise might be attributed to His genius. The truth is that genius is within our reach if we use the present to see the future, the negative to create the positive, and the simple to explain the profound.

The unlimited power of prayer. Jesus' teaching about prayer complements the creativity of His teaching. Behind the promise of the unlimited power of prayer are three limiting conditions. One is the *will of God.* A person cannot pray outside of that which God has said *"will come to pass"* (v. 23). His Word is the revelation of His will.

A second limitation is the *faith of the person who prays.* Doubt is a deterrent to answered prayer and unlimited power. To receive what you ask in prayer, you must *"believe that you receive them"* (v. 24).

A final limiting factor on unlimited power through prayer is the *failure to forgive* someone who has sinned against you. To go to prayer holding anything against anyone is to invite unanswered prayer and limited power.

Every time that Jesus speaks, He upsets the assumptions by which we live. For instance, we make creativity something beyond us and unlimited power a matter reserved for God's will. Neither assumption can stand before the example and teaching of Jesus. Our intellectual dullness is caused by a narrow and negative viewpoint and our spiritual impotency is the natural result of our failure to know the will of God, believe what He has promised, or refuse to forgive those who have sinned against us. If only we would understand His teaching and follow His example, the creative mind of Christ and the unlimited power of God would be unbelievably released in us.

NOTE

1. Anonymous, "The Best Loved Poems of the American People," in *Granger's Index to Poetry,* 5th ed. (Morningside Heights, NY: Columbia University Press, 1962), p. 819.

CHAPTER SIXTEEN

Finalizing His Authority

Mark 11:27—12:34

AUTHORITY OVER REASON

27 And they came again to Jerusalem. And as He was walking in the temple, the chief priests, the scribes, and the elders came to Him.

28 And they said to Him, "By what authority are You doing these things? And who gave You this authority to do these things?"

29 And Jesus answered and said to them, "I will also ask you one question; then answer Me, and I will tell you by what authority I do these things:

30 "The baptism of John—was it from heaven or from men? Answer Me."

31 And they reasoned among themselves, saying, "If we say, 'From heaven,' He will say, 'Why then did you not believe him?'

32 "But if we say, 'From men' "—they feared the people, for all counted John to have been a prophet indeed.

33 And they answered and said to Jesus, "We do not know." And Jesus, answering, said to them, "Neither will I tell you by what authority I do these things."

Mark 11:27–33

On His third trip to Jerusalem, Jesus continues to claim His Lordship by appearing in the Royal Cloister of the Temple's outer courts where rabbis teach and debate great ideas. His presence in this setting gives

His enemies the opening they need. Yesterday, when Jesus cleansed the Temple, they wanted to arrest Him, but drew back because of His popularity with the people. Today, He plays into their hands by walking and teaching in the courtyard where His religious credentials can be legitimately questioned without fear of a people's rebellion. A debate ensues in which Jesus demonstrates His authority over reason.

A subtle trap. Huddling together in a special meeting of the Sanhedrin, a rare coalition of chief priests, scribes, and elders comes together on a common question that they will address to Jesus. Usually, they are at odds with each other because the chief priests are jealous of their power, the scribes pride themselves on their intellect, and the elders never let either group forget the sacredness of tradition. Only a common enemy can cause them to put aside their differences long enough to bring their collective wisdom together on a question that will trap Jesus and justify His arrest. Each faction has its special reason for hating Him. He has exposed the unethical economic practices of the chief priests, embarrassed the scribes in debate, and repudiated the elders' position that the oral tradition equals God's Law. All of this hate now focuses in one event—the cleansing of the Temple. If Jesus gets away with this show of force in their sacred precincts, He can flaunt their authority at any time in any place. Still, the issue of raw power is too obvious. The question that they will ask Him must be spiritualized.

A spiritual coating for a sinful motive is a formidable defense. More than once, hate letters have come with the opening words, "God has told me. . . ." What more can be said? Divine authority has been evoked and debate is closed. The same idea strikes fire with the Sanhedrin. Jesus acted as if He were God in the sanctity of the Temple. Why not, then, devise a question that will force Him to declare whether His authority is spiritual or secular? On the surface, the question must be consistent with the Sanhedrin's responsibility to request credentials from an itinerant rabbi. At the same time, it must appear to be an unbiased and open-ended question befitting the climate of the debating porch. Whatever answer Jesus gives, He must be arrested. If He attests that His authority is from God, the charge is blasphemy. If He claims secular authority for His act of cleansing the Temple, the charge is insurrection.

Armed, then, with the dual question, *"By **what** authority are You do-*

*ing these things? And **who** gave You this authority to do these things?"* (v. 28),
a delegation from the Sanhedrin hurries to the porch, confident they
have the resolution to the Jesus question.

A strategic move. As a good debater, Jesus takes their question at
face value, thereby accepting the fact that authority constitutes the
key issue in their debate. He also acknowledges the legitimacy of
the questions, "What?" and "Who?" with reference to His authority.
When they ask, *"By what authority are You doing these things?"* (v. 28),
they know that Jesus cannot claim ordination by the chief priests,
academic degrees equal to the Sanhedrin, or religious ancestry recognized by the elders. Their question, *"And who gave You this authority to
do these things?"* (v. 28), leaves Jesus no alternative but to cite either
God or Himself.

If Jesus had answered their questions directly, He would have been
trapped. Instead, exercising His privilege under the rules of rabbinical
debate, He counters with His own question and makes an offer that
His opponents cannot refuse, *"Then answer Me, and I will tell you by
what authority I do these things"* (v. 29). Jesus' tactic puts the chief priests,
scribes, and elders on the spot. Because they initiated the debate,
chose the issue, and advanced an implicit charge, fairness dictates
that He has the right of asking for the first response. Like a life-
and-death chess game in which the player sets his strategy, Jesus
positions Himself for an early checkmate with just the push of a
pawn. Debate, which John Wesley called "the honest art," should
be a required course for Christian discipleship.

A specific case. Without deviating from the issue of the debate, Jesus
thrusts forward the challenge, *"The baptism of John—was it from heaven
or from men? Answer Me"* (v. 30). Not only has Jesus perceived the
substance of the issue as a choice of authority between heaven and
earth, but He appeals to the people by identifying Himself with their
martyred folk hero, John the Baptist. The worm has turned, and
the burden of proof rests heavily upon the shoulders of their chief
priests, scribes, and elders. Before answering Jesus' counterquestion,
they caucus to consider their alternatives and plan their next move.
All of their answers dead-end in defeat. If they admit that John's
authority came from heaven, Jesus will put them into opposition to
God by asking, *"Why then did you not believe him?"* (v. 31), but if they
even start to answer, *"From men"* (v. 32), shouts of the people will
never let them finish. What a posthumous honor to have Jesus risk

His life on John's integrity. Dare Jesus risk His life on the proof that the integrity of our witness and authority for our work comes from God, not from man?

A silent confession. Rather than conceding the debate, the delegates from the Sanhedrin retreat behind the false confession, *"We do not know"* (v. 33). Sometimes the answer, "We do not know," expresses honesty and humility. The chief priests, scribes, and elders know *too well.* As masters of theological and political argument, they are defeated at their own game. In a United States court of law, they would have taken the Fifth Amendment, saying, "I do not choose to answer on the grounds that it might incriminate me." Such an answer only deepens the suspicion that the defendant has something to cover up. In the parable that follows, Jesus addresses the cause of their guilt, but He also reveals the source of His authority.

Authority Over Rulers

1 And He began to speak to them in parables: "A man planted a vineyard, set a hedge around it, dug a place for the wine vat, and built a tower. And he leased it to vinedressers and went into a far country.

2 "And at harvesttime he sent a servant to the vinedressers, that he might receive from the vinedressers some of the fruit of the vineyard.

3 "And they took him, beat him, and sent him away empty-handed.

4 "And again he sent to them another servant, and at him they threw stones, wounded him in the head, and sent him away shamefully treated.

5 "And again he sent another, and him they killed; and many others, beating some and killing some.

6 "Therefore still having one son, his beloved, he also sent him to them last, saying, 'They will respect my son.'

7 "But those vinedressers said among themselves, 'This is the heir. Come, let us kill him, and the inheritance will be ours.'

8 "And they took him, killed him, and cast him out of the vineyard.

9 "Therefore what will the owner of the vineyard

do? He will come and destroy the vinedressers, and
give the vineyard to others.

10 "And have you not read this Scripture:
The stone which the builders rejected
Has become the chief cornerstone.
11 *This was the LORD's doing,*
And it is marvelous in our eyes' ?"

12 And they sought to lay hold of Him, but feared
the multitude, for they knew He had spoken the
parable against them. And they left Him and went
away.

Mark 12:1-12

By winning His debate with the delegation from the Sanhedrin,
Jesus earns His right to teach in the Royal Cloister reserved for the
rabbis. Mark tells us that He speaks more than one parable, but
His Gospel records only the story that is popularly known as "The
Parable of the Unjust Stewards." There, the similarity with His earlier
parables ends. In comparison with the peaceful, pastoral settings that
He chose for His earlier teachings, the Parable of the Unjust Stewards
is violent and bloody. His purpose is changed as well. Whereas He
had used the parable in His earlier teaching as a screening device
for serious seekers and as a prelude to teaching His disciples in private,
Jesus now screens out the crowd, but clearly and forcefully indicts
His enemies.

A sacred trust is given. The cast of characters in Jesus' parable reads
like the program for a dramatic performance:

Owner of the Vineyard .... God
The Vineyard .... House of Israel
Tenants of the Vineyard .... Rulers of Israel
Servants of the Owner .... Prophets of God, including
                                    John the Baptist
Son and Heir of Owner .... Jesus Christ

Landed estates of absentee owners who contract with tenants to
farm the land in return for a share of the profits are common sights
in Israel. The system works only when the owner and the tenant
trust each other implicitly. The owner trusts the tenant to manage
the estate, produce the crops, and share the profits just as if the
land belongs to him. In turn, the tenant trusts the owner to give

him full responsibility for the operation in his absence with only a schedule of shared dividends as accountability for his stewardship.

Isaiah sings of God's expectations in His trust relationship with Israel in the prophecy on which Jesus bases His parable: "Now will I sing to my wellbeloved a song of my beloved touching his vineyard. My wellbeloved hath a vineyard in a very fruitful hill" (Isa. 5:1, KJV).

God's singing expectations are not just romantic ditties. He carefully prepares every detail in His vineyard before turning it over to the tenant manager: "And he fenced it, and gathered out the stones thereof, and planted it with the choicest vine, and built a tower in the midst of it, and also made a winepress therein: and he looked that it should bring forth grapes, and it brought forth wild grapes" (Isa. 5:2, KJV).

A sacred trust violated. According to a typical contract between an absentee owner and a tenant manager, as many as five years are given for the land to produce a profit. Patience is backed up by the trust that the owner puts in his tenant manager. But when the time for the accounting comes, he sends his personal emissary to collect his share.

God has been so patient with the rulers of the House of Israel. In and out of season, He has stayed with them in the hope that they will finally produce the spiritual fruit which His vineyard promises. The time comes when He can wait no longer. Sending His prophets to call His leaders and people to accountability, the stewards usurp their role, persecute His servants and send them away emptyhanded. Perhaps, in reference to John the Baptist, the last servant who comes is killed.

A sacred trust perverted. To this point in the parable, Jesus is referring to past history. Now, the present bursts into full view as He refers to the owner of the vineyard sending His only Son with full authority to collect the rent or transfer the contract. God's motives are still the same. By sending His only beloved Son, He hopes against hope that the stewards of His trust will show Him the same respect that they would give to the Father, repent and rebuild the trust of the original contract. God's Son doesn't have a chance. Greedy to be owners in their own right, the tenant managers assume that the Son has come because the Father is dead. According to tenant law, if the owner dies and no heir remains to claim the land, the tenants themselves receive the inheritance. So, rather than respecting the Son, they kill Him and cast Him out of the vineyard.

By now, the chief priests, scribes, and elders who listen to the parable are fully aware of the authority that Jesus has claimed and the role that they will play in His death. They are the unjust stewards who have violated their trust and perverted their purpose.

A sacred trust lost. Jesus does not stop with the prediction of His death at the hands of the Jewish rulers. Moving from the historic present to the prophetic future, He reminds His hearers that God, the owner of the vineyard, is not dead. When He hears of the death of His Son, He will return and wreak judgment upon those whom He trusted. Isaiah also foresees this disaster as the Lord's response to wild grapes: ". . . I will tell you what I will do to my vineyard: I will take away the hedge thereof, and it shall be eaten up; and break down the wall thereof, and it shall be trodden down: And I will lay it waste: it shall not be pruned, nor digged; but there shall come up briers and thorns: I will also command the clouds that they rain no rain upon it" (Isa. 5:5, 6, KJV).

A sacred trust transferred. Judgment upon the unjust stewards of the vineyard Israel includes the transfer of trust. For the second time in two days, Jesus prophesies salvation for the Gentiles. The thought itself strikes fear into the heart. If we are now the stewards of God's purpose, are we faithful to our trust and returning to Him the fruit of His vineyard? The standards of accountability have not changed and His blessing or His judgment still depends upon our stewardship.

A sacred trust restored. With the truth of the parable digging into the conscience of the chief priests, scribes and elders of the Sanhedrin, Jesus clinches His case with an edge of sarcasm:

> "And have you not read this Scripture:
> *'The stone which the builders rejected*
> *Has become the chief cornerstone.*
> *This was the Lord's doing,*
> *And it is marvelous in our eyes'?"*
>
> (Mark 12:10, 11; Ps. 118:22, 23)

Another vivid word picture comes before our eyes. Builders are searching for the cornerstone that will finally support the arch that they are constructing. After examination, a stone is rejected, but when the arch is almost finished and the search for another cornerstone is futile, the builders return to the rejected stone and find that it fits perfectly. Caesar made the builders of Roman arches stand under their creation while the cornerstone was slipped into its place. If it fit, the arch stood; if not, the builder died under the crush of falling stones. Projecting one final step into the future, Jesus predicts His ultimate triumph, when all of history will fit around Him as Creator, Redeemer, and Lord

AUTHORITY OVER KINGDOMS

13 And they sent to Him some of the Pharisees and the Herodians, to catch Him in His words.

14 And when they had come, they said to Him, "Teacher, we know that You are true and care about no one; for You do not regard the person of men, but teach the way of God in truth. Is it lawful to pay taxes to Caesar, or not?

15 "Shall we pay, or shall we not pay?" But He, knowing their hypocrisy, said to them, "Why do you test Me? Bring Me a denarius that I may see it."

16 And they brought it. And He said to them, "Whose image and inscription is this?" And they said to Him, "Caesar's."

17 And Jesus answered and said to them, "Render to Caesar the things that are Caesar's, and to God the things that are God's." And they marveled at Him.

Mark 12:13–17

At last report, the delegation from the Sanhedrin *". . . went away"* (12:12) after suffering resounding defeat in debate with Jesus. They do not give up. Driven to frenzy by the sight of their own blood, the chief priests, scribes, and elders expand their unholy alliance to include the Pharisees and Herodians, bitterly opposed political opponents. As right-wing religionists, the Pharisees stand adamantly against compromise with Rome because Caesar claims to be a god. Herodians are Jews who might be classified as the "knee-jerk liberals" of their day. By taking the name of Herod, they let it be known that political expediency overrules religious convictions when survival is at stake. Hate flashes back and forth over the wide chasm between

242

the two groups until the defeated coalition from the Sanhedrin convinces them that their enmity will be better spent against their common enemy, Jesus.

Together, then, the Pharisees and Herodians concoct the perfect plot to snare Jesus. Even though the chief priests, scribes, and elders have failed, they know that they have to find a way *"to catch Him in His words"* (v. 13). Tacitly, at least, the enemies of Jesus acknowledge His words as the fulcrum upon which His credibility balances. Even His friends have been slow to come to that conclusion.

Consultation with the delegation from the Sanhedrin informs the Pharisees and Herodians that they will have to exercise two precautions: (1) the people must be appeased; (2) Jesus has to be forced to answer their charge. Flattery becomes the device to serve both purposes. They set up Jesus by acknowledging His authenticity, admitting His impartiality, and commending His courage to speak God's Truth without diversion. Hearing these glowing words, the people will be disarmed and Jesus will be obligated to answer their question.

As the final piece in their strategic puzzle, the Pharisees and Herodians need a relevant issue which demands an "either-or" answer. Naturally, the political issue that divides them meets the criterion. No Jew stands neutral on the question of resistance or accommodation to Roman rule. Instant anger and lasting antagonism divide political parties, religious orders, families and friends over the question. Its history goes back to A.D. 6, when Caesar put the rebellious Jews in Southern Palestine directly under his control. Since that time, Judea has been under Caesar's boot as an imperial province that pays for its military occupation with a poll tax that goes directly into the Emperor's coffers in Rome. Although the amount is small, the Zealots still mutter "No tribute to Caesar" from dark corners, Pharisees object quietly to paying a tax with a coin that bears the graven image of Caesar as god, and the Herodians reluctantly acquiesce to the system. So much emotion surrounds the issue that the political question gets lost in a theological and moral issue of first magnitude. Consequently, when the Pharisees and Herodians ask, *"Is it lawful to pay taxes to Caesar, or not?"* (v. 14), they really mean, "Is it right or wrong?" If Jesus answers "Yes," He will alienate the masses and give the Pharisees evidence for their charge of blasphemy. But if He answers "No" to the question about paying tribute to Caesar, the twisted allegiance of the Herodian Jews will speed the news to Roman authorities about the insurrectionist in their midst. Experience tells them that Roman

243

justice does not exist for a rebel. The smash of a fist, the flash of a spear, the thud of a nail, and Jesus will be silenced forever.

Jesus sees through the trap and calls the bluff of the Pharisees and Herodians. Mark puts the word *"hypocrisy"* (v. 15) into Jesus' mind; Luke is gracious enough to call their tactic "craftiness" (Luke 20:23). However their motives are assessed, the Pharisees and Herodians are guilty of tempting Jesus and siding with Satan.

Despite the fact that He sees through their hypocritical motives and cunning tactics, Jesus has no choice but to answer their question. Starting off on their terms, He asks them for the small coin that is used to pay the despised poll tax. A silver denarius is produced, valued at less than 25 cents in current exchange. Still on track of their question, Jesus asks them to identify the image and read the inscription on the coin. The image, they respond, is Caesar and the two-sided inscription is "Tiberius Caesar, divine Augustus, son of Augustus . . . Pontifex Maximus, High priest of the Roman nation." Unwittingly, their response enlarges the original question to this admission: Caesar exists, he occupies the land, he has his coinage, and he asks his tribute. Jesus now has a larger field in which to work. The question is not just taxes, but territory. How does the realm and rule of Caesar relate to the realm and rule of God? Jesus' answer sets lasting principles for Caesar-God, state-church relationships.

First, Caesar has a legitimate realm. By his statement, *"Render to Caesar the things that are Caesar's"* (v. 17), Jesus acknowledges the authority, function, and demands of the secular state, even when it is ruled by a pretender-god. Romans 13 expands upon the premise. Caesar gets his legitimate authority from God, his legitimate function is to preserve peace, and his legitimate demand is citizen responsibility, including the payment of taxes to support the peacekeeping function. Applied to the situation in Judea at that time, Caesar meets these conditions. He rules the land, keeps the peace, and deserves the tribute. Radicals of all ages will resist this premise, but it cannot be avoided in considering a Christian's responsibility to the state. Even now, a nuclear buildup in the United States in order to negotiate for peace from a position of strength is being protested by Christians who refuse to pay the portion of their income tax spent for defense. Even though peace through nuclear strength is a calculated risk involving millions of people, it does meet the primary condition for the realm of Caesar set by Jesus. The case has to be argued on other grounds.

Second, God has a legitimate realm. At first thought, it appears as if Jesus balances out the realms of Caesar and God by putting them side by side with interchangeable names for the same conditions. His positioning is intentional. God, too, has a legitimate authority, function, and demand which defines His Kingdom. Here, the similarity with Caesar stops. God's authority is sovereign, His function is redemption, and His demand is the tribute of total obedience to His will. No doubt remains about the responsibility of the religionists, such as the Pharisees, in failing to meet these conditions. Someplace in their search for righteousness, they have usurped God's sovereignty, narrowed His redemption, and limited their obedience. The conditions have not changed. As a preventive measure against Pharisaical attitudes, Christians must ask each day, "Is God sovereign in my life?" "Am I part of His redemptive function?" and "Does He have my total obedience?"

Third, the realms of Caesar and God cannot be confused. While Jesus makes room for both realms to coexist and cooperate with their own authority, function, and demand, He also keeps them separate. Neither a theocratic nor a totalitarian state is consistent with this principle. In a theocracy, the church assumes the authority of the state, taking over its protective and peacekeeping function. Inevitably, then, the lines of authority and function become confused. The sovereignty of the state merges into the "divine right of kings," and the spirit of redemption gets lost in the might and power required to protect people and preserve the peace. Conversely, a totalitarian state presumes upon the authority, function and demand of God. A man is made sovereign, citizenship equals redemption, and blind allegiance is the alternative to extermination.

In between these extremes, Jesus leaves room for Christians to enjoy or tolerate human systems of government. If the state stays within the boundaries of its legitimacy and permits freedom for the church to proclaim God's sovereignty, minister for human redemption, and expect full obedience to God's will from its members, the two realms need not be in conflict. In fact, Jesus implies that they can be mutually supportive.

Fourth, in the event of conflict between realms, God rules over Caesar. Drawing the distinction between Caesar and God, Jesus refutes the inscription on the denarius that Augustus is "divine," or that he reigns as "Pontifex Maximus." Although no doubt remains about the order of the realms, not even the Herodians can make the case for treason out of His words. God rules over Caesar, redemption transcends peace, and allegiance to God takes precedence over secular citizenship. The standards for Christian conscience are set. If Caesar must be worshiped, if redemptive witness must be forfeited for peace, and if the will of the state is imposed over the will of God, the believers must say, ". . . We ought to obey God rather than men" (Acts 5:29). Civil disobedience in the name of Christ is not out of the range of possibility for Christians, but only if and when the fundamentals of state-church relationships enunciated by Jesus are flaunted and denied. As long as the state permits the church the margin of freedom to be itself, Christians should be responsible citizens of the state. Spiritual paranoia which prematurely closes off the margin of freedom or political ambition that exploits the radical nature of the Kingdom of God is wrong. Jesus sees that the margin of freedom for the Gospel is still open under Roman rule and He will not have anything to do with the Zealots who try to advance their cause by violence in God's name. Contrary to those who might wish otherwise, Jesus knows that He can live with the demands of the Roman Empire, but He will die because of the sins of the Jerusalem establishment.

What choice do the Pharisees and Herodians have but to marvel at the astute answer given by Jesus? They cannot say that He avoids the issue, but neither can they find any self-incriminating words by which they can charge Him with blasphemy or treason. The secret rests in His ability to expand an "either-or" question into a "both-and" answer. God always thinks this way. Truth is a contradiction, a paradox, a forced choice for the human mind until seen from God's perspective. His thinking is never impaled on one horn or the other of an "either-or" dilemma. Both Caesar and God, like justice and mercy, are compatible from His eternal viewpoint if they stay within the boundaries of His sovereign authority, His redemptive purpose, and His Holy will.

AUTHORITY OVER LIFE

18 Then the Sadducees, who say there is no
resurrection, came to Him; and they asked Him, saying:
19 "Teacher, Moses wrote to us that if a man's

brother dies, leaves his wife behind, and leaves no children, his brother should take his wife and raise up offspring for his brother.

20 "Now there were seven brothers. And the first took a wife, and dying, left no offspring.

21 "And the second took her, and he died; nor did he leave any offspring. And the third likewise.

22 "And the seven had her and left no offspring. Last of all the woman died also.

23 "Therefore, in the resurrection, when they rise, whose wife will she be? For all seven had her as wife."

24 And Jesus answered and said to them, "Are you not therefore mistaken, because you do not know the Scriptures nor the power of God?

25 "For when they rise from the dead, they neither marry nor are given in marriage, but are like angels who are in heaven.

26 "But concerning the dead, that they rise, have you not read in the book of Moses, in the burning bush passage, how God spoke to him, saying, *'I am the God of Abraham, the God of Isaac, and the God of Jacob'*?

27 "He is not the God of the dead, but the God of the living. You are therefore greatly mistaken."

Mark 12:18-27

Wave after wave of religious shock troops launch their attacks on Jesus. Mark's factual statement, *"Then the Sadducees . . . came"* (v. 18), conveys the relentless pursuit after some flaw in Jesus' words that can be used against Him. Frustration has to run high for the Sadducees, despised by all religious factions and hated by the people, to carry the attack against Jesus on behalf of the Jews. True to form, their test lacks the immediate import of previous questions about Jesus' authority or Caesar's tribute. The best that they can do is expose their intellectual arrogance with an absurd theological question designed to discredit Jesus' position on the resurrection of the dead. In the interchange, we see how theological error is created, checked and corrected.

Creating theological error. The Sadducees question the immortality of the soul and reject the resurrection of the dead along with angels and spirits (Acts 23:8). To understand the Sadducees is to understand their doctrine. Although the sect constituted a small minority among the Jewish religious orders, its members controlled the priesthood of the Temple with an aristocratic air and accumulated wealth. Their sacred role did not keep them from being materialists whose attitudes toward power and possession are stuck, flat-footed, on earth.

Unexcelled educational credentials add to the power of the Sadducees. No one could match them for the intricacy of their arguments or the arrogance with which they approach the subject. Simple faith gives way, first, to inextricable reasoning and, finally, to unmitigated skepticism. It is not unfair to label the Sadducees as the rationalists of Jewish culture in the first century.

Surprisingly, the Sadducees also fit the category as the theological conservatives of their time. Pharisees are usually credited with the conservative designation because of their sticky interpretation of the Law and their unbending religious rituals. History, however, reverses the categories. The Sadducees limit the authority of Scriptures to the written canon with the highest order of revelation granted to the Pentateuch. This position on revelation puts them in opposition to the Pharisees, who add their own interpretation to the Scriptures and elevate the oral tradition to the level of God's Word. At least with respect to revelation, the Sadducees are conservative and the Pharisees are liberal. Their debates only serve to personalize their polarity and radicalize their doctrines. The Sadducees, for instance, are driven to the extreme of rejecting the resurrection of the dead because they reason that the belief cannot be found in the Pentateuch. Revelation that is stunted by conservatism or overgrown by liberalism suffers the same. Reasoning or ritual replace God's redemptive purpose.

Checks on theological error. The Sadducees' tactic complies with the rabbinical pattern for opening a theological discussion. Scriptural references are cited and illustrated by a story. They choose Deuteronomy 25:5–10, where the Mosaic Law provides for Levirate marriage: "If brethren dwell together, and one of them die, and have no child, the wife of the dead shall not marry without unto a stranger: her husband's brother shall go in unto her, and take her to him to wife . . ." (Deut. 25:5, KJV).

The intention of the Levirate law is to continue the family name if the widow and her second husband have children and to assure the line of inheritance for the family property. Leave it to the Sadducees. They create a hypothetical situation in which seven brothers

248

marry the same woman who remains childless in order to pose a question, *"In the resurrection, when they rise, whose wife will she be?"* (v. 23). To insult Jesus with this question requires unabashed intellectual arrogance. It belongs with the medieval game, "How many angels can dance on the head of a pin?" and the contemporary quip, "Where did Adam get his navel?" By reducing the doctrine of the resurrection to an absurdity, the Sadducees hope to stymie the unsophisticated bumpkin from the north country.

Jesus' response is appropriate to the occasion. Straight out, He tells the Sadducees that they are wrong and then proceeds to tell them why. Their theological error is caused by failing to know the meaning of the Scriptures and the power of God. The Sadducees err on the doctrine of the resurrection because they select the Scriptures and restrict the power of God to fit their frame of reference. How many other theological errors, historical and contemporary, can be traced along the same fault lines? To deny the deity of Christ requires a selective reading of the Word and a limitation on the power of God. The same faulty knowledge is behind the attempts to fuse Christianity with Marxism or to insulate the church from its social responsibility. If we are to avoid the Sadducees' theological error, we must invoke the twofold test: "Do we know the full and in-depth meaning of the Word of God?" and "Do we know from experience the unlimited power of God?"

Correcting theological error. Applying the two criteria to the false theology of the Sadducees, Jesus sets forth the doctrine of the resurrection which is true to the Word and the power of God. *First,* He accepts the Sadducees' tongue-in-cheek assumption about the resurrection of the seven brothers and one wife as an uncontested fact. By the power of God, the dead will rise. *Second,* Jesus corrects the Jewish misconception about the nature of life after death. Whereas persons will retain their identity and individuality in heaven, by the power of God, they will transcend the human ordinances that guided their relationships on earth. Marriage, the most sacred of these ordinances, prefigures the relationship of full communion which the resurrected will share with God and His angels. On earth, marriage sets necessary boundaries on human nature to sanctify sex, preserve the family, and seal the communion of couples by holy vows. Freed from that nature by the power of the resurrection, marriage, sex and family relationships will be transcended by perfect communion with God and among persons.

Turning from the power of God to the Scriptures, Jesus quotes a landmark passage from Exodus, a book of the Pentateuch to which the Sadducees attribute the highest revelation. Notably, the encounter between God and Moses at the site of the burning bush also involves Abraham, Isaac, and Jacob, patriarchs of the Pentateuch to whom the Sadducees pay highest esteem. Effectively using the Pentateuch and the patriarchs as entry points for His argument, Jesus points the Sadducees to the nature and the character of God as the ultimate test upon which the resurrection rests. When Moses hides his face from the brightness of the burning bush, God speaks: *". . . I am the God of Abraham, the God of Isaac, and the God of Jacob"* (Mark 12:26; Exod. 3:6).

Logic breaks through. If God is the "I am" of Abraham, Isaac, and Jacob, two facts follow. *First,* God is a Person who is alive, not dead, in the continuing present. *Second,* Abraham, Isaac, and Jacob are alive with Him in keeping with the covenant of life and love that He made with them. Moses is assured that God lives and keeps His covenant with all generations. Therefore, on the basis of God's living presence and His continuing covenant, Jesus draws the unequivocal conclusion, *"He is not the God of the dead, but the God of the living"* (v. 27). Jesus punctuates the point by His final word to the Sadducees, *"You are therefore greatly mistaken"* (v. 27). Like a geometrical theorem, the case for the resurrection of the dead is closed.

Our hope for the resurrection still rests upon the nature and character of God. Theologically, we would never say that "God is dead" or "He does not keep His promise." Yet, the tendencies to materialism, rationalism and conservatism that led to the Sadducees' error may still influence us. A Britisher has said, "In England, we say that God is dead, and pray to Him just in case. In America, they say that God is alive, but act as if He were dead." To believe in a personal God who lives in the continuing present should change the way we act as well as the way we believe.

Confidence in the character of God is our only hope for spiritual resurrection now and physical resurrection in the future. God has never wriggled one iota from this covenant of love that He gave to Abraham, Isaac, Jacob, Moses, and, through Jesus Christ, to all generations. Although I despise stickers on my bumper and buttons on my lapel, particularly those with gooey spiritual slogans, I would permit one that reads, *"You can count on the character of God."* Broken covenants are the bane of our secular existence. A witness to the consistent character of God's covenant love may well be the clarion call for which our world waits.

AUTHORITY OVER LAW

28 And one of the scribes came, and having heard them reasoning together, perceiving that He had answered them well, asked Him, "Which is the first commandment of all?"

29 And Jesus answered him, "The first of all the commandments is: *'Hear, O Israel, the* LORD *our God is one* LORD.

30 *'And you shall love the* LORD *your God with all your heart, with all your soul, with all your mind, and with all your strength.'* This is the first commandment.

31 "And the second, like it, is this: *'You shall love your neighbor as yourself.'* There is no other commandment greater than these."

32 And the scribe said to Him, "Well said, Teacher. You have spoken the truth, for there is one God, and there is no other but He.

33 "And to love Him with all the heart, with all the understanding, with all the soul, and with all the strength, and to love one's neighbor as oneself, is more than all the whole burnt offerings and sacrifices."

34 And when Jesus saw that he answered wisely, He said to him, "You are not far from the kingdom of God." And after that no one dared ask Him any question.

Mark 12:28–34

Glee must have welled up in ordinary people who witnessed Jesus' classic victory over the arrogant Sadducees. They might not have understood the intricacies of His argument, but no one could mistake the meaning of His words that reduced them to silence, "*. . . You are therefore greatly mistaken*" (12:27).

A scholar who observes the same exchange has another perspective. According to Mark, an expert in the Law arrives during the discussion and sees that Jesus answers the Sadducees with knowledge and skill. To an intellectual, a quick mind and a fair debate is admired as much as a clean victory. A scholar's respect, then, prompts the scribal expert in the Law to ask Jesus' opinion about the dilemma that he faces in his scholarly task. Jesus couches His profound answer in the simplest Truth and draws out of the scholar a spiritual insight that advances him to the threshold of the Kingdom of God.

The Scholar's dilemma. "Which is the first commandment of all?" (v. 28) is a typical scholarly inquiry; it has many roots. The primary task of the scribal expert is to interpret meaningfully the Law. In the process, a dilemma arises. Interpretation of the Law requires laws to explain the Law, thus creating an ever-expanding legal casebook. Meaningful interpretation of the Law, on the other hand, calls for the simplification which translates the Law into life. The split is between the complex interpretation and the simple meaning of the Law.

Scholars in every field of study share the dilemma. Research produces new knowledge that stimulates more research—on and on the ever-expanding cycle of knowledge goes. The other half of scholarly responsibility cannot be forgotten. To teach and apply their findings, scholars must be able to synthesize, order, and simplify knowledge. Otherwise, as one wag commented on the ever-expanding cycle of knowledge, "We know more and more about less and less, and soon we will know everything about nothing."

A scribe of the Pharisees would find it particularly difficult to make their laws simple and meaningful: 613 statutes comprise the oral law with 365 prohibitions to coincide with the number of days in the year and 248 commandments to equal the reputed number of generations of man. Attempting to make this morass meaningful, scribes divided the statutes into "weighty" and "light" categories and cross-classified them as "ritual" or "ethical" laws. The need for meaning in the Law also kept before them the challenge to develop a single, simple, working principle that would encompass all of the other statutes. When the scribal expert asked Jesus, *"Which is the first commandment of all?"* (v. 28), he must have had this challenge in mind. At least, Jesus' answer makes that assumption.

The simplest truth. Jesus' knowledge of the Law and its history keeps the scholar gasping. Reaching back to Deuteronomy 6:4, He confirms the foundational truth of the Shema which serves as the call to worship in the Jewish synagogue, "Hear, O Israel: The Lord our God is one Lord"(KJV). From this basic premise, He proceeds to the principle revealed in Deuteronomy 6:5: "And thou shalt love the Lord thy

God with all thine heart, and with all thy soul, and with all thy might" (KJV).

These are the words of the Mezuzah which are written on the doorpost of every Jewish home. Jesus then applies the principle by matching it with the commandment in Leviticus 19:18, ". . . thou shalt love thy neighbor as thyself . . ." (KJV). With scarcely a breath in between, Jesus has summed up the Law, the prophets and the Gospel so that He can say, *"There is no other commandment greater than these"* (v. 31).

"Oneness" is the theme around which Jesus wraps the simplest of truths. The "oneness" of God is His foundational premise. Throughout Jewish history, the struggle between monotheism and polytheism never abated. Pharaoh, Baal, Caesar, and many others joined the march of competing gods. Today, the battle of gods goes on, perhaps not with names and faces, but under the cover of ideas, attitudes and movements. Guerrilla action, not open warfare, blurs the battleground. Secular humanism, for instance, is a god of its own sort, ill-defined and misinterpreted most of the time, but nevertheless contending for sovereignty over the minds of men. To declare that our God is one God denies the deity of Baal, whether cast in stone and graven in image, whether breathed in spirit or embraced in ideas.

"Oneness" continues to be Jesus' theme as He identifies love as the dynamic agent in man's relationship to God. Ordinarily, one expects that power, not love, will rule the relationship between a sovereign God and submissive humanity. For pretender gods, this is the case. But for the God of Gods, self-giving love is the only explanation for the Creation, the Covenant, and the Christ. "Oneness" with God, then, presupposes a two-way relationship in which love engages heart, soul, mind, and strength to worship and obey God. No facet of human personality—affection, intellect, or will—is left untouched or untransformed by love for God. We are at "one" with Him and with ourselves when the commandment is freely and delightfully operative.

A dimension of "oneness" is missing if the love relationship is limited to communion between God and man. To make "oneness" complete, the same self-giving love must flow in person-to-person relationships. *"You shall love your neighbor as yourself"* (v. 31) is the point of proof that God is one God and that a person's heart, soul, mind and strength are transformed by love. Because the commandments to love God and to love your neighbor are separated in Old Testament

Scriptures, the Pharisees had an excuse to lower the priority of the second commandment. Jesus takes away their excuse by fusing into one simple and inseparable commandment what they believe about God, how they relate to Him, and how they treat their neighbor. Wherever and whenever there is the sin of separation in this commandment, Jesus calls again for the "oneness" with which He ended His answer, *"There is no other commandment greater than these"* (v. 31).

In what must have been one of the most satisfying moments in Jesus' teaching ministry, the scribe shows that he qualifies as a student as well as a scholar. Commending the thinking and admitting the Truth of Jesus' words, he summarizes the answer and relates it to the fatal issue which puts Jesus at odds with the Pharisees. By confessing that the love commandment *"is more than all the whole burnt offerings and sacrifices"* (v. 33), he walks away from his colleagues, but steps up to the threshold of the Kingdom of God.

Superior knowledge of the Word of God and superior wisdom in rabbinical debate has won out in Jesus' encounters with His enemies. The capstone comes when the expert in the Law asks, *"Which is the first commandment of all?"* (v. 28). After Jesus answers in a few short sentences the question that has absorbed centuries of scribal time and energy, His intellectual protagonists lose their daring and slink away, knowing that He will have to be faulted on something other than His words. From now on, no one will dare ask Him a question.

CHAPTER SEVENTEEN

Challenging His Enemies

Mark 12:35–44

THE THEOLOGICAL CHALLENGE

35 And Jesus answered and said, while He taught in the temple, "How is it that the scribes say that the Christ is the Son of David?
36 "For David himself said by the Holy Spirit:
'The LORD said to my Lord,
"Sit at My right hand,
Till I make Your enemies Your footstool." '
37 "Therefore David himself calls Him 'Lord'; how is He then his Son?" And the common people heard Him gladly.

Mark 12:35–37

When His enemies lose their daring for further debate, Jesus takes up the initiative and asks a question for Himself. He frames it by contradiction in the scribes' teaching. They teach that "Christ," the anointed One, is to be a direct descendant of David and that He will restore the Davidic kingdom upon His return as the Messiah. This line of reasoning feeds the prevailing false notion that the Kingdom of God is political rather than spiritual, and nationalistic rather than universal. To dispel this notion, Jesus puts into juxtaposition an equal and opposite truth. Deliberately noting that David writes under the inspiration of the Holy Spirit, He quotes the Messianic Psalm 110:1 (KJV), "The Lord said unto my Lord, Sit thou at my right hand, until I make thine enemies thy footstool." The conundrum

255

He creates is even clearer to the common people, *"Therefore David himself calls Him 'Lord': how is He then his Son?"* (v. 37).

Our five-year-old son came home from Sunday school with the same question. During his class, the subject of the Trinity came up. The teacher tried to explain God in three persons—Father, Son, and Holy Spirit. She left our son with a puzzling question that he did not ask until he got home:

> "Is God the Father God?" he asked.
> "Yes," I answered.
> "Is Jesus the Son God too?"
> "Yes."
> (A thoughtful pause.)
> "Well, if God the Father is God and Jesus the Son is God, how can Jesus be His own Father?"

Neither my son's father nor the scribes had a good answer to the question. We prefer to think in "either-or" terms.

Christ can be both the son of David and the Lord of David only through the Incarnation. Fully human and fully divine, there is no other way to resolve the apparent contradiction. Fatal flaws in scribal teaching resulted from the failure to understand the nature of Christ and the meaning of the Incarnation. By concentrating on genealogies of the house of David, they miss the prophetic fulfillment of the Son and Lord of David in the coming of Jesus Christ. Equally in error, they view the Kingdom of God through the tunnel vision of their own political and national interest. In contrast with their colleague whom Jesus has just commended, they are very far from the Kingdom of God.

THE MORAL CHALLENGE

38 And He said to them in His teaching, "Beware of the scribes, who desire to go around in long robes, love greetings in the marketplaces,
39 "the best seats in the synagogues, and the best places at feasts,
40 "who devour widows' houses, and for a pretense make long prayers. These will receive greater condemnation."

Mark 12:38–40

What we believe affects the way we act and how we act affects the way we believe. Jesus has just accused the scribes of interpreting Scripture to conform to their own perceptions of the Kingdom of God. Now, He indicts them personally for using their sacred office to promote their pride and cover unethical economic practices. No one who is guilty of these sins wants to know the whole Scripture and have it applied to their lives.

The pride of privilege. Jesus does not spare the details when He accuses the scribes of sinful pride. They are the original "power dressers" except that they wear long white linen robes with tassels on the fringe, rather than a three-piece navy blue pinstripe with a Phi Beta Kappa key chained across the vest. While clothes may not make the man, they certainly influence his behavior. A long white linen robe is good only for leisure, ceremony, or show. The scribes took full advantage of their dress by planned excursions through the streets and the marketplace just to see the rabble stand and hear them say, "Good morning, Master." The same robe gave them the first place of honor at the banquet table and special seats in the synagogue where they sat on a bench in front of the altar facing the congregation so that they could be seen by all people. Little wonder that they were despised by the common people.

Religious dress has been a question of controversy through the ages. Deference has been awarded a priest's collar, a nun's habit, a rabbi's cap, a pastor's robe, and a chaplain's cross. During recent times, the rebellion against established authority, the need for functionality, and the emphasis upon equality have reduced the wearing of these signs of spiritual office. If used only as showpieces for undue honor, wearing them should be reduced, if not eliminated. History, however, hints that they will return. Symbols are an inseparable part of human behavior. In proper perspective, they lend dignity to persons worthy of honor and meaning to the experiences of life worthy of remembrance. They can also be perverted into haughty signs of self-importance and abusive weapons against common people. In Jesus' time, the symbols of sacred office needed to be brought back into proper perspective. In our time, their meaning needs to be restored.

The hypocrisy of holiness. Sinful pride in their sacred office constitutes the lesser charge of Jesus against the scribes. Their greater sin is an outward show of holiness that conceals a pit of avarice. As one of their functions, scribes serve as consultants in estate planning for widows. Their role gives them the opportunity to convince lonely and susceptible women that their money and property should either be given to the scribe for his holy work or to the Temple for its holy ministries. In either case, the scribe gains personally. If he can convince a widow to become a patron of his work, a life of comfort is assured. If the widow prefers to contribute to the Temple, he determines the share that can be taken as his consulting fee. Of course, there is no better way to assure the confidence of widows than by a show of spirituality, whether with long prayers in the Temple or instant tears on television.

I personally share Jesus' rage against a sentimental show of spirituality to get money and property from lonely women and widows. My mother, left alone by divorce and stricken with leukemia, watched faith-healers on television in futile hope. On one of my last visits to her, I found the literature and plastic charm of a faith-healer whom I know to be a fraud. When I asked my mother about it, she told me that she had sent in a $10 contribution for the material. I bit my tongue because I could not take the slightest hope away from my mother, but I left in anger. My mother had great faith in God. Yet, she had succumbed to the wiles of a religious showman and given money for his support. I could only think about the millions of sick and lonely women and widows whose houses were being devoured by spiritual pretense.

Jesus reserves "greater condemnation" for holders of sacred office who use spiritual pretense for economic gain, particularly at the expense of the poor and vulnerable people. A tough police captain who took over a scandal-ridden department which housed a burglary ring of police officers called them "worse than thieves" because they had used their badges to commit a crime. Jesus voices the same biting condemnation for scribes who use their sacred office to prey upon defenseless widows. To Him, they and anyone who joins them are "worse than thieves."

The Spiritual Challenge

41 And Jesus sat opposite the treasury and saw how the people put money into the treasury. And many who were rich put in much.
42 And a certain poor widow came and threw in two mites, which make a quadrans.

43 And He called His disciples to Him and said to
them, "Assuredly, I say to you that this poor widow
has put in more than all those who have given into
the treasury;
    44 "for they all put in out of their abundance, but
she out of her poverty put in all that she had, her
whole livelihood."

Mark 12:41-44

Economics continues to be at the center of spiritual decision-making. Jesus has exposed the hypocrisy of the scribes in their scheme to bilk widows out of their money and homes. Now, by way of comparison, He pierces them with the arrow of shame by drawing attention to a widow, who gives her all.

Leaving the Royal Cloisters where He has been teaching, Jesus enters into the Court of Women which also houses the Treasury. Thirteen brazen receptacles shaped like trumpets line the walls. Worshipers put coins into one group of the trumpets and offerings of goods into others. As a people-watcher, Jesus observes *"how the people put money into the treasury"* (v. 41). Evidently, He notices the attitude with which they give as well as the amount of money they contribute. Do the faces of the rich show the pain of having to keep up their reputation for being generous? Does the widow look ashamed when she throws in her offering and hears only two "pings" as her mites hit the bottom of the trumpet? Who knows the difference between the offerings?

Jesus knows. Calling His disciples around Him, He repeats the lesson that He has taught so many times and in so many different ways. As she "out of her poverty put in all that she had, her whole livelihood" (v. 44), God asks that we give Him our all. Many axioms of giving can be developed from the widow's act:

Giving is to be measured
    —not by its count, but its cost
    —not by its amount, but its portion
    —not by what is given, but by what is kept
    —not by money, but by spirit

Fund-raising is one of the never-ending chores of a college president. I know why Jesus chose the Treasury as the place to learn about people. Giving is worse than death for some persons whom I have met. A woman whose annual earnings from stocks totaled more than one-half million dollars gave only $25.00 to a wildlife preserve. Misery, loneliness, and alcoholism stalked her existence. On the other extreme, I met a man whose genius had produced a multi-million-dollar empire. Although he had not been known as a generous giver, he responded affirmatively to an appeal for one large gift and then another. Not only did he learn the joy of giving, but a confidant said, "He's a changed man since he learned to give."

Giving is a conduit through which redemption flows. At the earliest age, a child should be taught to give tithes and offerings to God. Then, when the call comes to give the love of heart, soul, mind, and strength to God, the act will not be alien and the satisfactions will not be unknown. Through the insignificant sound of two "pings" in the bottom of the Treasury trumpet, the Truth is repeated: *"For whoever desires to save his life will lose it, but whoever loses His life for My sake and the gospel's will save it"* (Mark 8:35).

CHAPTER EIGHTEEN

Preparing for the Future

Mark 13:1–37

WEIGHING VALUES

1 And as He went out of the temple, one of His disciples said to Him, "Teacher, see what manner of stones and what buildings are here!"
2 And Jesus answered and said to him, "Do you see these great buildings? Not one stone shall be left upon another that shall not be thrown down."

Mark 13:1–2

By the time that Jesus finished cleansing the Temple and reducing His enemies to silence, the inside walls must have had a hollow ring. In fact, Matthew and Luke conclude the Temple experiences with Jesus' woeful pronouncement, "See! Your house is left to you desolate" (Matt. 23:38; Luke 13:35). The disciples feel this despair as they walk out of the Temple with Jesus. They cannot believe that one of the architectural wonders of the world has lost the grandeur of its spirit.

Visits to the monuments of the world confirm the fact that some are filled with the spirit of the place and others are barren except for the stones and the structure. I fell into silence and wept openly in the war memorial over the sunken battleship *Arizona* in Pearl Harbor. Few cathedrals in Europe or shrines in Israel had the same effect on me. A sense of the holy is not just a matter of structure. History must be alive with personal meaning, and in the case of spiritual places, God must still be present.

Perhaps feeling the spiritual emptiness of the Temple, one of the disciples looks back wistfully at the awe-inspiring view of the white marble with its gold overlay and, in a burst of optimism, exclaims, *"Teacher, see what manner of stone and what buildings are here!"* (v. 1). His hope is forgivable. Although Herod's Temple had been under construction for forty-six years (John 2:20), it still struck wonder in the eyes and heart of anyone who saw it. Ancient historians tell us that the southwestern view of the Temple which covered Mount Moriah and rose 200 feet over Jerusalem cast the image of dazzling whiteness from its marble walls and blinding fire from its golden dome. Some of the marble stones themselves weighed 100 tons and measured 37 feet long, 18 feet wide, and 12 feet high. Certainly, the awe of the external must mean that all is not lost in the spirit of the internal.

Sad as it may seem, Jesus holds out no hope for the Temple. Just as He had called the Pharisees "whitewashed tombs . . . full of dead men's bones . . ." (Matt. 23:27) and condemned Israel for being like a fig tree withered at the roots, He predicts the internal rot of the Temple will bring it to destruction.

Historical tragedy attests the accuracy of Jesus' prophecy of doom. In A.D. 70, Jerusalem fell to the Roman siege of Titus and suffered atrocities that exceed the Holocaust in comparative numbers and gruesome details. In his history *The Wars of the Jews,*[1] Josephus counts over one million inhabitants of the city who died by crucifixion, sword, or famine. He also records the actions of starving people who became murderers, animals, and cannibals in order to survive. As for the Temple, it was destroyed stone by stone just as Jesus had predicted. Except for some pieces of the stones that make up the Wailing Wall, nothing remains of Herod's Temple except the foundation.

AVOIDING PANIC

3 And as He sat on the Mount of Olives opposite the temple, Peter, James, John, and Andrew asked Him privately,

4 "Tell us, when will these things be? And what will be the sign when all these things will be fulfilled?"

5 And Jesus, answering them, began to say: "Take heed that no one deceives you.

6 "For many will come in My name, saying, 'I am
He,' and will deceive many.

7 "And when you hear of wars and rumors of wars,
do not be troubled; for such things must happen, but
the end is not yet.

8 "For nation will rise against nation, and kingdom
against kingdom. And there will be earthquakes in
various places, and there will be famines and troubles.
These are the beginnings of sorrows.

Mark 13:3–8

Jesus' private talk with four of His disciples regarding future events
is called either "The Olivet Discourse" because of its location or
"The Little Apocalypse" because of its eschatological nature. When
Peter, James, John, and Andrew are alone with Jesus on the Mount
of Olives, they ask Him for specifics about the destruction of the
Temple. Their question has two parts: "When" and "What?" They
want to know when Jesus' prediction will come to pass and what
advance sign they can expect as a warning.

Scholars agree that Jesus' answer to the disciples' question almost
escapes explanation. Too many intricate threads of meaning are interwoven in His words. The thread of Jewish prophecy seems to dominate, but does not fully account for the fact that Mark writes his
Gospel for Roman Christians who are under persecution. Another
thread is the personal identification with the sufferings of Jesus in
the future persecution of the disciples. Still another is the combination
of current, continuing, and end-time prophecies in the events which
Jesus describes. A scholar who can unravel all of these threads is
yet to be found. So, rather than trying to contribute to the analytical
literature on "The Olivet Discourse," our purpose is to ask about
the message that Jesus communicates in the four times that He warns
the disciples, "Take heed."

The first time that Jesus says, "Take heed," He warns the disciples
to *avoid early panic about the coming catastrophe.* Adopting His own principle,
". . . Sufficient for the day is its own trouble" (Matt. 6:34), Jesus
notes the three signs of God's judgment that are present in every
generation: (1) religious cultism, such as false prophets who claim
the authority and power of Christ's name for their predictions; (2)
social upheavals, such as wars and rumors of wars; and (3) physical
catastrophes, such as earthquakes and famine. Each of these phenom-
ena is tragic, but none is an exception to the natural events of human

history. Religious cultism is a natural result of man's search for spiritual meaning outside of God's will and Word; social upheavals are natural to human nature that is ruled by self-interest; and physical catastrophes follow the imbalances of natural law in the precarious ecological system of the universe. Because these natural traumas are present in every age, Jesus warns His disciples not to read them as signs of final judgment. Rather, He admonishes them, *"do not be troubled"* (v. 7) but accepts these events as necessary to the nature of things and prefigurative to end-time wrath.

Perish the thought that Jesus advises His disciples to become hardened stoics in the midst of religious cultism, social violence, and natural disaster. His other teachings leave no doubt that He expects them to be the first to counter false religion, condemn war, and show compassion to the victims of earthquakes and famine. In this teaching, however, He limits Himself to their specific inquiry about the "What?" and "When?" of apocalyptic events. *"Do not be troubled"* does not mean a lack of concern; it does mean to be free from the frenzy that is seen when a startled horse goes berserk. To let the periodic eruptions of human and natural history determine our prophetic reactions is to exhaust our energies and abort our mission in the throes of a continuing "startle effect."

Many contemporary, popular, and rich religious prophets lose their credibility under the criteria for reading the signs of the times that Jesus set forth. With the rise of every cult, the declaration of every war, and the announcement of every earthquake or famine, a new generation of prophets who take the name of Christ is born. Put to Jesus' test, they cannot survive, and if we yawn when they speak, they will not survive.

ENDURING PERSECUTION

9 "But watch out for yourselves, for they will
deliver you up to councils, and you will be beaten
in the synagogues. And you will be brought before
rulers and kings for My sake, for a testimony to them.
10 "And the gospel must first be preached to all
the nations.
11 "But when they arrest you and deliver you up,
do not worry beforehand, or premeditate what you

will speak. But whatever is given you in that hour,
speak that; for it is not you who speak, but the Holy
Spirit.

12 "Now brother will betray brother to death, and
a father his child; and children will rise up against
parents and cause them to be put to death.

13 "And you will be hated by all men for My name's
sake. But he who endures to the end will be saved.

Mark 13:9–13

Jesus' first caution to *"take heed"* involves the disciples' reading of
the time and signs of religious cultism, social violence, and natural
disaster. As traumatic as these events may be, the disciples are urged
to avoid panic because they occur in each human generation and
are preliminary, not final, signals of the end-time.

Suddenly, Jesus shifts from a large, cyclical view of world events
to the immediate, personal situation of the disciples when He says,
"But watch out for yourselves" (v. 9). The disciples must have been rocked
at their roots to hear that persecution in their lifetime is to be a
timely sign for coming destruction. In the days ahead, they can expect
five signs: (1) persecution by the Jews; (2) witness to the Gentiles;
(3) filling of the Spirit; (4) betrayal by families; and (5) hatred from
the public.

Persecution by the Jews. Betrayal and beatings at the hands of fellow
Jews await the disciples. The hidden tragedy is that their betrayal
will be perpetrated by the Sanhedrin, whose sacred trust is the preser-
vation of justice, and that their beatings will take place in the synagogue, which is supposed to be dedicated to the love of mercy. The
prophecy has a familiar ring to the ears of the disciples. Three times
in the prediction of His own Passion, Jesus says that He will be
"delivered up" into the hands of men, specifying the chief priests
and scribes who are pledged to see Him die. In His prophecy of
the disciples' passion, Jesus brings them into the ". . . fellowship
of His sufferings . . ." (Phil. 3:10), a role of highest honor.

Witness to the Gentiles. Betrayed, arrested, arraigned, condemned and
beaten by Jewish authorities, the disciples must also watch for the
sign of being brought before the secular authorities, rulers and kings
of the Gentile world. Jesus adds the beautiful phrase, *"for My name's
sake"* (v. 13), as the code of identification between Him and His disciples during the time of persecution. Later on, this thought, "for My
name's sake," will be on their lips as they take lashes, face lions,

hang on crosses, and burn at the stake. Jesus, however, does not prophesy the punishment that they will receive from the rulers and kings of the Gentiles. Rather, He foresees the privilege the disciples will have to testify before these authorities as a means for preaching the Gospel to all nations.

We do not like to think that persecution is a major vehicle for proclaiming the Gospel, but it is. Peter, James, John, and Andrew will prove the point themselves in the Acts of the Apostles and in the unwritten history of their missionary ventures and martyrdom. In all the classes, seminars, conferences, and congresses I have attended on the subject of world evangelization, no one has ever proposed "Proclamation Through Persecution" as the strategy for fulfilling the Great Commission. Of course, persecution cannot be planned, but the evidence keeps coming in that it is the Christian's most effective witness. We were visitors to South Korea in the early 1970s during the time that 125,000 soldiers sealed their new-found Christian faith in baptism. Anxious to find out why revival fires burned so brightly in the Korean church, I asked a pastor "Why?". Without hesitation, he explained, "You must remember that our people are less than one generation away from martyrdom." Few, if any, Christian families in Korea were missed in the martyrdom of the 1950s.

Across the world, it is estimated that 60 percent of those who profess the name of Christ are under persecution. While the other 40 percent have the knowledge, wealth, and technology to proclaim the Gospel to all nations, time and eternity will show that the persecuted majority, even if undereducated, poor, and underprivileged, is winning the world.

Filling of the Spirit. The third prophetic sign given by Jesus is the promise of the Holy Spirit speaking through the disciples when they stand before rulers and kings. No matter how self-confident a person is, terror takes over in the presence of royalty and power. Last week, I received my first gold-engraved invitation which reads, "The President of the United States requests your presence . . ." My secretary wanted to frame it immediately. I responded differently. Over and over in my subconscious mind, I turned the question, "What do you say when you meet the President?" More often than not, my rehearsed response in such situations comes out wrong. Finally, Jesus' words came back to me: *"Do not worry beforehand, or premeditate what you will speak. But whatever is given you in that hour, speak that; for it is not you who speak, but the Holy Spirit"* (v. 11).

Like the quieting of the storm at sea, Christ gave me the assurance that His Holy Spirit will speak through me, not for my ego, but for His sake and the President's good.

Betrayal by the family. Breakdown in the bonds of belief that tie people together can be expected from time to time. Blood ties, however, are expected to sustain their strength under any circumstances. My grandfather used to say, "Irish families may fight like cats and dogs, but let someone attack us from the outside and you'll see how strong we really are." Jewish families are known to be equally strong. To hear, then, Jesus' prophecy that a sign of the end-time is the betrayal of brother against brother, father against child, and children against parents has to be shocking. In our litigious society, court rulings are replacing family trust. Courts are hearing malpractice suits brought by children against parents who are accused of failing to provide everything that the child expected. Other precedent-setting cases are being brought by handicapped children who are suing their parents for permitting them to be born.

The betrayal within families of which Jesus speaks, however, involves the Gospel. Mirroring the betrayal of Judas as a member of the disciple family, Jesus forecasts the time when brothers will turn in Christian brothers, fathers will report Christian children, and sons and daughters will become traitors against Christian parents. Sordid history surrounding Titus' siege of Jerusalem in A.D. 70 makes the prophecy a fact.

Hatred by the public. Throughout Jesus' ministry to date, public opinion weighs heavily on His side. Common people form a buffer between Him and His archenemies. Wisdom, however, teaches Jesus that popularity is a fickle wind that blows in gusts and quickly changes direction. He, Himself, will soon hear the jubilant cheers of "Hosanna!" (11:9) turn into bloodthirsty yells, "Crucify Him! . . . Crucify Him!" (15:13–14). Jesus also knows that the disciples will be subjected to the same treatment. If the makers of public opinion are opposed to Christianity, they can manipulate the available information to turn love into hate and popularity into resentment. "Truth-twisters" exist in every age and Christians are often targets of distorted attitudes, but to be *"hated by all men for My name's sake"* (v. 13) is a rare moment that signals apocalyptic judgment.

Persecution cannot be enjoyed; it can only be endured. Resources beyond human grit must be mustered to withstand betrayal, beatings, inquisitions, and unrelenting hatred. Endurance comes from three sources: (1) *identification* with the Christ in which persecution is taken for His sake; (2) *commitment* to the mission of Christ in preaching the Gospel to all nations; and (3) *assurance* that *"he who endures to the end will be saved"* (v. 13). To Roman Christians who can put their own names and faces into the picture of the disciples' persecution, the encouragement to endure unto the end for the sake of Jesus and the Gospel is a special form of Good News.

Escaping Judgment

14 "But when you see the *'abomination of desolation,'* spoken of by Daniel the prophet, standing where it ought not" (let the reader understand), "then let those who are in Judea flee to the mountains.

15 "And let him who is on the housetop not go down into the house, nor enter to take anything out of his house.

16 "And let him who is in the field not go back to get his garment.

17 "But woe to those who are pregnant and to those with nursing babies in those days!

18 "And pray that your flight not be in winter.

19 "For in those days there will be tribulation, such as has not been from the beginning of creation which God created to this time, nor ever shall be.

20 "And unless the Lord had shortened those days, no flesh would be saved; but for the elect's sake, whom He chose, He shortened the days.

21 "And then if anyone says to you, 'Look, here is the Christ!' or, 'Look, He is there!' do not believe it.

22 "For false christs and false prophets will rise and show signs and wonders to deceive, if possible, even the elect.

23 "But take heed; see, I have foretold you all things.

Mark 13:14–23

Slowly, the veil lifts on the signs of the end-time. Jesus' third warning to *"take heed"* is a prophecy of the tribulation. After giving the signs that foretell the devastation of the Temple, Jesus informs the disciples that He has told them everything they need to know in order to escape destruction. The signs are: (1) sacrilege of the Temple; (2) urgency of flight; and (3) the ultimacy of destruction.

Sacrilege of the Temple. The sign that will signal the beginning of the Great Tribulation is to see the *"abomination of desolation"* violating the sacred altar of the Temple, or as Mark writes, *"standing where it ought not"* (v. 14). Jesus is not referring to violations of the Holy of Holies by Roman soldiers or unjust priests. Evil is personified in words which coincide with Daniel's prophecy: ". . . and they shall pollute the sanctuary of strength, and shall take away the daily sacrifice, and they shall place the abomination that maketh desolate" (Dan. 11:31, KJV).

Scholars believe that Daniel's prophecy of the apalling horror against the Temple refers to the sacrilege of Antiochus Epiphanes, the Seleucidian ruler, in 168 B.C. He tried to destroy Jewish religion by erecting an altar to Zeus over the altar of burnt offerings, sacrificing a pig, setting up brothels in the outer courts, and banning Judaism.

Looking forward to A.D. 40, the Emperor Caligula will advance the abomination by ordering a statue of his image to be built on the altar of burnt offerings for worship by the Jews. The greater abomination, however, will come from within the Jewish community. Josephus, the renowned historian of first century Jewish history, reports that Zealots occupied the Temple during A.D. 67–68, murdering Jewish brothers and piling up the dead in the Holy of Holies. Their acts of abomination climaxed with a ceremonial farce in which a clown named Phanni was installed as the chief priest of the Temple. Faithful Jews who heeded Jesus' warning read this sacrilege as ". . . the abomination that maketh desolate" (Dan. 11:31, KJV) and fled to the Peraean city of Pella just in time to escape the onslaught of Titus' armies.

Still further forward, when the wheel of prophecy turns again to signal the Great Tribulation, appalling horror will be fulfilled with the personification of Evil standing on the place of the Holy. Mark's Gospel infers that the sacrilege will be committed by a person, not by a social movement, a political ideology or a public attitude. Who the "Antichrist" will be, where he will stand, and when he will arrive are matters beyond our present knowledge, but not beyond Jesus' warning to *"take heed"* (v. 23) and flee.

Urgency of flight. Personal safety for His disciples during the tribulation is a primary concern of Jesus. Accordingly, He commands His friends to flee Jerusalem as soon as they see the man of sin standing in the Holy place. The state of urgency caused by the abomination becomes a sign as well as a test. Deterrents to flight will test the faithful. One deterrent is *possessions.* Time will be so short, Jesus says, that a person on a housetop will have to move as if escaping a burning building, taking the outside stairs instead of going through the house to pick up valuables. Laborers in the field must show equal speed, not even going back to the end of the furrow to retrieve an outer garment that was laid aside during the heat of the day. To let possessions reduce the urgency by a split second is to flirt with destruction.

Another deterrent to flight is *family obligations.* Pregnant women and nursing mothers will be unable to respond as fast as necessary because of the burden of children. Jesus knows that maternal instincts will prevail with mothers choosing death before risking an unborn baby or abandoning a new one. Jewish families who were being hunted down like animals by the Gestapo during Hitler's regime faced similar decisions. Escape frequently depended upon lightning speed in which every member of the family had to fend for himself or herself. More often than not, love overruled the natural instincts of survival so that families refused to leave behind the elderly, pregnant, young, or sick. Consequently, the Holocaust is a horror story of families being herded from their homes into boxcars, and then being forcefully divided into separate concentration camps to suit the Nazi purpose. The small room where Anne Frank and her family were hidden from the Nazis for years is a memorial to filial love. Sensitive to the reality of mother love and family loyalty, Jesus can only sigh "woe" for pregnant women and nursing mothers for whom a split-second delay will mean the difference between life and death.

The third deterrent to urgent flight before the sign of abomination is *physical nature.* Because the seasons are out of human control, Jesus speaks with resignation, *"pray that your flight not be in winter"* (v. 18). Floods which swelled the rivers, washed out bridges, and made roads impassable were standard for the Palestinian winter. If the force of destruction attacked at this time, flight from the city would be blocked. Again, timing is critical. In the winter of A.D. 68, the refugees who delayed their flight after Phanni's sacrilege in the Temple found the roads to Jericho washed away with the swelling of the Jordan.

The final deterrent to urgent flight from tribulation is *public pressure.* In the time of tribulation, desperate people grab for false hopes. Anyone who promises salvation becomes a savior, and public opinion will say, " 'Look, here is the Christ!' or 'Look, He is there!' " (v. 21). False

Christs who fool the people with signs and wonders deter the flight from destruction because of the human tendency to hold onto the thinnest thread of hope. Spectacular signs and wonders performed by false Christs add to the deception. As mentioned earlier, Kahn and Scalera, in their book *The Future of World Economic Development: Projections to the Year 2000 and Beyond,* see more ecstatic and exotic forms of religion arising as human worth and meaning get ground up in the depersonalizing processes of high technology. Magnified to the level of the Apocalypse, one can understand how deceptive saviors who do wondrous works can cause a person to pause . . . and die.

The ultimacy of destruction. In between Jesus' warnings against delaying the flight from destruction at the first sign of sacrilege in the Holy of Holies is an insight into the circumstances of the Great Tribulation. In the Greek, the word "tribulation" derives from the "winepress" for grapes and in the Latin, draws its meaning from the "threshing floor" for grain. Relating the analogy to people who go through tribulation, there is a fine line between "pressing" and "threshing." The thought of a bloody crushing or an unmerciful flailing just begins to encompass and fill in the meaning of total and unbearable devastation. Jesus goes even further when He tells His disciples that this tribulation will be unprecedented in human history and unequalled in the human future, *'such as has not been from the beginning of creation which God created to this time, nor ever shall be"* (v. 19). A remnant will remain, but only if God Himself intervenes to cut short the days of devastation for the sake of His elect people. Heavy symbolism weights His words. A remnant of the elect reaches back to the Old Testament promise of deliverance for the people of God (Dan. 12:1) and forward to the coming of the Son of Man when "His elect" will be gathered from the four winds and saved (13:27).

Modern man mixes apocalyptic anxiety with affluent ease. Multimillion sales of Hal Lindsey's books, such as *The Late Great Planet Earth,* is a symptom of our apocalyptic anxiety, but our actions do not follow our fears. At the same time that our guilt is piqued by dispensational prophecies, our "comfort zone" goes untouched. Historians may look back upon Christian behavior in our century with the tart comment by which native Hawaiians remember many missionaries to their islands, "They came to do good; and they did well."

Christian disciples must be alert for the sign of abomination that will precede the Great Tribulation and be prepared for urgent flight from judgment. No discernment of signs of the times is more difficult or delicate, and yet, Jesus concludes this section of His "Olivet Discourse" with the reminder, *"I have foretold you all things!"* (v. 23). Do we believe it? He has told us everything that we need to know about the forthcoming tribulation. It is up to us to *"take heed"* (v. 23).

Watching for His Coming

24 "But in those days, after that tribulation, the sun will be darkened, and the moon will not give its light;

25 "the stars of heaven will fall, and the powers in heaven will be shaken.

26 "And then they will see the Son of Man coming in the clouds with great power and glory.

27 "And then He will send His angels, and gather together His elect from the four winds, from the farthest part of earth to the farthest part of heaven.

28 "Now learn this parable from the fig tree: When its branch has already become tender, and puts forth leaves, you know that summer is near.

29 "So you also, when you see these things happening, know that it is near, even at the doors.

30 "Assuredly, I say to you, this generation will by no means pass away till all these things take place.

31 "Heaven and earth will pass away, but My words will by no means pass away.

32 "But of that day and hour no one knows, neither the angels who are in heaven, nor the Son, but only the Father.

33 "Take heed, watch and pray; for you do not know when the time is.

34 "It is like a man going to a far country, who left his house and gave authority to his servants, and to each his work, and commanded the doorkeeper to watch.

35 "Watch therefore, for you do not know when the master of the house is coming—in the evening, at midnight, at the crowing of the rooster, or in the morning—

36 "lest, coming suddenly, he find you sleeping.

37 "And what I say to you, I say to all: Watch!"

Mark 13:24–37

Coming to the grand denouement of human history, Jesus prophesies His personal return by giving the disciples the sign and seal of His coming. The sign will be unnatural disasters—not earthquakes and famine, but eclipses of sun and moon, falling of stars, and shaking of the heavens that defy human prediction or explanation. Astrologers and watchers of UFOs try to make a science of changes and disturbances in the heavens, but their efforts do not touch the prophecy of Jesus. When the sign of His coming is given, it will defy scientists and pseudoscientists, astronomers and astrologers, but there will be no way to misread its purpose. Even unbelievers *"will see the Son of Man coming in the clouds with great power and glory"* (v. 26). To the disciples who avoided panic, endured persecution, and fled from disaster, Christ's promise is fulfilled in His *parousia.* Power and glory belong to Him and to those who know Him and share the fellowship of His sufferings. As proof, He will send His angels to gather His elect from the four winds in a sweep that leaves no corner of heaven or earth untouched.

Although the immediate reference to "His elect" means the Jews, the coming of the Son of Man carries a timely message of hope for the Roman Christians to whom Mark writes. Jesus assures them that God is in ultimate control of the universe, of which Caesar is only a part. Furthermore, He assures them that their faith will be rewarded with salvation, and finally, that they will be among those raptured from the four winds to share the power and glory of Christ. Faithful Christians, under persecution in every age, discover the promise for themselves. Even when the tribulation is small and personal, rather than great and universal, Jesus' assurance of His coming is a daily claim.

In expectation of His "take heed" answer to the disciples' inquiry about the time and the signs for the destruction of the Temple, Jesus answers by two parables. One is the Parable of the Fig Tree, which He uses to seal the prophetic signs that He has given. No training in horticulture is needed to know that the leafy, tender branches of the fig tree forecast the coming of summer. In the same manner, anyone can see the signs that Jesus has given and know that the Son of Man is coming, but not until all of the signs are fulfilled, like the ripening of the fig tree.

No one can watch a fig tree grow, but never let the process be mistaken for the lack of fulfillment. As surely as the maturing of the fig tree predicts summer, most surely will the signs of Jesus' prediction bring His coming. With unmixed and unbridled confidence, He speaks, *"Heaven and earth will pass away, but My words will by no means pass away"* (v. 31). Throughout the centuries, this promise of the permanence of Christ's words has sustained Christians in time of trouble. Jesus Himself has just come through a time when His enemies attacked from every angle, trying to trap Him in His words. They failed, and so will all others who try to find a flaw in anything He says. Jesus has won His case. Having proven that His words are true, He can now say with equal assurance that they are eternally sure.

Jesus knows that the signs of His coming are sure, but the timing is not. In what must be a sequel to the Parable of the Vineyard, He relates the truth of timing to a homeowner who takes an extended trip, leaving his property, his authority, and his work in the hands of servants. This time, a new duty is added for servanthood. Doorkeepers are expected to remain constantly alert for the return of the Master at any hour. If they are caught sleeping upon His return, they betray their trust to Him, just as definitely as unjust servants who would forfeit the property, misuse their master's authority, or fail to do his work.

"Gatekeepers" has become a popular term for persons in key positions of leadership in organizations and communities. As the symbol suggests, there are persons who are on constant watch to protect social values that are entrusted to them. Sometimes the "gatekeeper" is a formal authority and sometimes it is a person who wields quiet, but powerful, influence. Nothing significant happens, however, without the approval of the "gatekeepers." Lyndon Johnson, one of the most successful of Presidents in getting his legislation through Congress, adopted the principle of "gatekeepers" as his strategy. Not wanting to waste his time and energy with peripheral people, he sought out the "gatekeepers" who were at the center of power, concentrated upon them, and rallied the votes to support his recommendations.

To be a "doorkeeper" or a "gatekeeper," on diligent watch for the coming of the Son of Man, is one of the most solemn duties in the Kingdom of God. Someone has to keep watch so that others can do their work. Executives in leadership roles carry this responsibility—reading the signs, interpreting the meaning, putting out warnings, setting the direction, and announcing the coming of the Master. What an awesome privilege! Jesus charges the disciples with the duty of "doorkeeping," making them responsible for the household of faith. If they fall asleep so that the household misses His coming, God will hold them responsible.

The "Olivet Discourse" is finished. Intricacies of the prophetic past, present and future are still being unraveled. "Take heed" to avoid panic, endure persecution, escape judgment and watch for the coming of the Son of Man came to factual fulfillment in the "little apocalypse," when Jerusalem was devastated in A.D. 70. Today, the same signs and warnings point toward the "great apocalypse" when the cycle of human history makes its final turn. No one knows when the time will be, but Jesus has us in mind when He speaks the valedictory warning from the Mount of Olives, *"And what I say to you, I say to all: Watch!"* (v. 37).

NOTE

1. Flavius Josephus, *The Wars of the Jews: The History of the Destruction of Jerusalem,* trans. William Whiston (Grand Rapids: Kregel Publications, 1960).

CHAPTER NINETEEN

Experiencing His Sacrament

Mark 14:1—15:47

CONSPIRACY AND PROMISE

> 1 After two days it was the Passover and the Feast
> of Unleavened Bread. And the chief priests and the
> scribes sought how they might take Him by trickery
> and put Him to death.
> 2 But they said, "Not during the feast, lest there
> be an uproar of the people."
>
> *Mark 14:1–2*

Mark begins his long and detailed Passion narrative by recording the time, tenor and circumstances of Jesus' final days in Jerusalem.

The time of Jesus' Passion. Two days after His prophetic discourse on
the Mount of Olives, Jesus is in Bethany on the eve of the great
Feast of the Passover which extended through to the lesser Feast of
Unleavened Bread as one continuous celebration. Passover, the Feast
of Redemption, commemorated the night in Egypt when the death
angel passed over the homes of the Israelites who had the blood of
a slain lamb on their doorposts. The Jews continued to sacrifice the
paschal lamb on the eve of the fourteenth day of their month Nisan
and feast on the meat the following day. Mark purposely introduces
the Passion narrative by noting that the time of the Passover has
come. Jesus is to be the paschal lamb and His blood is the price of
redemption.

The tone of Jesus' Passion. Festivity commingles with tension in the

276

tone for the Passion narrative. At the time of the Passover, Jerusalem bursts its seams with people as every man within a radius of fifteen miles seeks to meet the requirement to attend the feast in Jerusalem and every Jew in the world aspires to eat at least one meal of the paschal lamb in the Holy City during a lifetime. Josephus gives us some indication of the number of natives and pilgrims that swell the population of the city during the Passover, when he writes of an incident involving Nero around A.D. 65. The emperor's megalomania convinced him of the insignificance of Jewish religion and the ease with which it could be wiped out in Jerusalem. An adviser who felt otherwise proposed a count of the lambs that were sold for sacrifice during the Passover to illustrate the strength of the Jewish religion. By law, one lamb had to serve a minimum of ten people. The Romans counted the sale of 265,000 sacrificial lambs. Multiplying that number by a minimum of ten persons equals a Passover population bloated to almost three million celebrants in the city. The census of the lambs astounded Nero and forced him to change his mind about the insignificance of Judaism.

To contend with the tension of the masses, reinforcements were brought in for the Roman guard and stationed at strategic spots around the city to watch for the telltale signs of fomentation that Zealots could turn into rebellion.

The circumstances of Jesus' Passion. Masses of Passover celebrants caused trouble for the chief priests and scribes who had pledged themselves to kill Jesus. An influx of Galileans who claimed Jesus as a favorite son would never permit them to arrest Him without cause. Trickery remained their only alternative and, even then, they agreed to delay the plot until after the feast. If they were to deliver Jesus to Roman authorities for the sentence of death, they dared not risk a riot that might be blamed on them and, thus, alienate the Romans who were charged with the responsibility for keeping the peace. Masses of common people remain a formidable, but temporary, barrier between Jesus and His enemies.

Redemption never operates in a vacuum. Its joy is known in the presence of tension and despite the efforts of evil. As such, it prefigures the sacramental nature of Jesus' Passion. Life in the midst of death, love in the presence of hate, joy in the same setting as sorrow, justice in a mix with mercy—these are the signs and countersigns of God's redemptive process.

CRITICISM AND ANOINTING

> 3 And being in Bethany at the house of Simon
> the leper, as He sat at the table, a woman came having
> an alabaster flask of very costly oil of spikenard. And
> she broke the flask and poured it on His head.
>
> 4 And there were some who were indignant among
> themselves and said, "Why was this waste made of
> the fragrant oil?
>
> 5 "For it might have been sold for more than three
> hundred denarii and given to the poor." And they
> criticized her sharply.
>
> 6 But Jesus said, "Let her alone. Why do you
> trouble her? She has done a good work for Me.
>
> 7 "For you have the poor with you always, and
> whenever you wish you may do them good; but Me
> you do not have always.
>
> 8 "She has done what she could. She has come
> beforehand to anoint My body for burial.
>
> 9 "Assuredly, I say to you, wherever this gospel
> is preached throughout the whole world, what this
> woman has done will also be spoken of as a memorial
> to her."
>
> *Mark 14:3–9*

Jesus never ceases to amaze us. Foreknowledge of His imminent suffering and death is putting a crushing weight upon His mind and Spirit. Within hours, He will leave Bethany for the last time, walk the familiar path over the Mount of Olives, and enter the Holy City to celebrate the Passover in which He Himself will be the sacrificial lamb. How does Jesus choose to spend His last free hours? He goes to a party! According to Mark, Simon the leper hosts a Passover Eve dinner at his home with Jesus as the honored guest. Nothing is known about Simon except that he once had leprosy. If this fact is combined with the act of gratitude shown by the anonymous woman guest, we may surmise that the dinner served as a reunion for the close friends of Jesus who had been touched and changed by Him in one way or another. Is Simon perchance the leper whom Jesus cleansed at the beginning of His servant ministry?

A diplomat languished as a hostage in a South American prison for months. When he arrived home after his release, reporters asked him what he wanted to do first with his freedom. His answer? "Three simple things: eat a good meal, read a good book, and talk with good friends." Jesus makes a similar choice with His final hours. Imagination sees Him spending a day with the Word of God before heading to Simon's house to eat a good meal and talk with good friends. One thing is sure. No cloud of pessimism hangs over the party. Jesus will not allow it. Light banter aids their digestion and genuine gratitude graces their conversation. All goes well until a woman's act of love bursts the boundaries of propriety. By custom, she would show hospitality and honor to a distinguished dinner guest by sprinkling His head with a drop or two of nard, a pure and expensive perfume imported from the banks of the Ganges River in India. Her gratitude to Jesus does not fit within these boundaries. Breaking the neck of the alabaster flask, she pours all the perfume over Jesus' head.

Who is this woman? John's record of the same incident identifies her as Mary, sister of Martha and Lazarus. If so, we can understand her gratitude as well as her grief. Jesus has no closer friends than Mary, Martha and Lazarus. In the privacy of their home, He finds respite from public pressure. Probably He also confides in them His prophecy of suffering and premonition of death. Mary has already shown unusual sensitivity to spiritual Truth when she becomes so enthralled with Jesus' teachings that she forgets to help Martha fix dinner one evening. Above and beyond all, Jesus has raised Mary's brother, Lazarus, from the dead. For this miracle, she can never give adequate thanks. So, when love, understanding, and gratitude merge as one, Mary cannot contain herself. By breaking the flask and pouring the oil, she creates a crisis of intuitive love, provokes the disciples' ritual criticism, and prompts Jesus to match her devotion with a lasting memorial in her honor.

A woman's act of intuitive love. Most of our love is channeled through routines of duty and standard patterns of expression—and well it should be. On rare and grand occasions, however, the spontaneity of love breaks out of channels and skyrockets across the sky in a spectacular display. A child, for instance, catches a mother by surprise with a clean room or a bouquet of dandelions. Mother's typical reaction is, "What have you done wrong?" The child answers, "Nothing, this time. I just want to say I love you." Mary didn't have to break the flask and pour the perfume over Jesus. Her spontaneous act surprises everyone, including her. Love is sometimes extravagant. When ordinary acts do not suffice to express one's feelings, an extraordinary show of love is in order. People whom Christ redeems from gross sin are often the most extravagant Christians. Converts in the Wesleyan revival, for instance, were converted from the gross sins of drunkenness, brawling, sloth, profanity, and adultery. In the joy of their redemption, they sang and shouted the praises of God and were ridiculed as "enthusiasts" by the hierarchy of the established church. There are times when spontaneous and extravagant love is appropriate.

The disciples' barrage of ritualistic criticism. A wet blanket falls over the party when the woman breaks the flask and pours the perfume over Jesus' head. The disciples, led by Judas, launch a barrage of personal invectives against her. Thinking that they know the mind of Jesus, they register two complaints. First, the fragrant oil is wasted. Second, the expensive oil could have been sold with the proceeds going to the poor. Both criticisms are valid if spiritual truth is limited to ritualistic limits. In a ritual, a drop is as good as a flaskful because it is the symbol that counts. Logically, the disciples reason that the opportunity to anoint many heads is better than one. A ritualistic mind also fixes upon tradition. On the eve of the Passover, custom dictated the giving of alms to the poor. Mary's act makes that practice impossible, so Judas and the other disciples attack her on the principles of stewardship and compassion. Indirectly, they also attack Jesus because He accepts the anointing.

Criticism is a dangerous and delicate instrument. Like a scalpel, it can cut to heal or it can cut to harm. Only in the hands of the most skilled and best-motivated practitioners can it heal. More often than not, harm is done because critics cannot keep persons separate from issues. Mark notes that the disciples start their attacks against principles, but transfer them to criticism of the woman as a person. The NKJV translation, *"And they criticized her sharply"* (v. 5) is not biting enough. In the original Greek, the word for criticism is *embrimaomai*— a verb that is used in other instances to describe the snorting of horses.

Criticism frequently tells more about the critic than it does about the person who is criticized. In the case of the disciples, and Judas in particular, criticism exposes their motives. Neither concern about wasted resources nor compassion for the poor really counts with them. Their criticism stems from a value system that will not let go of a Messianic dream built out of earthly wealth and human power. Under the pretense of pure love, they lay bare their unadulterated selfishness.

For Judas, leader of the critics, his arrogance and avarice prove to be fatal.

Jesus' response of eternal tribute. An insight into the maturity of Jesus is to see His gift for matching gratitude with gratitude. It is a gift for which I pray. Today, my son and I were playing tennis. A woman came to watch us. During a break between games, she asked, "How old is your son?" "Thirteen," I answered. "He plays very well," she complimented me. Instead of saying, "Thank you, I'm proud of him," I apologized, "Oh, he's just a beginner." Afterward, I berated myself when I realized that I had rejected her compliment and insulted my son. Jesus does just the opposite. He rejects the disciples' criticism and matches the woman's gratitude.

Point for point, Jesus rejects the disciples' criticism. First, He describes the woman's act as *beautiful* rather than *wasteful*. Mark translates the Greek word *kalos* as "a good work" (v. 6), but in its larger meaning, it conveys a sense of beauty that gives goodness and artistic glow beyond its instrumental value. Debate over the waste of beauty never lets up. Works of fine art are considered wasteful by some people and yet others find their souls cleansed by visiting an art gallery, listening to a symphony, seeing a play, or reading great literature. Jesus puts Himself on the side of artists, musicians, dramatists, and poets when He commends the beauty in the woman's impractical and nonproductive act of devotion. Sunsets are wasteful, too.

Jesus goes on to counter the disciples' criticism of the woman's insensitivity to the needs of the poor. His response is so often quoted out of context. Rather than justifying a fatalism toward the *"poor [who are] with you always"* (v. 7), Jesus credits the woman's perception of a timely and appropriate act of devotion. Under no circumstances is He reducing our obligation to the poor and needy. In fact, he reinforces our responsibility when He says, *"And whenever you wish you may do them good"* (v. 7). On this occasion, however, the time of Jesus's Passion has come. Tomorrow, the opportunity for acts of love will be lost. Mary has the timely compassion that the disciples lack. The poor can count upon her to respond to their needs because she senses Jesus' need. As the "poorest of the poor," He needs her gift of timely compassion, at that moment, more than anyone on earth.

Jesus counters the disciples' criticism by putting a world of meaning into the commendation, *"She has done what she could"* (v. 8). One hears the widow's two mites "pinging" into the Treasury trumpets all over again. How many times does Jesus teach that the total gift of giving one's self in love to your neighbor is the sum and substance of all the commandments? Indirectly, Jesus tells the disciples, "You have not yet given your all and done what you can do. Don't criticize someone who has." That's the danger of criticism. Behind the self-protective screens from which we attack the spiritual efforts of other people, we hide our failure to live and give up to our own potential.

Enough for the critics. Jesus turns to match the woman's gratitude with His own. In response to her love, Jesus etches her act into a lasting tribute that will extend through and around the world wherever and whenever the Gospel is preached. Twenty centuries later, as these words are being written, her memorial is erected once again.

Not knowing it, Mary memorializes Jesus' burial by anointing His body with the perfume. A gripping fact is that she is telling Jesus through her act that He will die as a criminal because only criminals' bodies are denied anointing with aloes, spices, and perfume after death. Her act of love will sustain Him in His darkest moment of disgrace.

Mark does not add or delete words without a purpose. The fact that he does not name the woman who breaks the alabaster flask and pours the perfume over the head of Jesus has to be significant. Is he not saying what we often sing:

> . . . For not with sword's loud clashing,
> Nor roll of stirring drums;
> With deeds of love and mercy,
> The heav'nly kingdom comes.[1]

BETRAYAL AND FULFILLMENT

10 And Judas Iscariot, one of the twelve, went to the chief priests to betray Him to them.
11 And when they heard it, they were glad, and promised to give him money. And he sought how he might conveniently betray Him.

Mark 14:10–11

Mark's prelude to Jesus' Passion interlaces three events: the plot by the chief priests and scribes, the anointing by the unnamed woman, and the betrayal by Judas. By putting an act of love between the nefarious plot and the infamous betrayal, Mark accentuates the contrasting beauty and ugliness in the people whose decisions and motivations made history. For comparison and contrast, each participant makes a voluntary not a forced decision, acts out of internal not external motivation, and leaves a lasting memorial to their honor or dishonor. Judas' treachery gives us a base from which to draw the comparison.

A voluntary decision. Mark reports that Judas "went" to the chief priests to betray Jesus to them. Earlier, we learned that the chief priests were forced to delay their plot against Jesus because of the crowds of people in Jerusalem at the time of the Passover. How would Judas know their intent? John, in his Gospel (John 11:57), tells us that the chief priests put out a command reserved in our day for fugitives from justice, "Anyone knowing the whereabouts of this person is to inform authorities at once." Surely, Judas gets the word and makes the decision to turn informer. Sheer glee greets him when he offers himself to the chief priests. To have "one of the twelve" volunteer to find a "convenient" time to betray His Master goes beyond their wildest expectations.

An internal motivation. Although Mark does not state the reason for Judas' betrayal, the lingering question "Why?" remains in our minds. Many motives have been advanced. *Money* is one. Matthew says that Judas went to the chief priests asking how much they were willing to pay for the betrayal (Matt. 26:15).

Embezzlement is a second possible motive. Closely related to Judas' denial is John's report that he criticized Mary's waste of perfume because he had been pilfering from the bag which he held for Jesus and the disciples, not because he cared for the poor.

A third motive is *demon-possession.* Both Luke and John report that the Devil entered into Judas (Luke 22:3; John 13:27). This does not assume that Judas becomes the innocent victim of satanic takeover. The Devil needs either an empty or an evil heart for his possession.

Fourth, there is speculation that Judas is motivated by his *nationalism.* This theory says that Judas does not want Jesus to die, but hopes to force Him into a militant stance against the Jews.

Mark's placement of Judas' betrayal following the woman's anointing seems to favor the money and power motives. As an embezzler of the disciples' money, Judas sees personal gain being poured out in perfume worth three hundred denarii—a year's pay for the average person of that time. Still, his avarice does not seem adequate to anticipate betrayal. Something had to be building within him for a long time. My opinion is that Jesus' public rejection of his leadership in criticizing the woman's act of devotion became the "moment of truth" when Judas' ambition for wealth and power in an earthly Messianic Kingdom shatters at his feet. He realizes that Jesus sees through his avarice and his thievery. It is only a matter of time before he will be exposed. The survival instinct takes over as Judas decides, "It's He or I; it's now or never." Sin as well as grace leads us to ultimate decisions.

A lasting memorial. The conspiracy of the chief priests leaves a blot on the cause of justice that is studied in case law as a precedent for the "kangaroo court." The woman's act of anointing is remembered worldwide as an active example of love in its highest form. Judas, too, has his legacy. No greater insult can be given than to call someone "Judas." His name is spit from the tongue with a detestation that is reserved for traitors. To add to the disgrace, the "Judas tree" is shaped by branches fit only for hanging. In contrast with the woman whose deed is honored wherever the Gospel is preached, Judas' evil act also follows the Gospel as a worldwide memorial of dishonor.

Mark has played out the prelude of Jesus' Passion. Conspiracy and treachery will take Him to a criminal's death, but not without the anointing of love which will assure His dignity and the fulfillment of His mission.

EXPOSURE AND RESOLUTION

12 And on the first day of Unleavened Bread, when they killed the Passover lamb, His disciples said to Him, "Where do You want us to go and prepare, that You may eat the Passover?"

13 And He sent out two of His disciples and said to them, "Go into the city, and a man will meet you carrying a pitcher of water; follow him.

14 "And wherever he goes in, say to the master of the house, 'The Teacher says: Where is the guest room in which I may eat the Passover with My disciples?'

15 "And he will show you a large upper room, furnished and prepared; there make ready for us."

16 And His disciples went out, came into the city,

and found it just as He had said to them; and they prepared the Passover.

17 And in the evening He came with the twelve.

18 And as they sat and ate, Jesus said, "Assuredly, I say to you, one of you who eats with Me will betray Me."

19 And they began to be sorrowful, and to say to Him one by one, "Is it I?" And another said, "Is it I?"

20 And He answered and said to them, "It is one of the twelve, who dips with Me in the dish.

21 "The Son of Man indeed goes just as it is written of Him, but woe to that man by whom the Son of Man is betrayed! It would have been good for that man if he had never been born."

Mark 14:12–21

The time of Passion has closed in on Jesus. Simon's party is behind Him and the Passover feast is just ahead. As He had done once before in preparation for the triumphal entry, Jesus takes control of the plans for the Passover supper. Acting like the leader of a guerrilla band, He sends two disciples with coded instructions to find a man carrying a water pot who will lead them to the master of the house who has prepared the room where they will celebrate the Passover meal. Then, the disciples are to complete the elaborate and symbolic details of the lamb, the unleavened bread, salt water, bitter herbs and spicy paste, and four cups of wine which make up the Passover meal. Why the secrecy? Treachery shadows the final hours. Jesus must protect Himself by limiting His confidence to two disciples who will know the time and place for the Passover feast.

For years, I have worked with a President's Cabinet that includes my vice presidents, the chairman of the faculty council, and the student body president. At the beginning of the relationship, the confidentiality of our conversations is stressed. Once the lines of confidence are clear, an atmosphere of personal growth and professional effectiveness is created. Only once in twenty-one years has that confidence been breached. After that, all of our relationships changed. Items on the agenda were selected to avoid confidential matters and conversations became guarded for fear of disclosure. Misery replaced camaraderie in our relationships and distrust almost tore us apart.

Jesus' last appeal. Misery and distrust because of Judas' treachery cloud the dinner that Jesus should have enjoyed with His disciples on the eve of the Passover. Until He clears the air, Jesus cannot celebrate the full meaning of the feast. When He can no longer contain Himself, He speaks one last word of *appeal* to Judas, *"Assuredly, I say to you, one of you who eats with Me will betray Me"* (v. 18). Somehow, Judas also betrays himself. Whether by action or word, he telegraphs the signal of his guilt which Jesus intercepts and reads.

The closer one is to a person, the easier it is to know when something is wrong. Husbands and wives do not need objects thrown through the air to know when trouble is brewing at home. The whole atmosphere flashes the news of a troubled relationship.

Jesus' perception that He has a traitor among the Twelve is often credited to His supernatural knowledge. Without denying His divine nature for one moment, I doubt that Jesus needs the supernatural to know that Judas is a turncoat. With His sensitivity to human nature, His closeness to His friends, and His knowledge of the prophecy in Psalm 41:9 (KJV), "Yea, mine own familiar friend, in whom I trusted, which did eat of my bread, hath lifted up his heel against me," omniscience is unnecessary.

Judas' final choice. In response to Jesus' last appeal, Judas joins the other disciples in their sadness as they ask, "Is it I?" The pretense of innocence means that Judas intends to play the ruse to the bitter end. Jesus therefore becomes more specific by narrowing the number down to one of the two or three who are dipping bread into the same dish with Him. What starts out as an appeal turns into a warning. Judas is identified and the margins for confession are slim. Still, there seems to be a choice as Jesus says, *"The Son of Man indeed goes just as it is written of Him, but woe to that man by whom the Son of Man is betrayed!"* (v. 21). The message is clear. What is inevitable for Jesus is not inevitable for Judas. No alternative to the cross is open to Christ, but Judas does not have to be the betrayer. Divine sovereignty and human freedom are held in tension at this moment. God's foreknowledge which sees Judas as the traitor does not foreordain his act. To the very last moment, Jesus works for his redemption and Judas has a choice.

At the same time that Jesus tries to turn Judas by appeal and warning, He feels the finality of his treacherous choice. "Woe" is the word that Jesus uses to describe a person or a situation when love can no longer make a difference. A sense of failure must have shuddered through Him as He speaks the verbal epitaph for the man who betrays his friend, the Christ, *"It would have been good for that man if he had never been born"* (v. 21). Judas had much to offer or he would never have been selected as a disciple. But as the poet Whittier says, "Of all sad words of tongue or pen, the saddest are these: 'It might have been.'"[2]

SACRIFICE AND CELEBRATION

22 And as they were eating, Jesus took bread,
blessed it and broke it, and gave it to them and said,
"Take, eat; this is My body."
23 And He took the cup, and when He had given
thanks He gave it to them, and they all drank from
it.
24 And He said to them, "This is My blood of the
new covenant, which is shed for many.
25 "Assuredly, I say to you, I will no longer drink
of the fruit of the vine until that day when I drink
it new in the kingdom of God."
26 And when they had sung a hymn, they went
out to the Mount of Olives.

Mark 14:22–26

Jesus takes over the ritual of the last supper to fulfill God's purpose and symbolize His role in the new covenant. Reaching back to His statement about fulfilling the written will of God and advancing forward to the singing of the final hymn of the Passover meal, Jesus shows us the dimensions of His own will at work: understanding the *determinative* will of God, speaking the *declarative* will of God, and choosing the *discretionary* will of God.

The determinative will of God. Jesus expresses His understanding of the determinative will of God when He says, *"The Son of Man indeed goes just as it is written of Him . . ."* (14:21). An eternal question balances between "determinism" and "free will." If Jesus is following the will that is written for Him, does He have a valid choice to die or not to die? Or is He a puppet dancing on the strings of divine purpose with God being the puppeteer? What is the determinative will of God which Jesus understands and accepts?

Gordon Allport, the renowned Harvard psychologist, pictures a person on a bluff looking down on a river far below. From the perspective of the bluff, he sees a man rowing a boat on the river. His view from the heights also lets him see around the bend, where the rower cannot see, to a swift current that flows over a falls and into the white water and rocks below. Allport uses the picture to suggest how God sees man. Does the fact that He sees the man rowing and the danger ahead mean that the man's fate is settled? In this case, we would say "No." For God to see the future is not to say that God predetermines the future. Until the current of the river makes disaster inevitable, the man still has a choice, just as Jesus tried until the very last moment to get Judas to change his course. Jesus, too, still has the freedom to choose and change His course. Call it blind trust, if you wish. Jesus submits Himself to the determinative will of God, trusting that His ultimate purpose is good even if the path leads through suffering and death.

The declarative will of God. Jesus uses the eating of the unleavened bread and the drinking of the bitter wine to celebrate God's purpose. *"Take, eat; this is My body"* (v. 22) and *"This is My blood of the new covenant, which is shed for many"* (v. 24) is His declaration to do the will of God freely and fully.

Man is neither an ape nor an angel. An ape is a creature of physical instincts neither good nor bad. An angel is a creation of spiritual instincts—knowing only God. Suspended in between apes and angels is man—capable of immense good or insufferable evil.

Man has a will and is free to make choices. He also has an intelligence that directs his decision toward some specific purpose. These two dimensions of will—freedom to choose and purpose of choosing—represent the unique elements of God's image which He creates in us. Jesus shares the dilemma of our will with us because He is fully man and He is fully God. He is free to choose and He chooses according to purpose.

Just recently, a man who was a minister, the son of a minister, and the husband of a minister's daughter, complained, "My whole life has been dictated by the church. I have never had the freedom to choose." Presumably, then, to demonstrate his freedom, he left the ministry, divorced his wife, married a woman half his age, and joined a liturgical church just opposite his evangelical upbringing. In our next conversation, he said, "I am now free of my past. For the first time, I have made my own decision." Time will determine whether or not his declaration of a free and purposeful will is consistent with the will of God.

Jesus takes the opposite course. Accepting what is written for Him, He freely and purposely declares His intention to suffer a broken body and shed His blood for the redemption of man.

The discretionary will of God. After His disciples have shared the bread and wine with Him, Jesus answers, *"I will no longer drink of the fruit of the vine until that day when I drink it new in the kingdom of God"* (v. 25). Here is an expression of the discretionary will of God. Contrary to some expectations, all aspects of God's will are not signed, sealed, and delivered. In the making of His determinative purpose which we can understand and His declarative purpose which we can celebrate, is His discretionary will which gives us many options for choice. Jesus can choose or not choose to drink wine again until the day when He will drink it new in the Kingdom of God. Is He setting a symbol for Christian discipline? Is He deferring to the immediacy of suffering that will not permit Him opportunity to drink the fruit of the vine? Or is He saying that He prefers to go to His suffering with a clear head and undulled senses? Is His choice symbolic, timely, or practical? God gives us the opportunity to make discretionary choices which may not be life and death matters, but do reflect our desire to do His will. For these open choices, Jesus sets the example. He chooses to honor God.

Whenever the call to communion comes, these three dimensions of will are engaged. Communicants are asked to trust the *determinative* will of God as good, even though all of the outcomes cannot be traced. To come to the table of the Lord, eat the bread and drink the wine is to celebrate the *declarative* will of God as it is revealed to us. And wherever the *discretionary* will of God gives us open options for choice, our decision is to honor Him.

DESERTION AND REUNION

27 And Jesus said to them, "All of you will be made to stumble because of Me this night, for it is written:
'I will strike the Shepherd,
And the sheep will be scattered.'
28 "But after I have been raised, I will go before you to Galilee."
29 But Peter said to Him, "Even if all are made to stumble, yet I will not be."

30 And Jesus said to him, "Assuredly, I say to you
that today, even this night, before the rooster crows
twice, you will deny Me three times."
31 But he spoke more vehemently, "If I have to
die with You, I will not deny You!" And they all said
likewise.

Mark 14:27–31

After singing the final hymn of the Passover feast, Jesus and His
disciples leave the city under cover of darkness to return to the Mount
of Olives where Jesus often prayed. On the way, Jesus reveals another
hurt of His heart. He knows that He must die alone. Realistically,
this means that His small band of friends, upon whom He counts
to win the world, will desert Him in the crisis.

Three sobering facts characterize the disciples' denial of Jesus. *One*,
"all" of them will deny Him. Judas has already been singled out as
the traitor, but each of them is a coward at heart. We, too, find the
same potential for treachery and cowardice waiting within us, so
much so that we must share Thomas Carlyle's confession when he
saw a criminal standing on the scaffold, "There but for the grace of
God go I."

Two, the disciples will deny Jesus because they are "offended" at
Him. The reason for their denial is stated in a word that will become
part of a key phrase in future apostolic writing. *Skandalizō* generally
means to be offended, but specifically means to "stumble over an
obstacle," "fall into a trap," or be "impaled on a stake." The more
vivid meanings will fix themselves in the disciples' minds when they
finally understand why they deny Jesus. It is the cross, an obstacle
over which they cannot climb, a trap into which they will fall, a
shaft that will penetrate clear through them. Does Peter have this
moment in mind when he extols Christ as the "chief cornerstone,"
precious to those who believe, but a "stone of stumbling and a rock
of offense" to the disobedient (1 Pet. 2:7–8)? Paul is more specific
when he pleads with the Galatians to resist the Judaizers who would
cancel the "offense of the cross." Throughout ensuing ages, the scandal of crucifixion has been the object which stands in the way of
human ambition and easy salvation.

Charles Schulz, creator of the "Peanuts" cartoon strip, draws a tree
which invariably snarls the string of Charlie Brown's kite every time
he tries to put it into the air. But in a reflective moment, he admits

that the same tree which is his nemesis, shades him from the sun, keeps the rain off his head, and when all else fails, is "very good to lean against." So it is with the cross of Christ—at one and the same time, nemesis to our lofty ambitions and sole hope for our salvation.

Three, the disciples will be scattered like sheep which have lost their shepherd. Stumbling over the cross and having Jesus' personal leadership temporarily lifted, the disciples disintegrate into a chaotic, fumbling band of cowards. They deny their Lord—not just by rejecting the scandal of the cross, but by the show of confusion and incompetence. To borrow some terms which are in vogue, the friends of Jesus honor or deny Him by either their "orthodoxy"—what they believe, or by their "orthopraxy"—what they do.

Peter still nurses a superior air that puts his head above the other disciples. Thus, it becomes necessary for Jesus to let him know that he, too, is vulnerable to denial. Fact piles upon fact as Jesus predicts that Peter will be the worst offender of all—

> today . . .
> even this night . . .
> before the rooster crows twice . . .
> you will deny Me three times. . . .

The Truth only stokes the fires of Peter's fervor. Even "more vehemently," he puts his life on the line in a loyalty pact to die with Jesus before he will deny Him. In unison, every disciple echoes the pledge.

We must admit that we do not know ourselves. Surface intentions pledge loyalties that are motivated by love and sincerity. Our problem is that we do not know how we will act under extreme pressure. American soldiers who were imprisoned during the Korean War were subjected to brainwashing. Some survived, others did not. The difference was an inner quality of strength bolstered by an inner core of conviction that buffered the worst of the blows and the most subtle of the temptations. Yet, it is difficult to predict these strengths and convictions in advance. Not until the pressure rises to the breaking point can we know what is in the depths of our soul.

Jesus agonizes over denial by His closest friends. If He cannot count on them, who's left? To die alone is the death of deaths. His only assurance is the unfulfilled promise of God that He will be raised again for a glorious reunion with His disciples.

AGONY AND ACCEPTANCE

32 And they came to a place which was named Gethsemane; and He said to His disciples, "Sit here while I pray."

33 And He took Peter, James, and John with Him, and He began to be troubled and deeply distressed.

34 And He said to them, "My soul is exceedingly sorrowful, even to death. Stay here and watch."

35 And He went a little farther, fell on the ground, and prayed that, if it were possible, the hour might pass from Him.

36 And He said, "*Abba,* Father, all things are possible for You. Take this cup away from Me; nevertheless, not what I will, but what You will."

37 And He came and found them sleeping, and said to Peter, "Simon, are you sleeping? Could you not watch one hour?

38 "Watch and pray, lest you enter into temptation. The spirit truly is ready, but the flesh is weak."

39 And again He went away and prayed, and spoke the same words.

40 And when He returned, He found them asleep again, for their eyes were heavy; and they did not know what to answer Him.

41 And He came the third time and said to them, "Sleep on now and take your rest. It is enough; the hour has come; behold, the Son of Man is being betrayed into the hands of sinners.

42 "Rise up, let us go. See, he who betrays Me is at hand."

Mark 14:32–42

In preparation for the inevitable cross, Jesus retreats to His usual place of prayer in the Garden of Gethsemane on the Mount of Olives. The name Gethsemane is a forewarning in itself. Synonymous with "tribulation," it means "press," connoting the stomping of the grape to squeeze out the blood of the vine.

Jesus expects Gethsemane to be a time of final communion with His Father in preparation for the cross. Even though He has predicted that all the disciples will deny Him, He takes His inner circle of Peter, James, and John with Him to the place of prayer, hoping that their denial will be delayed until the very last moment. In other words, Jesus counts upon communion with God and fellowship with friends to sustain Him until the moment of betrayal. He does not expect His friends to continue with Him beyond that point, but His Father is different. Surely He will stay beside Him through an ordeal which no man had ever suffered before, and no one will ever suffer again.

Our experiences do not permit us to probe the depths of Jesus' emotions in the Garden of Gethsemane. His foreknowledge of suffering and His sensitivity of spirit take His anguish deeper than we have ever known. Even then, Jesus is not prepared for the shock of reality which overcomes Him in the Garden. Mark says, *"He began to be troubled and deeply distressed"* (v. 33). The English translation is not strong enough to carry the full impact of His feelings. A more literal translation is, "He began to be terrified and disoriented." Sheer terror strikes at His soul as He faces for the first time the reality of unbridled evil.

Robinson Crusoe found himself on a desert island. When darkness fell, he retreated to the beach, built a fire and huddled close to it. The range of security extended only to the outer edge of his campfire's light. Beyond that, as he peered into the darkness toward the jungle, icy fingers of terror caused his soul to shudder, knowing that if he stepped beyond the flickering light of his campfire, his terror would be compounded by the distress of being out of his realm and not knowing how to cope with the situation.

In effect, Jesus stepped beyond the circle of light cast by God's presence into pitch blackness in the jungle of evil. Before this moment, He had theoretically accepted the responsibility for bearing the sins of the whole world. Now, terror tells Him what it really means. Also, before this moment, Jesus has enjoyed unbroken fellowship with His Father. Now, He realizes that He must die alone, His friends will deny Him, and His Father will have to leave Him. The combined weight of sin and loneliness is almost more than He can stand, so to His disciples He confesses, *"My soul is exceedingly sorrowful, even to death"* (v. 34). Terror, disorientation, and depression are now so severe that death is the preferable alternative. Jesus, who thought that He knew what to expect and how to handle His Passion, is drinking the "wine of astonishment" (Ps. 60:3) from the "cup of trembling" (Isa. 51:17) and choking on the dregs.

Each day we should thank God for restraining evil and continuing

His presence in our lives. Only the mind of John, the revelator, can comprehend the cosmic devastation, and only the heart of Jesus can absorb the personal fury that would follow if God lifted His hand from our world. How false it is to assume that a society can be organized as if God does not exist. How crucial it is for Christians to declare the presence of God in the affairs of men and nations. Jesus wrung dregs from the cup of fury which we must pray that we will never know.

Leaving Peter, James, and John behind to keep watch, Jesus goes a short distance, falls on His face and pleads like a little child before His Father for release from His compact to drink the cup of suffering. His actions, which are criticized by psychiatrists trying to prove Jesus' mental imbalance, are consistent with His emotions. To fall face down on the ground in prayer is appropriate to His anguish and to pray, *"Abba, Father"* (v. 36) as a desperate child is in line with His helplessness. No longer is Jesus the self-sufficient adult, teacher, and miracle-worker. He who teaches that we must become as a little child to inherit the Kingdom finds His words coming full cycle back to Him. At the end of His reliance on human and supernatural resources, Jesus falls back into the love of the Father, His first and last center of trust.

Jesus also falls back onto the will of God as the only way in which He can accept the intense suffering into which He has entered. Reason has no answer, experience is not sufficient, feeling is out of control, and human will lacks the strength to "tough it out."

Piece by piece, every layer of Jesus' self-reliance is peeled off until nothing remains except an unshakable desire to do the will of God at all costs, *"Not what I will, but what You will"* (v. 36). How often do we say this prayer without knowing what Jesus poured into its content? Crushed in the "press," His blood has begun to flow.

With this prayer of resolve on His lips, Jesus has to check on His disciples who are watching for Him. They have fallen asleep, perhaps victims of the intensity and exhaustion that emanated from Jesus during the past few hours. Now, however, the scene reverses itself. When Jesus enters the Garden, He experiences terror, disorientation, and depression that take Him to the edge of death. His disciples are stronger than He, so He asks them to "watch." Returning from prayer, Jesus is in full control of His mind, emotions, and will. It is the disciples who have broken down. As proof of His objectivity,

Jesus breaks the gloom of the Garden with a bit of wry humor, *"Simon, are you sleeping?"* (v. 37). Of course, he is sleeping. For Jesus to ask the question is like the person who calls on the telephone in the middle of the night and asks, "Oh, I'm sorry. Were you asleep?" If the mind is quick enough, the best answer is, "No, no problem. I had to get up and answer the telephone anyway." Peter has no answer; pledged to die for Him, he cannot stay awake for Him. Jesus digs no deeper. Asking them again to watch, He adds a word of understanding from His own immediate past experience, *"The spirit truly is ready, but the flesh is weak"* (v. 38).

Jesus returns to pray again. It takes time to work through all of the facets of life-and-death decisions. Do the sleeping disciples add another bit of unexpected reality to His suffering? Does Jesus see the torchlights of the betrayer's band moving across the valley below? Prayer is never simple, quick, and easy. The price is too high, the issues are too great, and the results are too far-reaching. When prayer reaches life-and-death levels, it is complex, prolonged, and hard.

On the third time that Jesus returns from prayer and finds His disciples in sleepy stupor, He knows that the hour of His betrayal has come. Prayer is in the past. His mind is clear, His emotions are strong, His will is set. With the dignity and valor of a king who goes to his death with honor, Jesus commands His disciples, *"Rise up, let us go. See, he who betrays Me is at hand"* (v. 42). The initiative belongs to Jesus.

ARREST AND PEACE

43 And immediately, while He was still speaking, Judas, one of the twelve, with a great multitude with swords and clubs, came from the chief priests, the scribes, and the elders.

44 And he who was betraying Him had given them a signal, saying, "Whomever I kiss, He is the One; take Him and lead Him away safely."

45 And as soon as He had come, immediately he went up to Him and said to Him, "Rabbi, Rabbi!" and kissed Him.

46 And they laid their hands on Him and took Him.

47 And one of those who stood by drew his sword and struck the servant of the high priest, and cut off his ear.

48 And Jesus answered and said to them, "Have you come out, as against a robber, with swords and clubs to take Me?

49 "I was daily with you in the temple teaching, and you did not take Me. But the Scriptures must be fulfilled."

50 And they all forsook Him and fled.

51 And a certain young man followed Him, having a linen cloth thrown around his naked body. And the young men laid hold of him,

52 and he left the linen cloth and fled from them naked.

Mark 14:43–52

All emotions are pushed to extremes in the Garden confrontation. In the middle of His command to the disciples, "Rise up, let us go . . ." (14:42), Jesus sees Judas coming and announces His own betrayal. From here, the emotions of the players in the drama called "Gethsemane" escalate to a fever pitch. The crowd comes after Jesus with *provocative intent*, Judas betrays his Lord with *depraved deceit*, Peter reacts with the slash of a sword from *foolish love*, Jesus responds to the threat of violence with *consummate peace*, and a young man, probably John Mark himself, flees the scene in *wild fear*.

The crowd—a mob with provocative intent. Judas comes to Jesus leading *"a great multitude with swords and clubs"* (v. 43). What started out as a small, well-armed squad of the Temple guard charged with the responsibility for controlling domestic disturbances among the Jews has picked up a vigilante band of brutes and hoodlums who grab the nearest weapon on the way. The stage is set for violence.

Scholars differ on the legality of the arrest. Some are quick to say that officers from the Sanhedrin carry a warrant for Jesus' arrest. If so, what is the charge? Blasphemy? Sabbath violation? Disturbing the peace? No charge is made against Jesus. His rights are not read to Him. Other students of the Law suggest that the Jews purposefully enlisted a crowd of rowdies to provoke the violence that would give them cause to send Jesus to the Romans on the charge of treason and insurrection. Whatever their intent, the situation is almost out of hand. Judas holds the key. Sensing the volatility of the situation, he takes command with the signal of a kiss, the instruction to take only Jesus, and the warning to make sure of His safe conduct to the Sanhedrin. The clarity and firmness of Judas' leadership of a crowd with provocative intent adds its own note of tragedy for his lost potential in the Kingdom of God.

Judas—a beloved disciple with unmitigated gall. Deceit has a way of compounding itself until a person is capable of perfidious actions beyond the range of their own expectations. Judas offered to betray Jesus to the Sanhedrin by locating Him at a "convenient" time and place away from the crowd. Leaving the upper room before the end of the Passover meal, he goes to the chief priests, scribes, and elders with his plan. Knowing the devotional pattern of Jesus' life, he proposes that the silence and isolation of the Garden of Gethsemane in the middle of the night be the place for the arrest.

Our pattern of life tells a lot about us. In a given week, people know when to find us worshiping in church, playing with the children, jogging along the street, lunching at a service club, shopping for groceries, sitting under a hair dryer. Would anyone know when to find us at our usual place of prayer?

The Sanhedrin concurred with Judas' plan and authorized him to lead the arresting squad to Jesus. On the way, the traitor outlines a plan that includes the signal of a kiss to identify Jesus as the person to be taken. Judas intends at all costs to avoid armed conflict which might permit Jesus to escape during the skirmish. He also wants to make sure that Jesus gets delivered safely to the Sanhedrin so that he will earn his blood money.

The kiss indicates the depth of Judas' deceit. When he informs the officers of the Sanhedrin of his plan to kiss Jesus, he uses the word *philein,* signaling a kiss of courtesy given by a disciple to a Master. But when the actual moment of betrayal comes, emotion overwhelms Judas. Summoning up all the emotions of his long relationship with Jesus, Judas greets Him like a long-lost friend whom he deeply loves. Doubling his greeting, *"Rabbi! Rabbi!"* (v. 45) as if to say, "Beloved Master!," he enfolds Jesus with a kiss that can only be given in the name of love. Mark's word is *kataphilein*—a fervent kiss reserved to show the deepest of affection. Crushed under the turning wheel of his own depravity, Judas would never have thought that he was capable of such an act when the betrayal began.

Peter—a defender with foolish love. Mark does not identify the disciple who draws his sword and cuts off the ear of the high priest's servant.

In the Gospel of John, however, we are informed that Peter is the culprit and Malchus is the victim (John 18:10). Luke takes the incident to its conclusion when he tells us that Jesus ". . . touched his ear and healed him" (Luke 22:51).

Peter is doing what he can to live up to his oath that he will die with Jesus. As usual, his impulsive love is misdirected. In this context, it is foolish. Despite Jesus' total rejection of physical violence and earthly might for advancing the Kingdom of God, Peter arms himself, reacts with rage, and endangers the mission of Jesus as well as the life of the company. A fine line runs between his act in the Garden and the woman's devotion during the dinner at Simon the leper's house. Both are motivated by impulsive love, but hers is timely and appropriate. Peter's intent meets the test of good motivation, but his timing is atrocious and his method borders on the fatal.

Jesus—an example of consummate peace. Standing in the midst of provocation, deceit and impulse, Jesus is the picture of serenity. His response to the turmoil speaks for itself. Like pouring oil over troubled waters, His first words are a question that settles the scene, *"Have you come out, as against a robber, with swords and clubs to take Me?"* (v. 48). His pride is hurt because they are treating Him as a criminal. Furthermore, He reminds them that there will be no resistance. After all, He was open to arrest every day while teaching in the Temple. Why is this necessary? He answers His own question from the perspective which He has gained again and again in His prayer of resolution. All this is a part of God's will for the fulfillment of Scripture.

A plaque on an office wall reads, "If you have peace when everyone around you is in panic, maybe you don't understand the problem." What an insight into the consummate peace of Jesus! He had peace in the midst of panic—and He alone understood the problem. This is the legacy of the Garden of Gethsemane which Jesus bequeaths to us for the time of turmoil: "Peace I leave with you, My peace I give to you; not as the world gives do I give to you. Let not your heart be troubled, neither let it be afraid" (John 14:27).

John Mark—a young man with wild fear. Only Mark includes the parenthesis about a certain young man who follows Jesus to witness the events of His arrest and escape naked with his life. No one knows for sure whether or not the young man is John Mark, the author of the Gospel. Whatever evidence we have, however, points directly to him. Acts 12:12 tells us that his mother's house served as the Jerusalem headquarters for the Apostles and, by inference, may have been the site for the last supper. Is it possible that a young man's enthusiastic devotion to Jesus prompted John Mark to fall into step behind the mob heading for Gethsemane?

His expensive linen cloth, which the young man left behind in his flight for life, also hints at the affluence which John Mark enjoyed. Who else would have known such details as the "linen cloth" and a "naked body"? John Mark is the logical choice. If so, Mark has a message even in a parenthesis. As an art lover who searches for the signature, initials, sign or number of the artist in the corner of a painting, I like the idea that John Mark put his imprimatur in the corner of his work.

In the Garden experience, Jesus learns the agony of denial, decision and deceit. The consequence is to know that He will suffer alone without the communion of the Father or the fellowship of friends. Coleridge edges up to that emptiness when he writes:

> Alone, alone,
> All, all alone;
> Alone on a wide, wide sea.[3]

Cut adrift from all divine and human supports, Jesus goes to trial all, all alone.

Trial and Confidence

53 And they led Jesus away to the high priest; and with him were assembled all the chief priests, the elders, and the scribes.

54 And Peter followed Him at a distance, right into the courtyard of the high priest. And he sat with the servants and warmed himself at the fire.

55 And the chief priests and all the council sought testimony against Jesus to put Him to death, and found none.

56 For many bore false witness against Him, but their testimonies did not agree.

57 And some rose up and bore false witness against Him, saying,

58 "We heard Him say, 'I will destroy this temple that is made with hands, and within three days I will build another made without hands.' "

59 And not even then did their testimony agree.

60 And the high priest stood up in the midst and asked Jesus, saying, "Do You answer nothing? What is it these men testify against You?"

61 But He kept silent and answered nothing. Again the high priest asked Him, saying to Him, "Are You the Christ, the Son of the Blessed?"

62 And Jesus said, "I am. And you will see the Son of Man sitting at the right hand of the Power, and coming with the clouds of heaven."

63 Then the high priest tore his clothes and said, "What further need do we have of witnesses?

64 "You have heard the blasphemy! What do you think?" And they all condemned Him to be guilty of death.

65 And some began to spit on Him, and to blindfold Him, and to beat Him, and to say to Him, "Prophesy!" And the officers struck Him with the palms of their hands.

Mark 14:53–65

An eternity ago, Jesus began the longest night of His life with the Passover meal where he announced Judas' betrayal and celebrated the symbols of His own death. The trip from the upper room out of the eastern gate and across the valley of Kedron has included the painful prediction that all His disciples will desert Him. Even though He prays otherwise, the prediction comes to pass during His agonizing hours in the Garden of Gethsemane. What He hadn't predicted also came true. Communion with God the Father will be broken if He is to be a sufficient sacrifice to bear the sins of all mankind. Betrayal follows with the repulsion of a passionate kiss and the indignity of a criminal's capture.

The fatal night holds more. Jesus' captors usher Him into the presence of the distinguished Sanhedrin council which is gathered at the home of the high priest, Caiaphas, in the middle of the Passover night to sit as a grand jury to indict Jesus. At the same time, according to Mark's record, Peter, still acting on his pledge to die with Jesus, sits in a lower chamber warming his hands at the fire of the high priest's servants.

Because the events of Jesus' trial and Peter's denial are simultaneous,

Mark introduces them at the same time, but records them in sequence. A legal mind may find technicalities which justify the proceedings of the Sanhedrin from Jesus' arrest to His conviction. For those with a more simple sense of justice, the actions of the council are without justification.

First, the arrest in the Garden had to be illegal because the hearing before the Sanhedrin is set to determine the charge against Jesus. He was arrested without charge.

Second, the Sanhedrin cannot consider the case of a capital offense on a feast day, according to its own rules. Yet, it meets during the Passover with one intention in mind, to convict Jesus of a capital offense.

Third, by the same rules, the council cannot make final judgments if it meets at night or outside its sacred chambers in the Temple. Darkness greets the members as they gather at Caiaphas' house to finalize the condemnation of Jesus.

Fourth, the condemnation of death requires the unanimous testimony of at least two witnesses. On no account can they get the witnesses, who bring trumped-up charges against Jesus, to agree. Perjury, not truth, pervades the courtroom.

Fifth, when all else fails, Caiaphas, the high priest, president of the Sanhedrin, puts aside his sacred trust as the guarantor of justice and assumes the role of prosecutor, asking leading questions of the defendant, which he himself would never permit in an ordinary trial.

Sixth, after failing to get an incriminating answer to the charge that Jesus threatened to destroy the Temple, Caiaphas resorts to the tactic of leading the witness and forcing Him either to condemn Himself with the court or discredit Himself with the people. *"Are you the Christ, the Son of the Blessed?"* (v. 61). He leaves Jesus no alternative to an incriminating answer. Caiaphas has undermined the quality of justice which he is sworn to protect.

Seventh, after Jesus confesses His claim to be the Messiah, in answer to Caiaphas' leading question, no test of the claim follows. Caiaphas leaps to the verdict of blasphemy and the council concurs with the unanimous "Aye" condemning Jesus to death.

Eighth, in direct violation of its principle calling for patience in cases of capital offense, the Sanhedrin does not wait twenty-four hours between the hearing and the sentence in Jesus' case. Exercising the rarest of exceptions which permits immediate action on the death penalty to serve as a deterrent against other crimes, the Sanhedrin arrests, arraigns, tries, convicts, and sentences Jesus within the matter of an hour or two.

Ninth, even though the spitting, beating, and mocking that the blindfolded Jesus receives at the hands of the Sanhedrin and its officers may be commensurate with the condemnation to death, no court of mercy can condone the fulfillment of Isaiah's prophecy, ". . . his visage was so marred more than any man, and his form more than the sons of men" (Isa. 52:14, KJV). At the hands of His own people, Jesus' face is beaten to a pulp.

Only as we understand the mounting evidence of gross injustice in His rigged trial before the Sanhedrin can we understand why Jesus chose to incriminate Himself in response to Caiaphas' leading question. Enough is enough. Any hope for a fair trial that Jesus might have nourished has been dashed. Justice cannot prevail when the arbiters of due process have already come to a conclusion. Whatever legal or extralegal means must be invoked, the chief priests are determined that Jesus will be condemned to die. Only one alternative remains. Jesus can die on the false charge of destroying the Temple or on the true charge that He claims to be the Messiah. He chooses to die on the self-incriminating confession that He is the Christ, the Son of the Blessed, but not without the reminder that He will come again as the Son of Man to judge those who are now judging Him.

Caiaphas jumps at the opportunity to seal his case. Without calling for a test of the claim, he tears off His clothes, screams for a verdict, and accepts a unanimous vote for Jesus' death. With just a twist in the charge of blasphemy, he knows that he can convince Pilate, the Roman prefect, that Jesus professes to be a king dedicated to the overthrow of Caesar and the Roman empire. Confidence exudes from the high priest as he pronounces the death sentence and anticipates its confirmation by Pilate the next day. In a show of triumph, he leads the officers of the Sanhedrin with the first blow to Jesus' face.

Legal systems are only as just as the integrity of the judges who make decisions. Despite constitutions and principles of law, there is always room for interpretations which are influenced by the political persuasion of the judges and the social pressure of the times. Sandra Day O'Connor, the first woman justice of the United States Supreme Court, withstood public pressure to declare her position on such a controversial issue as abortion, stating only that she would have to judge the merits of each case according to the Constitution. She took a noble stand for justice, quite in contrast with Caiaphas, who violated the tenets of his oath and the principles of his office in order to serve his own perverted purpose. Let the lesson be fixed in our minds. Whenever the standards of justice and mercy are cast aside for personal gain, the Son of Man will be the victim and the judge.

Denial and Repentance

66 And as Peter was below in the courtyard, one of the servant girls of the high priest came.

67 And when she saw Peter warming himself, she looked at him and said, "You also were with Jesus of Nazareth."

68 But he denied it, saying, "I neither know nor understand what you are saying." And he went out on the porch, and a rooster crowed.

69 And the servant girl saw him again, and began to say to those who stood by, "This is one of them."

70 But he denied it again. And a little later, those who stood by said to Peter again, "Surely you are one of them; for you are a Galilean, and your speech shows it."

71 But he began to curse and swear, "I do not know this Man of whom you speak!"

72 And a second time the rooster crowed. And Peter called to mind the word that Jesus said to him, "Before the rooster crows twice, you will deny Me three times." And when he thought about it, he wept.

Mark 14:66–72

Destiny stalks through Caiaphas' house on the night that the Sanhedrin meets in an upper room to condemn Jesus to death. In a lower courtroom, Peter joins the circle of Caiaphas' servants around a warming fire while waiting for the verdict. Before he hears what happens to Jesus, another fateful prediction comes true. Peter denies his Lord three times.

Peter is hard to condemn and impossible to dislike. He fits into the category of the bold, blithe and irrepressible people who are always on the verge of trouble. As children, they balance on the parapets of a bridge; as adults, they drill for oil and risk everything they have on an idea that usually makes them millionaires. They scare us, but we admire them. Like Peter, they are stuff out of which heroism is born—and sometimes cowardice is made.

Denial in part. Peter's denial is not an isolated event; it has a past, rooted in Peter's personality. When Peter hears Jesus predict the flight and denial of all the disciples before the night passes, extreme and contradictory motives of love and arrogance burst to the surface in protest. *". . . Even if all are made to stumble, yet I will not be"* (14:29). To dispel his arrogance, Jesus gives Peter the details of his denial. Thinking that he knows himself better than his Master, Peter literally explodes in a declaration of love, *". . . If I have to die with You, I will not deny You! . . ."* (14:31). Within minutes, the same love lies exhausted in drowsy stupor—a partial denial of Jesus, who has only asked that he stay awake. No more than an hour or two later, Judas and his gang appear to arrest Jesus. Wide awake now, Peter sees his chance to redeem his pledge. Reacting in the rage of blind love, he draws a concealed sword and slashes at Malchus' head, only to get an ear. With the swing of the sword, Peter repudiates everything that Jesus has taught him about the spirit of love, except total commitment. Then, after forsaking Jesus and fleeing with the others, Peter returns and follows the arresting party back to Caiaphas' house. Distance is its own form of denial. Peter has weakened, but he has not broken. In his mind, at least, the pledge to die with Jesus is still intact.

A denial in full. While Peter is warming his hands at the fire of Caiaphas' servants, a maid spots him as a stranger in their group. Studying his face in the flickering flame, she recognizes him as a person whom she has seen with Jesus. Whether he knows it or not, Peter has become a public figure identified as a disciple of Jesus Christ. From now on, every moment, every action, every word will be identified with Christ and claimed as public property.

Three unmistakable clues tip Peter's identity to the maid and other servants. The same clues speak volumes about any of us. *First,* we are recognized by *the leader whom we follow.* Prominent people have an aura which reflects in their followers. Aides to congressmen, assistants to presidents, consorts to royalty, and attachés to diplomats might never be recognized in their own right, but gain their identity through their leader. Is it possible that the servant girl is trying to pay Peter a compliment by identifying him as someone who had been with

Jesus? If so, his denial comes from shame as well as from fear. *Second,* we are recognized by the *group with whom we associate.* Consciously or unconsciously, we take on the traits, demeanor, dress, and gestures of the people who surround us in our homes, jobs, schools, and churches. As a people watcher at hotels where professional meetings are being held, I can usually distinguish the doctors from lawyers, the professors from the preachers, and the secretaries from the salesmen. Something about their dress and demeanor as they gather in the lobby sorts them out. What is it about Peter's dress and demeanor that causes the servant girl to exclaim, *"This is one of them"* (v. 69)? *Third,* we are recognized by *the language we speak.* Irony of ironies, Peter's own words of denial betray him, leaving no shadow of doubt about his identity with Jesus. Earlier, in the Temple, chief priests, scribes, Pharisees, Sadducees, and Herodians tried to trap Jesus in His own words. They failed. Peter trips, however, over his Galilean accent. A professor friend of mine prides himself on his ability to recognize the section of the country from which a person comes by his or her accent. In test after test, he has not failed yet. We should not be surprised, then, when Peter's speech betrays his identity as a disciple to a curious servant girl. It is to Peter's credit that he has taken on the identity, demeanor and speech of Jesus; it is to his shame that he denies his Lord with an oath.

Repentance in perspective. Little needs to be added to Mark's description of Peter's response to the second crowing of the cock, *"And when he thought about it, he wept"* (v. 72). Authenticity rings through these words, assuring us that Peter indeed is the narrator of Mark's Gospel. Who else can know that he "thought" about Jesus' prediction? Tears must have filled his eyes when he confesses his denial to Mark all over again.

Repentance is both intellectual and emotional. Peter has a lifetime of mastering any situation with an impulsive show of emotion. A vehement pledge, a stuporous sleep, a violent act, a cursing oath— these are the characteristics of the man. Like the prodigal son in the pig pen, he needs cold, hard facts to bring him to his senses. Perhaps for the first time, Peter reasons rather than reacts. He sees his arrogance, his cowardice, his sin against the perspective of truth which he has never before faced. Guilt and shame burst through the charade of his toughness, and he weeps—not with the hysteria of another impulsive action, but with the remorseful tears of an awakened mind and a broken heart. Together, they will lead to repentance.

For the Roman Christians to whom Mark writes, Peter's denial is a warning and a promise. For those to whom identity with Christ and His church is to invite death, denial is a daily temptation. Some rely on their pledge of love to hold them in their faith. Peter's experience is a warning that such a pledge, however strong the person and sincere the heart, will not remove the cowardice that is within them. For those who have fallen, Peter's willingness to confess his sin and repent is an encouraging promise. All is not lost because Jesus will not give up on Peter, on them, or on us.

SENTENCING AND SILENCE

1 And right away, in the morning, the chief priests held a consultation with the elders and scribes and the whole council, and bound Jesus, led Him away, and delivered Him to Pilate.

2 And Pilate asked Him, "Are You the King of the Jews?" And He answered and said to him, "It is as you say."

3 And the chief priests accused Him of many things, but He answered nothing.

4 And Pilate asked Him again, saying, "Do You answer nothing? See how many things they testify against You!"

5 But Jesus still answered nothing, so that Pilate marveled.

6 Now at the feast he was accustomed to releasing one prisoner to them, whomever they requested.

7 And there was one named Barabbas, who was chained with his fellow insurrectionists, who had committed murder in the insurrection.

8 And the multitude, crying aloud, began to ask him to do just as he had always done for them.

9 But Pilate answered them, saying, "Do you want me to release to you the King of the Jews?"

10 For he knew that the chief priests had delivered Him because of envy.

11 But the chief priests stirred up the multitude, so that he should rather release Barabbas to them.

12 And Pilate answered and said to them again, "What then do you want me to do with Him whom you call the King of the Jews?"

13 And they cried out again, "Crucify Him!"

14 Then Pilate said to them, "Why, what evil has He done?" And they cried out more exceedingly, "Crucify Him!"

15 Then Pilate, wanting to gratify the crowd, released Barabbas to them; and he delivered Jesus, after he had scourged Him, to be crucified.

16 And the soldiers led Him away into the hall called Praetorium, and they called together the whole band.

17 And they clothed Him with purple; and they twisted a crown of thorns, put it on His head,

18 and began to salute Him, "Hail, King of the Jews!"

19 And they struck Him on the head with a reed and spat on Him; and bowing the knee, they worshiped Him.

20 And when they had mocked Him, they took the purple off Him, put His own clothes on Him, and led Him out to crucify Him.

Mark 15:1–20

A relentless march toward death has begun for Jesus. He goes willingly, but His steps are speeded by the motives of men. Players in the Roman phase of Jesus' trial include the chief priests of the Jewish Sanhedrin, Pontius Pilate, prefect of the Roman province of Judea, the crowd of Barabbas' defenders, and the Roman soldiers who make sport of their doomed victim. Mark keeps the facts of the Roman proceedings sketchy, in comparison with the accounts of Luke and John. His intention is the difference. Writing to Roman Christians, Mark wants to convey to them Jesus' response in suffering under the *studied malice* of the chief priests, the *political expediency* of Pilate, the *incited fury* of the crowd, and the *debased humor* of the soldiers.

Studied malice—the chief priests' motive. Of all the indignities that Jesus suffers, the cold and calculated hate of the chief priests must have been the most difficult to bear. As soon as the dawn breaks, they call the Sanhedrin back together in order to legitimize the legal travesty of the night hours. According to their own code, council decisions made at night are invalid. Also, no sentence of capital punishment can be pronounced until a grace period of twenty-four hours separates the verdict from the sentence, in the event that new evidence might be presented.

Malice has its own code. In order to transfer Jesus' sentence of death to Roman authorities and be assured of swift execution, the chief priests have to get their case to Pilate during his early morning working hours. Otherwise, they will have Jesus on their hands for another day because Roman prefects hold office only during the hours before the sun turns the city into an oven. Later on, Pilate will be unavailable, indulging his leisure.

Quickly, then, the chief priests rework their charge of blasphemy against Jesus in order to make it fit a crime for capital punishment according to Roman law. How devious is the malicious mind. In answer to Caiaphas' leading question, *"Are you the Christ, the Son of the Blessed?,"* Jesus said, *"I am"* (14:61–62). "Christ" is synonymous with "Messiah" and, in the Jewish mind, equal to the "King of the Jews." With just another slight twist, then, "King of the Jews" can be interpreted as a challenge to Roman power and Caesar's sovereignty. Devilish triumph must have danced in the eyes of the chief priests as they presented their proposal to the assembled Sanhedrin. By His own confession, *"I am,"* Jesus is charged with high treason against Rome, a charge that means immediate execution if confirmed by Pilate.

Political expediency—Pilate's motive. During the Passover season when tempers run high, Pilate takes personal command of the Roman troops by moving temporarily to Jerusalem. Tradition has it that he established his headquarters in either Herod's Palace or the Tower of Antonia. To one of these places, the chief priests bring Jesus and formally charge Him with treason because of His own confession to be the "King of the Jews."

Roman procedure requires that Pilate conduct his own hearing with the defendant. When he asks Jesus directly, "Are You the King of the Jews?", he gets the answer, *"It is as you say"* (v. 2). Does Jesus confirm His guilt or repeat Pilate's question? His answer will never condemn Him in a court of law. The chief priests, then, accuse Him *"of many things"* (v. 3), some of which are specified in Luke 23:2: ". . . We found this fellow perverting the nation, and forbidding to pay taxes to Caesar, saying that He Himself is Christ, a King."

Pilate has no use for Jews. His reputation for brutality includes slaughtering Galileans and mixing the blood with their sacrifices (Luke

13:1). Yet, in the circumstances of Jesus' hearing, he carefully follows the procedure of asking the defendant if He has anything to say for Himself. As He has done before, Jesus refuses to answer false charges. Pilate senses that he is dealing with a trumped-up charge, but he has never known a defendant who refuses to respond when the perjured testimony is so obvious. At this point, Pilate runs into a conflict between his responsibility for legal justice and his penchant for political expediency. No longer can he be neutral or innocent.

Political expediency wins out. In a false show of generosity, he decides to shift the verdict to the masses, assuming that Jesus' innocence will be chosen over the proven guilt of the insurrectionist and murderer, Barabbas. Sarcasm fills his voice, *"Do you want me to release to you the King of the Jews?"* (v. 9). He has no doubt that the chief priests' charge stems from their envy, not Jesus' treason.

Incited fury—the crowd's motive. A leader makes a fatal error when he turns his authority for decision-making over to the masses. He may default on his authority, but he can never escape his responsibility.

Crowds are unreliable decision-makers because they are so easily manipulated. Again, with studied malice, the chief priests move through the masses, inciting them to fury. Mark's words, *"stirred up"* (v. 11), derive from the same root as "earthquake." What did the chief priests say to produce an eruption that buried reason, justice and mercy in the white heat of mass hysteria? For one thing, the crowd is already predisposed to Barabbas. Many sermons have been preached about the fickle crowd that shouted, "Hosanna!" during the Triumphal Entry and "Crucify Him!" five days later. Most likely, we are dealing with two different crowds. One is the band of people who joined with Jesus on His pilgrimage to Jerusalem; the other is the mass of militants who idolized the rebellious and murderous Zealot, Barabbas. Molten rage boils just beneath the surface of their milling and muttering movement. All the chief priests have to do is put out the word that Jesus has betrayed the nationalistic hopes of the Jews and mass hysteria takes over. No matter that Pilate gives them a choice or calls for proof of His guilt, the crowd stamps and screams, "Crucify Him!" Pilate has lost control. Unless he frees Barabbas and crucifies Jesus, not even the disciplined Roman guard can quell the riot that will follow.

Mass hysteria is a frightening phenomenon that paralyzes traditional systems of control in society. Orson Welles' radio broadcast, "The War of the Worlds," is used as the classic case of teaching sociology students about mass hysteria. On a peaceful evening in the 1930s, Welles introduced his fictional drama with an official-sounding announcement that Martians had invaded earth. News of the emergency alert produced an eruption of hysteria that the nation has never known before or since. The line between mass communications and mass hysteria is very thin, particularly when emotions of anger, hostility, and fear are seething just beneath the surface.

Equal guilt is placed upon the chief priests who manipulated the masses for their own malicious intent and upon Pilate who forfeited his responsibility for justice to the instability of public opinion.

Debased humor—the soldier's motive. Once Pilate succumbs to political expediency, his Roman instincts take over. Human life means little and a Jewish life means nothing. With a casual turn of the thumb, he condemns Jesus to scourging, followed by crucifixion. As he has forfeited his decision for justice to a frenzied crowd, he passes on the responsibility for mercy to bored and brutal Roman soldiers.

Herod's palace is a planned stop for walking tours from the reputed site of Jesus' trial along the Via Dolorosa and up to the Church of the Holy Sepulchre. On the stone floor in the Praetorium Hall of Herod's Palace is an etched figure of a scorpion with a crown on its head. The guide informs visitors that Roman soldiers played a game that might be called "King for a Day" with prisoners who were condemned to die by crucifixion. The crown symbolizes the ghoulish motive of the Roman soldiers who made sport of life and the scorpion signifies crucifixion, the death with a thousand stings. Whether concocted or true, the sight of the crowned scorpion is never forgotten. Debased humor accompanies the atrocities of depraved humanity. Hitler, for instance, had the reputation for being a master teller of Jewish jokes. To laugh at brutality and make sport of death is degradation unmatched. As the butt of Roman burlesque, Jesus drank with silent dignity the hemlock of human nature.

Roman Christians who were being ground under Nero's heel could see themselves in the suffering of Jesus. The same vicious motives of studied malice, political expediency, incited fury, and debased humor pushed them toward the arena and the stake. Mark also wants his readers to feel Jesus' response. His silence speaks for itself. With a peace that causes Pilate to marvel and a dignity that cannot be broken by the mockery of the soldiers, Jesus is the suffering servant who sets the example and fulfills the prophecy, "He shall not cry, nor lift up, nor cause his voice to be heard in the street" (Isa. 42:2, KJV).

EXECUTION AND SUBSTITUTION

21 And they compelled a certain man, Simon a Cyrenian, the father of Alexander and Rufus, as he was coming out of the country and passing by, to bear His cross.

22 And they brought Him to the place *Golgotha,* which is translated, the Place of a Skull.

23 And they gave Him wine mingled with myrrh to drink, but He did not take it.

24 And when they crucified Him, they divided His garments, casting lots for them to determine what every man should take.

25 And it was the third hour, and they crucified Him.

26 And the inscription of His accusation was written above:

THE KING OF THE JEWS.

27 And with Him they crucified two robbers, one on His right and the other on His left.

28 And the Scripture was fulfilled which says, *"And He was numbered with the transgressors."*

29 And those who passed by blasphemed Him, wagging their heads and saying, "Aha! You who destroy the temple and build it in three days,

30 "save Yourself, and come down from the cross!"

31 Likewise the chief priests also, together with the scribes, mocked and said among themselves, "He saved others; Himself He cannot save.

32 "Let the Christ, the King of Israel, descend now from the cross, that we may see and believe." And those who were crucified with Him reviled Him.

Mark 15:21–32

Mark wastes neither time nor words in describing persons, places and events leading up to the crucifixion after the soldiers have scourged and mocked Him. Christians in Rome do not need to know the details. Crosses upon which criminals hung until death were a common sight for Roman citizens. Caesar believed that the public show of slow, agonizing death served as an effective deterrent against crime. Mark, therefore, casts the Roman soldiers charged with the task of execution into the nameless and faceless category, "they." In rapid succession, "they"

—*compelled* a certain man . . . to bear His cross
—*brought* Him to the place Golgotha
—*gave* Him wine mingled with myrrh
—*divided* His garments, casting lots
—*crucified* Him
—*crucified* two robbers (with Him)

Only at the beginning (v. 21) and the end (v. 28) of these running events does Mark stop for notation.

Personal notations. As Jesus staggers along the tortuous and humiliating path of the Via Dolorosa, His beaten body gives way under the weight of His cross, *"And they compelled . . . Simon a Cyrenian, the father of Alexander and Rufus . . . to bear His cross"* (v. 21). Mark, we have learned, does not add details without a purpose. Speculation about the identity of Simon the Cyrenian as a black man, a pilgrim attending the Passover, or a wealthy Cyrenian Jew living in Jerusalem, continues until the present day. Mark's interest, however, is the fact that Simon is the father of Alexander and Rufus, names which must have been known in Rome. Paul's later letter to the Romans concludes with greetings to ". . . Rufus chosen in the Lord, and his mother and mine" (Rom. 16:13). Is this the same Rufus who is the son of Simon the Cyrenian? The fact cannot be substantiated except by circumstantial evidence. Mark is saying to the Roman Christians, "You have a personal line of relationship with the sufferings of Jesus through someone who was there, someone you know." He may also be saying that their inheritance in suffering follows the line through Simon, who helped Jesus bear His cross. One thing is sure. When the Roman Christians read Mark's Gospel, they find encouragement to bear and to share the weight of the cross which they are compelled to carry.

At the other end of the sequence of events that leads to the cross, Mark stops to note that Jesus' two companions in crucifixion were "robbers" or, more likely, "terrorists." Theft itself did not qualify as a capital offense in Roman law. If, in combination with insurrection, a person committed a crime of theft or violence, crucifixion could be the penalty. To explain this moment of disgrace, Mark informs us that the Scripture is fulfilled, ". . . and He was numbered with the transgressors . . ." (Isa. 53:12, KJV). Although the Roman Christians would not have the same interest in prophetic fulfillment as Jewish Christians, Mark uses this example to remind them that all of the sufferings of Jesus are forecast in Scripture. When "they" offer Jesus wine mingled with myrrh as a sedative for suffering, Mark might have inserted Psalm 69:21 (KJV), "They gave me also gall for my meat; and in my thirst they gave me vinegar to drink." Or after reporting the soldiers dividing Jesus' garments and casting lots for them, he might have quoted Psalm 22:18 (KJV), "They part my garments among them, and cast lots upon my vesture." Although the nameless and faceless soldiers do not know it, "they" are acting on the pivot point of human history. All prophetic revelation of the Scriptures comes into focus and fulfillment on the cross of Christ.

Prophetic taunts. Prophecy is not only fulfilled in Mark's account of the Crucifixion, it is advanced. The author returns to a detailed report of the blasphemy and the mockery thrown at Jesus as He hangs on the cross. Although the bitter invectives from passersby, chief priests and scribes must have pained Him more than the nails through His hands and feet, Jesus hears His future predicted and His purpose reinforced in the jibes.

Passersby revile Him with blasphemous words, taunt Him with wagging heads, and jeer at Him with a devilish "Aha!" Like the Roman soldiers in the parody of Jesus as King, these persons try to make Him the laughingstock of the world. Unlike the Roman soldiers, they are not spiritually ignorant and insensitive. Remembering His prediction about the destruction of the Temple and its rebuilding in three days, they jab at His complete helplessness as He hangs on the cross. If He has the miraculous power to destroy and rebuild the Temple, surely He has the power to save Himself and come down from the cross. Aha! Their blasphemy turns against them. Unwittingly, they become prophets of the Resurrection. Through them, Jesus hears His words come back to Him in the promise of His Father. The temple of His body will be destroyed, but by the power of God, in three days it will be raised in the newness of life. What starts out as ridicule turns into reinforcement. If anything, Jesus feels a wave of peace pass over His being and, for just a moment, override the pain.

Any relief that Jesus feels from the jibes of those who passed by

leaves quickly when He hears the familiar voices of the chief priests
and scribes mocking Him. They have their wish. Why add to His
misery? Evil has an insatiable appetite. Once the chief priests choose
to become part of the conspiracy against Jesus, they continue on
their self-degrading course into treachery, perjury, and murder. Now,
in their mockery, their religious sophistication makes them especially
vicious. The debased humor of the Roman soldiers who made a burlesque of Jesus as King is nothing compared to the chief priests'
and scribes' parody of His Lordship. First, they praise Him for saving
others, but stab Him because He lacks the power to save Himself.
Next, they honor Him as the Christ, the King of Israel, but call for
Him to break free from the nails, come down from the cross, and
stand whole before them. In final mockery, they promise to believe
in Him if He proves His miraculous power on His own behalf.

It is a wonder that the heavens did not break open at that moment
with a show of force that would make the chief priests and scribes
eat sand. Jesus certainly had to be humanly tempted to pray that
God would make the moment of His coming with power and glory
an immediate event. Instead, He remembers the cup from which He
must drink in order to be the ransom for the sins of many. If He
saves Himself, others He cannot save. In their blindness, the chief
priests and scribes become prophets of redemption. In their mockery,
"He saved others; Himself he cannot save" (v. 31), Jesus hears His purpose
come back to Him, "For even the Son of Man did not come to be
served, but to serve, and to give His life a ransom for many" (10:45).
With equal strength, He hears God speak through the co-opted prophets of the Sanhedrin, ". . . You are My beloved Son, in whom I
am well-pleased" (1:11). To remain on the cross and bear the sins
of many is to fulfill God's purpose for His life, ". . . that whoever
believes in Him should not perish, but have eternal life" (John 3:16).
They are too deaf to hear it, but when the chief priests and scribes
say, *"that we may see and believe"* (v. 32), they speak not for themselves,
but for all humankind.

Robbers on each side of Jesus pick up the taunts of His enemies.
Again, the chief priests will be responsible for inciting them to blasphemy just as they are responsible for stirring up the crowd to crucify
Jesus. Nothing the robbers say is new and Jesus probably includes
them among those for whom He asks forgiveness because they do
not know what they are doing. Condemnation passes to the leadership
of the chief priests and scribes. Because their mockery may have

kept one of the robbers from the Kingdom of God, it would have been better for them never to have been born.

DEATH AND FULFILLMENT

33 And when the sixth hour had come, there was darkness over the whole land until the ninth hour.

34 And at the ninth hour Jesus cried out with a loud voice, saying, *"Eloi, Eloi, lama sabachthani?"* which is translated, *"My God, My God, why have You forsaken Me?"*

35 And some of those who stood by, when they heard it, said, "Look, He is calling for Elijah!"

36 And someone ran and filled a sponge full of sour wine, put it on a reed, and offered it to Him to drink, saying, "Let Him alone; let us see if Elijah will come to take Him down."

37 And Jesus cried out with a loud voice, and breathed His last.

38 And the curtain of the temple was torn in two from top to bottom.

39 And when the centurion, who stood opposite Him, saw that He cried out like this and breathed His last, he said, "Truly this Man was the Son of God!"

40 There were also women looking on from afar, among whom were Mary Magdalene, Mary the mother of James the Less and of Joses, and Salome,

41 who also followed Him and ministered to Him when He was in Galilee; and many other women who came up with Him to Jerusalem.

Mark 15:33–41

Other writers of the Synoptic Gospels emphasize the last words of Jesus on the cross. Mark chooses to center upon four distinctive signs that sum up the purpose of Jesus' death.

The eschatological sign. Three hours of unnatural darkness covers the land from the sixth hour of the day until the ninth hour when Jesus dies. Amos prophesied hours of blackness during these final, fatal hours: "And it shall come to pass in that day, saith the Lord God, that I will cause the sun to go down at noon, and I will darken the earth in the clear day" (Amos 8:9, KJV).

Darkness is the sign for God's judgment throughout the Scriptures. The plague of darkness in Egypt served as the final warning for Pharaoh before God sent the death angel to slay the firstborn of every household (Exod. 10:21–23). Jesus Himself announced that the coming of the Son of Man in judgment will be signaled by the sun being darkened, the moon not giving its light, and the stars of heaven falling (13:24–25). Thus, three hours of darkness preceding Jesus' death aligns the Crucifixion with the Passover and the Second Coming as a sign of God's judgment preceding His redemption.

The Christological sign. For Jesus, the three hours of darkness mean hell on earth. What He had foreseen in the Garden becomes reality. The shock of learning that He will be made sin and separated from His Father almost took His life at Gethsemane. Now, on Golgotha, He experiences what He had foreseen. For three hours, sin in its universal and unadulterated form penetrates His soul until finally He becomes sin itself. At that moment, God's nature demands justice. He has to break the lines of unfettered communion, leaving Jesus all alone as the Man of Sinners under the Judgment of God. No other suffering can break Jesus' silence, but to be separated from His Father brings death imminent and provokes the loud cry, *"My God, My God, why have You forsaken Me?"* (v. 34).

Jesus has gone beyond the range of our knowledge and our experience. Rationally, it is impossible for us to reconcile the questions, "Did God forsake Jesus?" or "Did Jesus' faith fail?" Experientially, we who are sinners cannot understand what it means for Jesus, who knew no sin, to be made sin on our behalf. Nor can we who have so often broken communion with God feel the trauma of separation that is not of Jesus' choosing. Only our Christology can rescue us. Jesus is at once fully God and fully man, free from sin and sin itself, one with the Father and all alone. His Person resolves our rational paradox and His purpose answers our experiential dilemma. Unless Jesus is made sin which separates Him from communion with His Father, there is no hope for our justification.

Something in the nature of Jesus' cry tells the waiting crowd that the end is near. Mistaking the pain-filled sound of *"Eloi, Eloi"* for the name of Elijah, some of the bystanders think that they hear Him calling for help. Someone else runs to fill a sponge with sour wine, puts it on the end of a reed, and stretches it up to offer Jesus a drink. Cruel curiosity, not compassion, motivates the move. Liquid in Jesus' dehydrated body will keep Him alive a while longer, giving them a chance to *"see if Elijah will come to take Him down"* (v. 36).

It is too late. With another great cry, Jesus expires—a sign of a violent death, but sudden for a crucifixion. The insight into separation from His Father, which almost killed Him in the Garden, speeds His death on the cross. But then again, we must ask whether His quickened death is a matter of the Father's mercy. Just a glimpse of hell is all that is necessary to know its full impact. Therefore, even though God the Father has to break communion with His Son because of sin, He does not have to forsake His mercy. Critics of Mark say that he leaves Jesus to die with the words of desolation on His lips. It is true that Mark does not add the words, "It is finished" or "Into Thy hands I commend My Spirit" which we read in the other Synoptic Gospels, but he has made his point. For Roman Christians who face death momentarily, a prayer for God's mercy is still appropriate.

The revelational sign. Simultaneously with Jesus' last breath, the curtain of the Temple is *"torn in two from top to bottom"* (v. 38). Scholars take sides on the question of whether the split curtain hung in the outer chamber of the Temple which preserved the area of the priests or the inner chamber of the Temple which guarded the Holy of Holies. Consensus favors the inner curtain even though it is not in public view. Inner or outer curtain, public or private view, the revelational sign is most important. At its roots, revelation means "unveiling." With the death of Christ, then, the tearing of the Temple curtain signifies the unlocking of the mystery, which as Paul wrote, ". . . has been hidden from ages and from generations, but now has been revealed to His saints" (Col. 1:26). The mystery is out: Jesus is the final revelation and the Holy of Holies is open to all people, including the Gentiles.

The redemptive sign. Jesus' last breath also brings the confession from the centurion's lips, *"Truly this Man was the Son of God!"* (v. 39). If anyone can make a judgment about the character of Jesus, the Roman centurion can. Most likely, he has been in charge of the prisoner since the chief priests turned Him over to Roman authorities. He has seen Jesus falsely accused by the chief priests, unfairly condemned by the frenzied mob, brutally scourged just short of death, grotesquely mocked by his own troops, utterly humiliated on the forced march along the Via Dolorosa, nailed to the cross, mocked by passersby, and crucified as a common criminal. Nothing is new in this crucifixion except the Man on the cross. By His demeanor in death, Jesus witnesses to His righteousness, even to a case-hardened officer of the Roman guard who confesses that his victim is the Son of God.

Mark has closed the second loop in his purpose to write, "The beginning of the gospel of Jesus Christ, the Son of God" (1:1). After presenting the case for Jesus as the ministering Servant, Peter's confession, "You are the Christ" (8:29), brings the first half of the Gospel to a conclusion. From then on, everything that Mark writes is pointed toward the Passion of Jesus, the Suffering Savior. However theologically inadequate the Roman centurion's confession may be, he closes the Passion narrative with the evidence that Jesus has proved Himself to be the Son of God to a pagan. For Roman Christians, his confession has a personal and prophetic ring to it. Personally, they are encouraged that their witness in suffering will not be in vain. Roman soldiers can believe. Prophetically, the centurion's confession attests to the redemption of Gentiles as well as Jews.

From a lawyer's standpoint, Mark might rest his case. On the basis of the evidence, Peter has confessed that Jesus is the Christ and the Roman centurion has acclaimed Him as the Son of God. One conclusive truth is missing. Mark declares in his original purpose that he will present the case for "the beginning of the gospel of Jesus Christ, the Son of God." With the faithful women who followed and ministered to Jesus from Galilee to Golgotha, we await the final evidence that the Gospel is the Good News.

BURIAL AND EXPECTATION

42 And now when evening had come, because it was the Preparation Day, that is, the day before the Sabbath,

43 Joseph of Arimathea, a prominent council member, who himself was waiting for the kingdom of God, coming and taking courage, went in to Pilate and asked for the body of Jesus.

44 And Pilate marveled that He was already dead; and calling the centurion to him, he asked him if He had been dead for some time.

318

45 And when he found out from the centurion, he
granted the body to Joseph.

46 And he bought fine linen, took Him down, and
wrapped Him in the linen. And he laid Him in a tomb
which had been hewn out of the rock, and rolled a
stone against the door of the tomb.

47 And Mary Magdalene and Mary the mother of
Joses observed where He was laid.

Mark 15:42–47

Humiliation for Jesus does not stop at death. Crucified as a criminal
for high treason, the Romans prefer to let His body rot on the cross
as food for vultures or drop to the ground to be torn apart by scavenging dogs. If the family of the criminal had the courage to claim the
body for burial, Roman authorities would usually grant the request
just to rid themselves of the nuisance. There was one exception. In
cases of death for high treason, only the prefect of the province could
approve the petition. Unless Pilate granted permission to remove the
body of Jesus, His humiliation would continue.

Jewish Law further complicated the issue. According to Deuteronomy 21:23: "His body shall not remain all night upon the tree, but
thou shalt in any wise bury him that day; (for he that is hanged is
accursed of God;) that thy land be not defiled . . ." (KJV).

In obedience to this commandment, Jews took it upon themselves
to petition for crucified bodies so that they could take them down
and bury them before darkness on the day of death. Under no circumstances could a body remain hanging on a tree over the Sabbath
day. Criminals presented a special problem. If no one claimed them,
they were consigned to a common grave in what we now call the
"Potter's Field."

Time creates a crisis over Jesus' body. Dying at the ninth hour
on Preparation Day, He must be buried by the twelfth hour before
darkness falls and the Sabbath begins. Where is Jesus' family? His
mother Mary and his aunt Mary, wife of Clopas, were present at
the cross (John 19:25). Where are the disciples? Even though they
had all forsaken Him and fled, John admits that he stood by the
cross. At least a partial answer to these questions is implied in Jesus'
commitment of His mother to John's care. Her grief and helplessness
went deeper than His own pain. Jesus made sure that His mother
had the continued strength of a loving son after His death. The re-

sponsibility for burial then shifts to John, but he is a fugitive cowering under fear and probably disguised as he stands by the cross. A criminal's unmarked grave appears to be the final humiliation for Jesus.

God is full of surprises. Out of anonymity steps Joseph of Arimathea to petition Pilate for Jesus' body in order to bury Him before sundown and honor Him by commitment to a newly hewn tomb. Joseph of Arimathea is a man of destiny. As a *"prominent council member"* (v. 43) of the Sanhedrin, he refused to be a part of the conspiracy and the charge that led to Jesus' death (Luke 23:51). Matthew adds the fact that Joseph is a "rich man" and "a disciple of Jesus" (Matt. 27:57). Regrettably, however, he kept his discipleship secret for fear of the Jews (John 19:38).

Joseph of Arimathea is a prototype of the "closet Christian." In a personal survey of the leadership of a large city, I found a substantial core of prominent persons who professed Christ if pressed for an answer. Publicly, however, their reputation for integrity and participation in community service constituted the limit of their Christian witness. At a luncheon of these leaders, one squinted across the table at a person who served as a member of his board of directors and exclaimed, "I had no idea that you are a Christian." After the luncheon, I concluded that the city could be won for Christ if we could only get its leaders "out of the closet."

Two qualities of Joseph of Arimathea brought him out. One is his *spirit of expectation* as a person *"waiting for the kingdom of God"* (v. 43). The other is his *show of courage* to put aside his fear, and go directly to Pilate and ask for Jesus' body. He risks everything with his petition. Members of the Sanhedrin will probably expel him. Pilate might well reject him or find reason to take out his spite on the Sanhedrin by including Joseph in the charge of treason. Certainly, the crowds will mix a special potion of scorn at the sight of a wealthy and powerful Jew taking down the body of Jesus and carrying it to burial. But his greatest risk will be spiritual uncleanness on the Sabbath after touching the dead body. Do not condemn Joseph for a belated act of open commitment. When he steps into Pilate's presence, his power, wealth, reputation, and salvation are on the line. Joseph has only his expectation for the coming of the Kingdom of God to hold him, but he is willing to take the risk.

Imagine the faith that is required to believe that a dead body is the key to eternal life. Hope, not despair, makes Joseph bold to petition Pilate, arrange a burial of honor, and provide a newly hewn tomb fit for a King. By action rather than words, Joseph of Arimathea joins the Roman centurion in the confession that Jesus is truly the Son of God. Through Him, God keeps alive the expectation of life, even in the presence of death. For Roman Christians, Joseph is proof that death does not still their witness, but speeds it to the highest councils of the land. For every one who dies, many who are moving toward the Kingdom of God will come forward to carry the witness.

NOTES

1. Ernest W. Shurtleff, "Lead On, O King Eternal," in *Hymns of the Living Faith* (Winona Lake, IN: Light and Life Press, 1951), p. 358.

2. John Greenleaf Whittier, "Maude Muller," in *Bartlett's Familiar Quotations*, p. 513, #14.

3. Samuel Taylor Coleridge, in *Bartlett's Familiar Quotations*, p. 434, #26.

CHAPTER TWENTY

Celebrating His Triumph

Mark 16:1–20

THE RESURRECTION VERIFIED

1 And when the Sabbath was past, Mary Magdalene, Mary the mother of James, and Salome bought spices that they might come and anoint Him.

2 And very early in the morning, on the first day of the week, they came to the tomb when the sun had risen.

3 And they said among themselves, "Who will roll away the stone from the door of the tomb for us?"

4 And when they looked up, they saw that the stone had been rolled away—for it was very large.

5 And entering the tomb, they saw a young man clothed in a long white robe sitting on the right side; and they were alarmed.

6 And he said to them, "Do not be alarmed. You seek Jesus of Nazareth, who was crucified. He is risen! He is not here! See the place where they laid Him.

7 "But go your way, tell His disciples—and Peter—that He is going before you into Galilee; there you will see Him as He said to you."

8 And they went out quickly and fled from the tomb, for they trembled and were amazed. And they said nothing to anyone, for they were afraid.

Mark 16:1–8

All other evidence that Mark has marshaled to substantiate his claim that Jesus is the Christ, the Son of God, falls short of being the Good News without the conclusive fact of the Resurrection. Therefore, he reports the event through the eyes of the women, Mary Magdalene, Mary the mother of James, and Salome, who have also been firsthand witnesses of Jesus' crucifixion and burial. Although the word of women lacks credibility among the Jews, the corroboration of the three cannot be disclaimed, particularly when they come to the tomb with doubt and leave with fear, telling no one what they have seen.

The physical facts. Mary Magdalene, Mary the mother of James, and Salome are doubters and worriers. After the Sabbath day has passed, they take the responsibility to minister to Jesus one more time by anointing His head with spices that will counter the smell of physical decomposition. Despite their devotion, they expect His death to be permanent. They also worry all the way to the tomb, asking each other, *"Who will roll away the stone from the door of the tomb for us?"* (v. 3). Obviously, their expectations do not include a miracle. Otherwise, they would never have approached the tomb with their heads down, a sign of doubt and worry as well as grief.

Physical proof of the Resurrection begins to unfold before their eyes when they look up to see that the massive stone has been rolled away. Entering the tomb, they find it empty except for a young man clothed in a long, white robe sitting on the right side of the stone bench where Jesus' body had been. Through their alarm, they hear him speak the fact that they are seeking Jesus of Nazareth who was crucified, but now is risen. The tomb is empty, and they can see for themselves the empty place where Jesus lay.

No supernatural happening, such as the Resurrection, can ever be proven by natural evidence; it can only be inferred by physical facts that are consistent with the event, even though incomplete. The Shroud of Turin, for instance, continues to baffle scientists. To date, every analytical technique confirms the fact that the shroud is not a fake. No scientific explanation can account for the facial impressions in the shroud and the blood stains of a crucified man. Yet, no one assumes that scientific analysis can produce incontrovertible evidence that it is the linen cloth in which Joseph of Arimathea wrapped the body of Jesus and the one that lay in the tomb for the women to see. When all the available facts are in, some people will believe that it is the Shroud of Jesus and others will not.

The physical facts of the Resurrection are in. Jesus, who was crucified on Friday, is gone from the tomb on Sunday. Three women who expected to find a decomposing body in a tomb sealed by a stone too heavy for them to move are eyewitnesses to an empty tomb, an empty bench, and an empty shroud.

The revelational facts. Faith in the Resurrection must take over where physical facts leave off. Empirical evidence that can be scientifically verified is only one way of seeking and finding the truth. Intuition is a way of knowing that is equally reliable for the truths expressed in art, literature, and music. But for the leap of faith by which a person believes in the Resurrection, God gives us His Word as the way of knowing His Truth. Neither empirical facts nor intuitive knowledge can finally verify such Truths as the Creation, Incarnation or Resurrection. His Word is our basis for belief. So, as proof of Jesus' Resurrection, God sends His messenger to speak His word. *"He is risen!"* (v. 6) is all that God needs to say. Centuries of natural, historical, and prophetic revelation peak in these three words. Angels bow, demons flee, and humans tremble before the Truth. This is the Good News—Jesus Christ is alive and our hope is not in vain. ". . . even so in Christ all will be made alive" (1 Cor. 15:22). As Mark promises in his preamble, He has not only delivered the Good News to the Christians at Rome, but He has put it into the headline edition, **He is risen!**

The prophetic facts. Wherever the disciples are hiding, they must have remembered Jesus' prediction time and time again: "All of you will be made to stumble because of Me this night, for it is written: 'I will strike the Shepherd, And the sheep will be scattered' " (Mark 14:27).

Grief and shame will hardly permit the daring thought that the other half of Jesus' prophecy might still come true, "But after I have been raised, I will go before you to Galilee" (14:28).

God keeps His word. Immediately after the angel announces the Resurrection, He sends the women away with a personal message from the risen Christ to His fallen disciples, *"Tell His disciples—and Peter—that He is going before you into Galilee; there you will see Him as He said to you"* (v. 7). As another proof of the Resurrection, Jesus intends to bring His disciples back together in a relationship that will be stronger than ever. He begins by letting them know that He looks forward to seeing them, even though they have forsaken Him. To illustrate His forgiveness, He mentions Peter by name. Not by surprise, Mark's Gospel is the only one that singles out Peter for a special invitation to the meeting in Galilee. John relates at length the story of Peter's restoration around the campfire in Galilee. Sometimes, though, a single word carries as much meaning as a long story. If I were Peter, beating myself with guilt in some grubby hiding place, and then were to hear that the risen Lord has invited me by name to meet with Him in Galilee as He had promised, I would know that He still loved me and would break every record to get to His side. Of all the proofs of the Resurrection, forgiveness is the indisputable evidence that we can understand.

Poor women! Rather than following the angel's instruction to "go" and "tell," they are so stunned by the incredulous Truth that they say nothing. Their silence lends its own authenticity to the proofs of the Resurrection. If they are just hysterical women fantasizing out of frustration, why do they not talk? Anyone who has stood in the presence of God loses the glibness of a smooth and ready tongue. Trembling hands, whirling mind, and faltering heart—these are the after-effects of meeting God face to face. Fear so ties their tongues that Jesus will have to confirm the fact of His Resurrection by personal appearances rather than by spoken word.

THE RESURRECTION PERSONIFIED

9 Now when He had risen early on the first day of the week, He appeared first to Mary Magdalene, out of whom He had cast seven demons.

10 She went and told those who had been with Him, as they mourned and wept.

11 And when they heard that He was alive and had been seen by her, they did not believe.

12 After that, He appeared in another form to two of them as they walked and went into the country.

13 And they went and told it to the rest; they did not believe them either.

14 Afterward He appeared to the eleven as they sat at the table; and He rebuked their unbelief and hardness of heart, because they did not believe those who had seen Him after He had risen.

15 And He said to them, "Go into all the world and preach the gospel to every creature.

16 "He who believes and is baptized will be saved; but he who does not believe will be condemned.

17 "And these signs will follow those who believe:
In My name they will cast out demons; they will speak
with new tongues;
18 "they will take up serpents; and if they drink
anything deadly, it shall not hurt them; they will lay
hands on the sick, and they will recover."

Mark 16·9–18

The end of Mark's Gospel is a matter of dispute. Scholarly consensus is that verses 9–20 are a later addendum to the original writing. The question deserves discussion, but because this commentary emphasizes communication rather than criticism, it is preferable to proceed on the assumption that the final verses have value for communication purposes.

At the close of the angel's announcement of the Resurrection, he sends the message through the women to the disciples that they will see Jesus in Galilee just as He has promised. Two other appearances precede that meeting, according to the Marcan text. First, Jesus appears to Mary Magdalene to *reward her faithfulness.* John tells us that outside the tomb Jesus appears to her as she weeps out of fear that the body of Jesus has been stolen, not resurrected. Mary believes that she is talking to the gardener. Whether her eyes are blinded by tears, or Jesus remains so nondescript that she does not recognize Him, we do not know. But when Jesus speaks her name, Mary sees and believes. Her faithfulness as one of the women who did not abandon Jesus is rewarded. How significant that the risen Lord chooses to appear first to a woman out of whom He cast seven devils and from whom He received the ministry of love. The Resurrection confirms the purpose that He set at the very onset of His public ministry, "Those who are well have no need of a physician, but those who are sick. I did not come to call the righteous, but sinners, to repentance" (2:17). Mary tries to tell the Good News to the others, but they refuse to believe her.

Jesus' second personal appearance comes to the men who have given up hope of the Resurrection and are heading back to their home in Emmaus. *He reveals Himself to restore their confidence.* Luke gives us the story in detail, but an intriguing phrase is used in the Gospel of Mark, *"He appeared **in another form** to two of them as they walked and went into the country"* (v. 12). Luke infers that the two men mistake Jesus as a fellow-traveler who does not know what has happened in Jerusalem during recent days. His purpose in this appearance is to restore the confidence of the two disciples whose mourning has turned to despair. As Luke informs us, they recognize Jesus in the breaking of the bread and run to tell the rest of the disciples the Good News that they have seen Jesus alive. To reject the woman's testimony is understandable because of Jewish custom, but to scoff at two fellow disciples whose unanimous word is a credible testimony by Jewish Law means that the disciples need to see for themselves before they will believe. Jesus restores the confidence of the two Emmaean men, but no one else believes them.

In His third and final appearance, Jesus comes into the room where the eleven remaining disciples are reclining at dinner, still refusing to believe the reports of those who had seen Jesus alive. For them, Jesus appears to *renew their commission*. After rebuking them for their unbelief and hardness of heart, Jesus goes directly to the purpose of His appearance. He gives the Great Commission for world evangelization along with the promise of salvation to those who believe and with the power to do miracles. So much dispute centers around this montage of the spiritual signs of casting out demons, speaking in tongues, handling snakes and healing the sick that it is difficult to say more about them. A wise person suggests that these signs will follow those who believe, but none of them should be made a cardinal doctrine that diverts us from the central Truth of the Great Commission which is the message of Good News. In this context, the addendum is consistent with the purpose and the spirit of Mark's Gospel.

THE RESURRECTION RATIFIED

19 So then, after the Lord had spoken to them, He was received up into heaven, and sat down at the right hand of God.
20 And they went out and preached everywhere, the Lord working with them and confirming the word through the accompanying signs. Amen.

Mark 16:19–20

As part of the divine-human paradox, the Resurrection of Jesus is a revealed fact that stands alone. It needs no human action for its proof. At the same time, if the Resurrection is to be the Good

News of the Gospel, it will be ratified by the proof of redemption through human agents who carry out the Great Commission. Appropriately, then, the Gospel of Mark concludes with the follow-up report on Jesus and His disciples.

Jesus' ascension into heaven is Good News. His redemptive mission is complete, His full glory is restored, and His position at the right hand of God assures His power for those to whom He has entrusted the Gospel. Mark's case is closing. The ascension into heaven is part of the final evidence presented on behalf of the original proposition to show ". . . Jesus Christ, the Son of God" (1:1).

Complementing the proof of the ascension is the continuing interaction between Jesus and His disciples. Accepting His commission, *"they went out and preached everywhere"* (v. 20). True to His Word, Jesus continues *"working with them and confirming the word through the accompanying signs"* (v. 20). Paul outlines this relationship between Jesus' Resurrection and the Apostle's preaching when he writes to the Corinthians, "And if Christ is not risen; then our preaching is vain, and your faith is also vain" (1 Cor. 15:14). Conversely, the Resurrection is ratified by the ongoing evidence of effective preaching and redemptive faith. No greater testimony of the living and reigning Christ can be presented than to have each generation of Christians show the evidence attributed to the church after Pentecost, "And with great power the apostles gave witness to the resurrection of the Lord Jesus. And great grace was upon them all" (Acts 4:33). Great power and great grace in the continuing witness of Christ's disciples are ratifying signs of the Resurrection and the final proof of the original proposition that Mark's Gospel is written as "The beginning," not the end of the Good News.

With the thought of the Good News as the continuing ratification of the Resurrection through the redemptive power and grace of Christian witness, a perspective on the dispute over the ending of Mark's Gospel comes into view. To assume that Mark ends His writing at verse 8 with trembling, stunned, mute and fearful women seems inconsistent with the carefully constructed case that the author presents throughout the Gospel. After entering so deeply into Mark's mind, a closing argument is expected. Is the abrupt ending intentional or accidental? Some say that he intends to leave his Roman readers trembling, stunned, mute, and fearful before the awesome power of God. Others surmise that the final page of Mark's writing got lost in transition.

Biblical translators of the second or fourth centuries tried to complete the Gospel of Mark with two other endings. One is the lengthy addendum of the King James Version which is first found in second-century manuscripts. The other is the short summary which appears in fourth-century manuscripts and is added as an option in the Revised Standard Version: "But they reported briefly to Peter and those with him all that they had been told. And after this, Jesus himself sent out by means of them, from east to west, the sacred and imperishable proclamation of eternal salvation" (Mark 16:9, RSV).

Neither the long nor the short ending adequately fits the spirit and style of Mark's writing. If a choice has to be made, let Mark be known as "The Unfinished Gospel" with verse 8 as the last, but not final, word. After all, Mark only promises to write "the *beginning* of the gospel of Jesus Christ, the Son of God." The ending is up to us.

Bibliography

Achtemeier, P. J. *Mark.* Proclamation Commentaries. Philadelphia: Fortress, 1975.

Alexander, J. A. *Commentary on the Gospel of Mark.* London: Banner of Truth Trust, 1960.

Allen, W. C. *The Gospel According to St. Mark.* The Oxford Church Biblical Commentary. New York: Macmillan, 1915.

Bacon, B. W. *The Gospel of Mark.* New Haven: Yale University Press, 1925.

Barclay, W. *The Gospel of Mark.* Philadelphia: Westminster Press, 1956.

Barnes, A. *Notes on the New Testament: Matthew and Mark.* Grand Rapids: Baker Book House, 1950.

Bartlet, J. V. *St. Mark.* Century Bible. New York: H. Frowde, 1922.

Best, E. *The Temptation and the Passion: The Marcan Soteriology.* Cambridge: University Press, 1965.

Blunt, A. W. F. *The Gospel According to St. Mark.* Clarendon Bible. Oxford: Clarendon Press, 1929.

Branscomb, B. H. *The Gospel of Mark.* The Moffatt New Testament Commentary. New York: Harper, 1937.

Bratcher, R. G., and Nida, E. A. *A Translator's Handbook on the Gospel of Mark.* London: E. J. Brill, 1961.

Bruce, A. B. *The Synoptic Gospels.* The Expositor's Greek Testament, vol. 1. London: Hodder and Stoughton, 1897–1910.

Burkill, T. A. *New Light on the Earliest Gospels.* Ithaca, NY: Cornell University Press, 1972.

Church, I. F. *A Study of the Marcan Gospel.* New York: Vantage, 1976.

Clark, K. S. L. *The Gospel According to St. Mark with Notes and Commentaries.* London: Darton, L & T, 1973.

Cranfield, C. E. B. *The Gospel According to St. Mark.* Cambridge: University Press, 1963.

Dewey, J. *Disciples of the Way: Mark on Discipleship.* Cincinnati: Women's Division of Board of Global Ministries, United Methodist Church, 1976.

Dorris, C. E. W. *A Commentary on the Gospel According to Mark.* New Testament Commentaries. Nashville: Gospel Advocate Co., 1975.

Doudna, J. C. *The Greek of the Gospel of Mark.* Philadelphia: Society of Biblical Literature and Exegesis, 1961.

Earle, R. *Mark.* The Wesleyan Bible Commentary, vol. 4. Grand Rapids: Eerdmans, 1964.

Erdman, C. R. *The Gospel of Mark.* Philadelphia: Westminster Press, 1928.

Farmer, W. R. *The Last Twelve Verses of Mark.* New York: Cambridge University Press, 1974.

Farrer, A. *A Study in St. Mark.* Westminster: Dacre Press, 1951.

Finegan, J. *Mark of the Law.* Richmond, VA: John Knox, 1972.

BIBLIOGRAPHY

Grant, F. C. *The Gospels, Their Origin and Their Growth.* New York: Harper, 1957.
—— and Luccock, H. E. *The Gospel According to St. Mark.* The Interpreter's Bible, vol. 7. New York: Abingdon-Cokesbury Press, 1951–57.
Green, H. B. *The Gospel According to Mark.* London: Oxford University Press, 1957.
Gutzke, M. G. *Plain Talks on Mark.* Grand Rapids: Zondervan, 1975.
Hargreaves, J. *A Guide to St. Mark's Gospel,* rev. ed. London: SPCK, 1970.
Hendriksen, W. *Exposition of the Gospel According to Mark.* Grand Rapids: Baker, 1975.
Hiebert, D. E. *Mark: A Portrait of the Servant.* Chicago: Moody Press, 1974.
Hobbs, H. H. *An Exposition of the Gospel of Mark.* Grand Rapids: Baker, 1970.
Hunter, A. M. *The Gospel According to St. Mark.* London: SCM Press, 1948.
Jensen, I. L. *Mark: A Self-Study Guide.* Chicago: Moody Press, 1972.
Kee, H. C. *Community of the New Age, Studies in Mark's Gospel.* Philadelphia: Fortress, 1977.
Lane, W. L. *The Gospel According to Mark.* Grand Rapids: Eerdmans, 1974.
Lenski, R. C. H. *The Interpretation of St. Mark's Gospel.* Minneapolis: Augsburg, 1951.
Lightfoot, R. H. *The Gospel Message of Mark.* Oxford: Clarendon, 1950.
Maclear, F. G. *The Gospel According to St. Mark.* Cambridge Greek Testament. Cambridge: University Press, 1889.
Martin, R. P. *Mark: Evangelist and Theologian.* Exeter: Paternoster Press, 1972.
Menzies, A. *The Earliest Gospel.* London: Macmillan and Co., 1901.
Meye, R. P. *Jesus and the Twelve: Discipleship and Revelation in Mark's Gospel.* Grand Rapids: Eerdmans, 1968.
Miller, S. *The Adult Son. A Study of the Gospel of Mark.* Des Moines: Miller Books, 1974.
Minear, P. S. *The Gospel According to Mark.* The Layman's Bible Commentary. Atlanta: John Knox Press, 1977.
Mitton, C. L. *The Gospel According to St. Mark.* London: Epworth Press, 1957.
Moule, C. F. D. *The Gospel According to Mark.* Cambridge Bible on the N.E.B. London: Cambridge University Press, 1965.
Nineham, D. E. *St. Mark, 1963.* New York: Seabury Press, 1963.
Phillips, J. B. *Peter's Portrait of Jesus.* London: Collins and World, 1976.
Rawlinson, A. E. J. *Saint Mark.* Westminster Commentaries. London: Methuen and Co., 1925.
Redlich, E. B. *St. Mark's Gospel.* London: G. Duckworth, 1948.
Robertson, A. T. *Studies in Mark's Gospel.* Nashville: Broadman, 1958.
Robinson, James. *The Problem of History in Mark.* Naperville, IL: Allenson, 1957.
Schweizer, E. *The Good News According to Mark.* Richmond, VA: Knox, 1970–71.
Scroggie, W. G. *The Gospel of Mark.* Grand Rapids: Zondervan, 1976.
Smith, T. G. *The Mighty Message of Mark.* Winona, MN: St. Mary's College Press, 1973.
Stedman, R. C. *The Servant Who Rules.* Waco, TX: Word Books, 1976.
——. *The Ruler Who Serves.* Waco, TX: Word Books, 1976.
Stonehouse, N. B. *The Witness of Matthew and Mark to Christ.* Grand Rapids: Eerdmans, 1963.
Swete, H. B. *The Gospel According to St. Mark.* Grand Rapids: Kregel Publications, 1972; London, Macmillan and Co., 1898.
Taylor, V. *The Gospel According to St. Mark.* London: Macmillan, 1952.

Wesley, J. *Explanatory Notes on the New Testament.* New York: G. Lane & C. B. Tippett, 1845.

Whiston, L. A. *Power of a New Life.* Relational Studies in Mark. Waco, TX: Word Books, 1976.

————. *Through Suffering to Victory.* Relational Studies in Mark. Waco, TX: Word Books, 1976.

Wuest, K. S. *The New Testament, An Expanded Translation.* Grand Rapids: Eerdmans, 1956.